Rocko's Modern AfterLife ™

kaboom!

Series Designer
MICHELLE ANKLEY

Collection Designer
JILLIAN CRAB

Editor
MATTHEW LEVINE

kaboom!™

nickelodeon

ROCKO'S MODERN AFTERLIFE, January 2020. Published by KaBOOM!, a division of Boom Entertainment, Inc., 5670 Wilshire Boulevard, Suite 400, Los Angeles, CA 90036-5679. © 2020 Viacom International Inc. All Rights Reserved. Nickelodeon, Rocko's Modern Life and all related titles, logos, and characters are trademarks of Viacom International Inc. Originally published in single magazine form as ROCKO'S MODERN AFTERLIFE No. 1-4. © 2019 Viacom International Inc. Created Joe Murray. KaBOOM!™ and the KaBOOM! logo are trademarks of Boom Entertainment, Inc., registered in various countries and categories. All characters, events, and institutions depicted herein are fictional. Any similarity between any of the names, characters, persons, events, and/or institutions in this publication to actual names, characters, and persons, whether living or dead, events, and/or institutions is unintended and purely coincidental. KaBOOM! does not read or accept unsolicited submissions of ideas, stories, or artwork.

BOOM! Studios, 5670 Wilshire Boulevard, Suite 400, Los Angeles, CA 90036-5679. Printed in China. First Printing.

ISBN: 978-1-68415-488-3, eISBN: 978-1-641-44646-4

Rocko's Modern Afterlife ™

Created by
JOE MURRAY

Written by
ANTHONY BURCH

Illustrated by
MATTIA DI MEO

Colors by
FRANCESCO SEGALA

Letters by
JIM CAMPBELL

Cover by
IAN McGINTY

Colors by **JOVEN PAUL**

Special Thanks To
**JOAN HILTY, LINDA LEE,
JAMES SALERNO, ALEXANDRA MAURER,**
AND THE WONDERFUL TEAM AT **NICKELODEON.**

CHAPTER
ONE

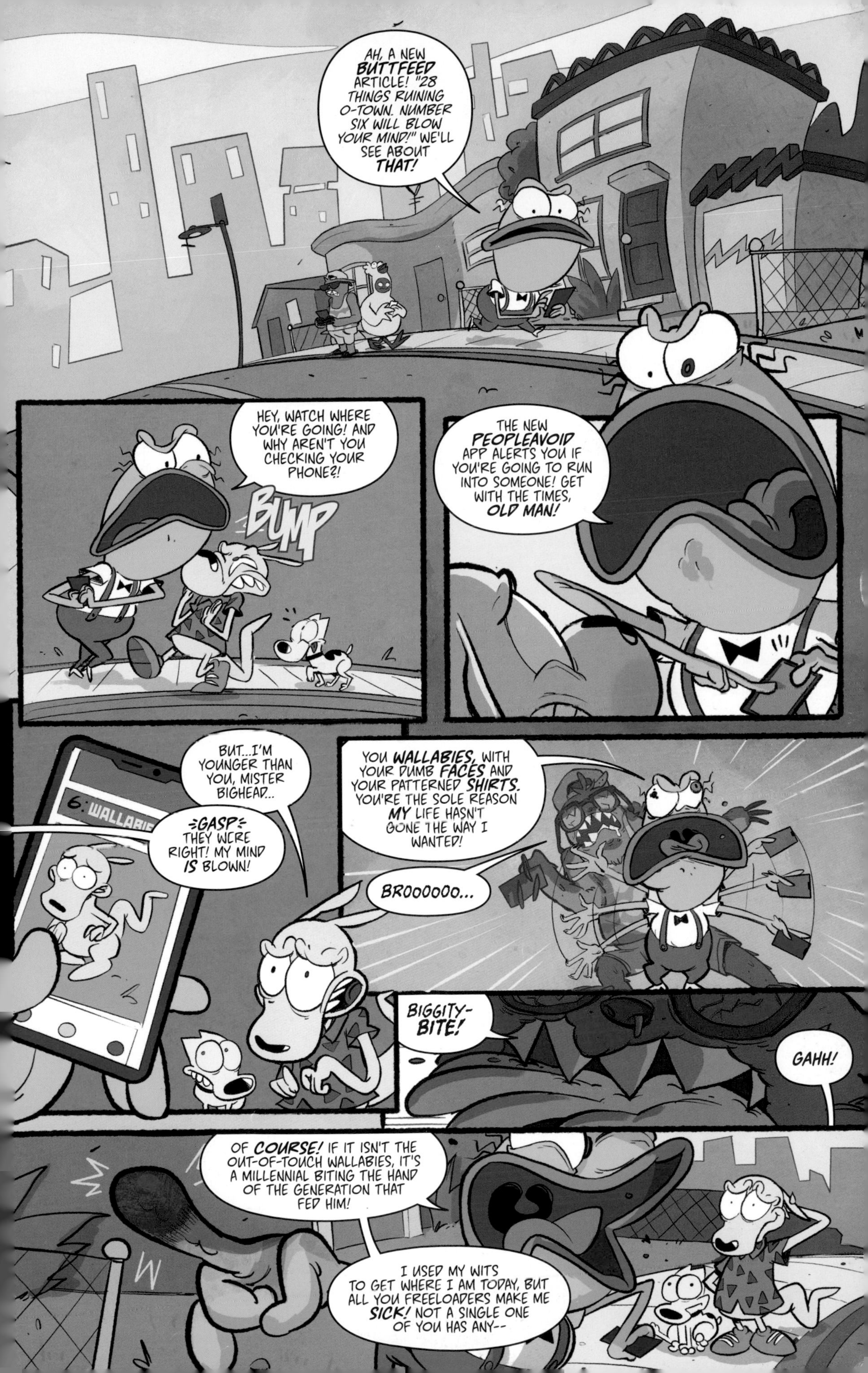
AH, A NEW BUTTFEED ARTICLE! "28 THINGS RUINING O-TOWN. NUMBER SIX WILL BLOW YOUR MIND!" WE'LL SEE ABOUT THAT!
HEY, WATCH WHERE YOU'RE GOING! AND WHY AREN'T YOU CHECKING YOUR PHONE?!
BUMP
THE NEW PEOPLEAVOID APP ALERTS YOU IF YOU'RE GOING TO RUN INTO SOMEONE! GET WITH THE TIMES, OLD MAN!
BUT...I'M YOUNGER THAN YOU, MISTER BIGHEAD...
6: WALLABIE
GASP THEY WERE RIGHT! MY MIND IS BLOWN!
YOU WALLABIES, WITH YOUR DUMB FACES AND YOUR PATTERNED SHIRTS. YOU'RE THE SOLE REASON MY LIFE HASN'T GONE THE WAY I WANTED!
BROOOOOO...
BIGGITY-BITE!
GAHH!
OF COURSE! IF IT ISN'T THE OUT-OF-TOUCH WALLABIES, IT'S A MILLENNIAL BITING THE HAND OF THE GENERATION THAT FED HIM!
I USED MY WITS TO GET WHERE I AM TODAY, BUT ALL YOU FREELOADERS MAKE ME SICK! NOT A SINGLE ONE OF YOU HAS ANY--

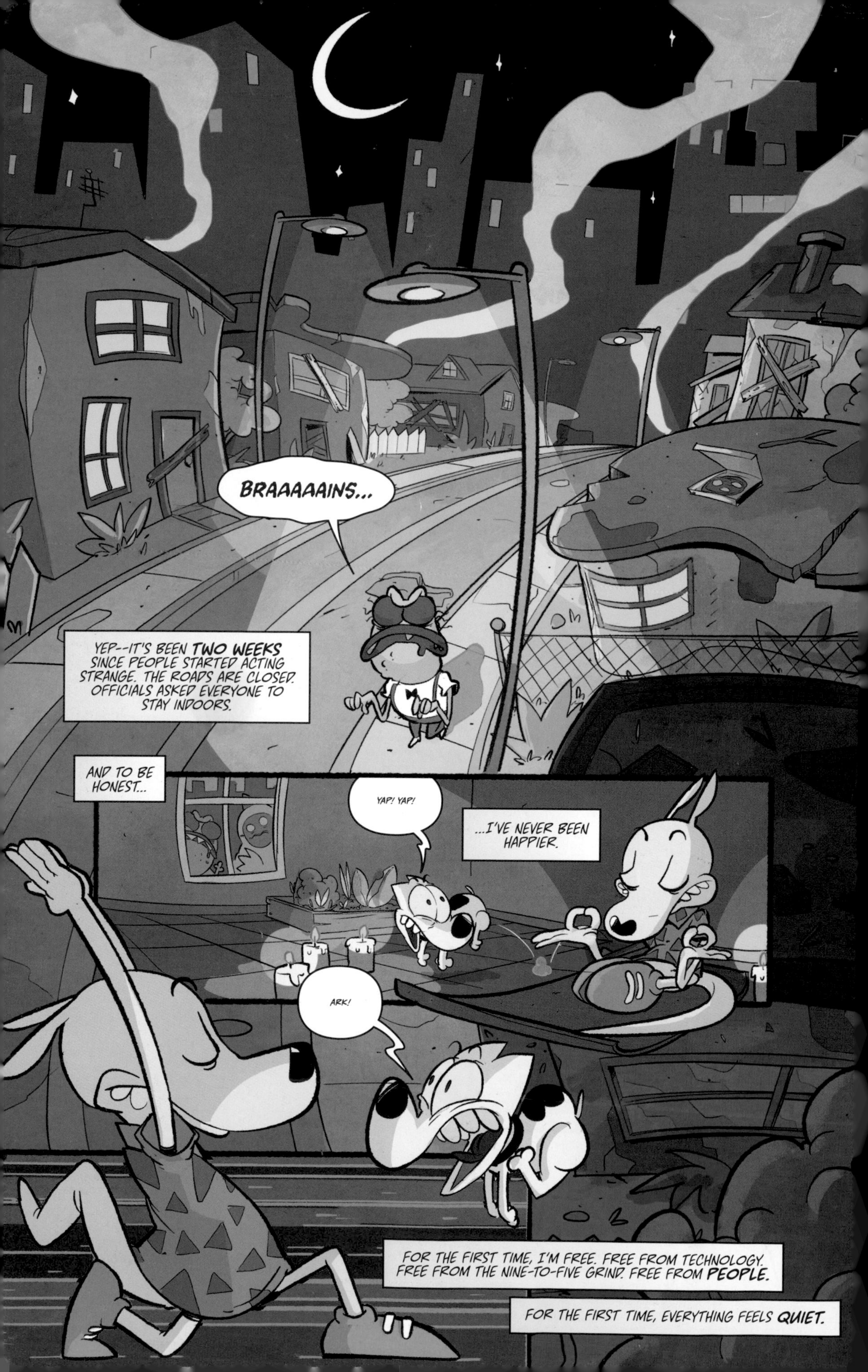

BRAAAAAINS...
YEP--IT'S BEEN TWO WEEKS SINCE PEOPLE STARTED ACTING STRANGE. THE ROADS ARE CLOSED. OFFICIALS ASKED EVERYONE TO STAY INDOORS.
AND TO BE HONEST...
YAP! YAP!
...I'VE NEVER BEEN HAPPIER.
ARK!
FOR THE FIRST TIME, I'M FREE. FREE FROM TECHNOLOGY. FREE FROM THE NINE-TO-FIVE GRIND. FREE FROM PEOPLE.
FOR THE FIRST TIME, EVERYTHING FEELS QUIET.

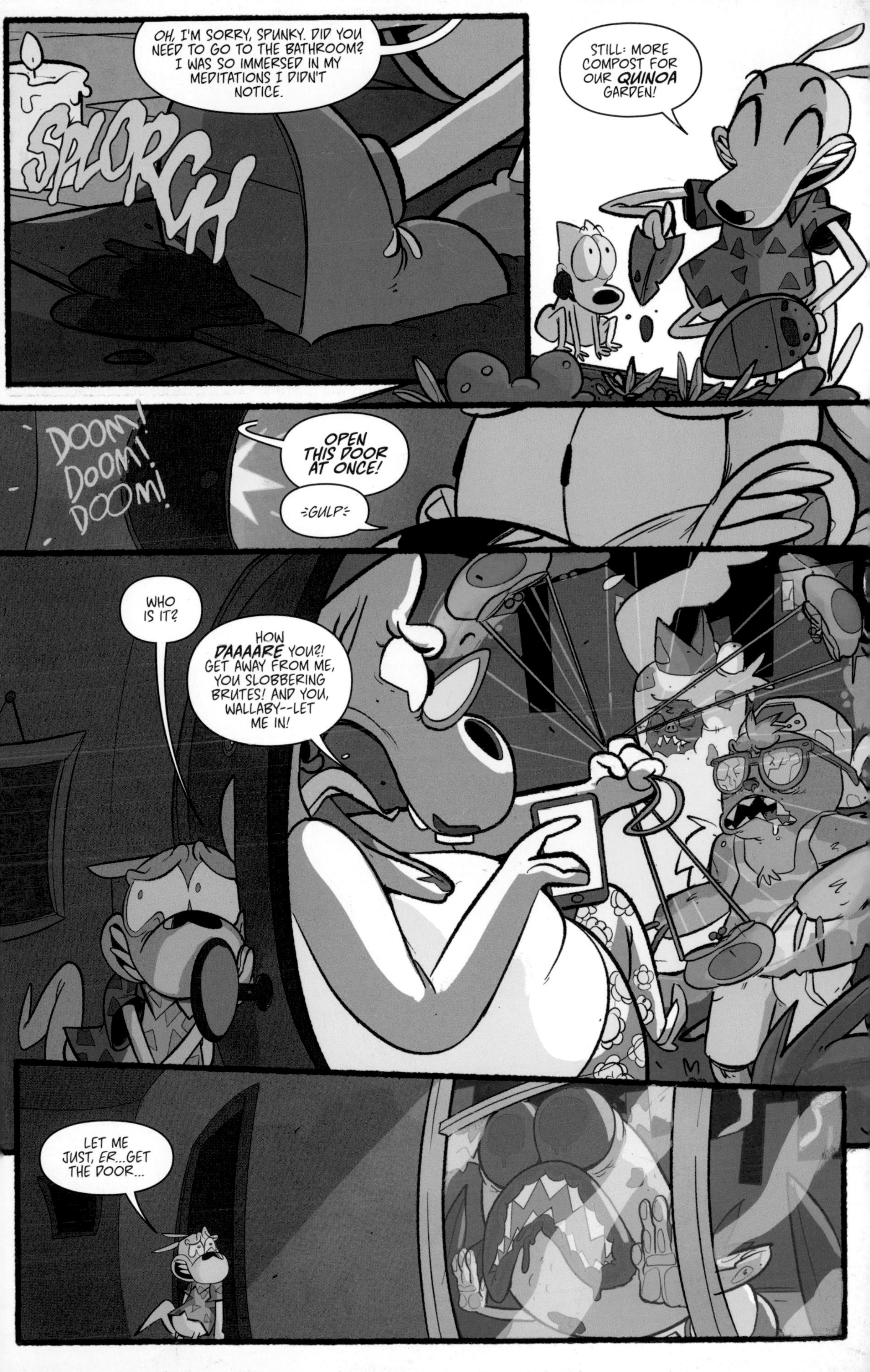

OH, I'M SORRY, SPUNKY. DID YOU NEED TO GO TO THE BATHROOM? I WAS SO IMMERSED IN MY MEDITATIONS I DIDN'T NOTICE.
SPLORCH
STILL: MORE COMPOST FOR OUR QUINOA GARDEN!
DOOM! DOOM! DOOM!
OPEN THIS DOOR AT ONCE!
GULP
WHO IS IT?
HOW DAAAARE YOU?! GET AWAY FROM ME, YOU SLOBBERING BRUTES! AND YOU, WALLABY--LET ME IN!
LET ME JUST, ER...GET THE DOOR...

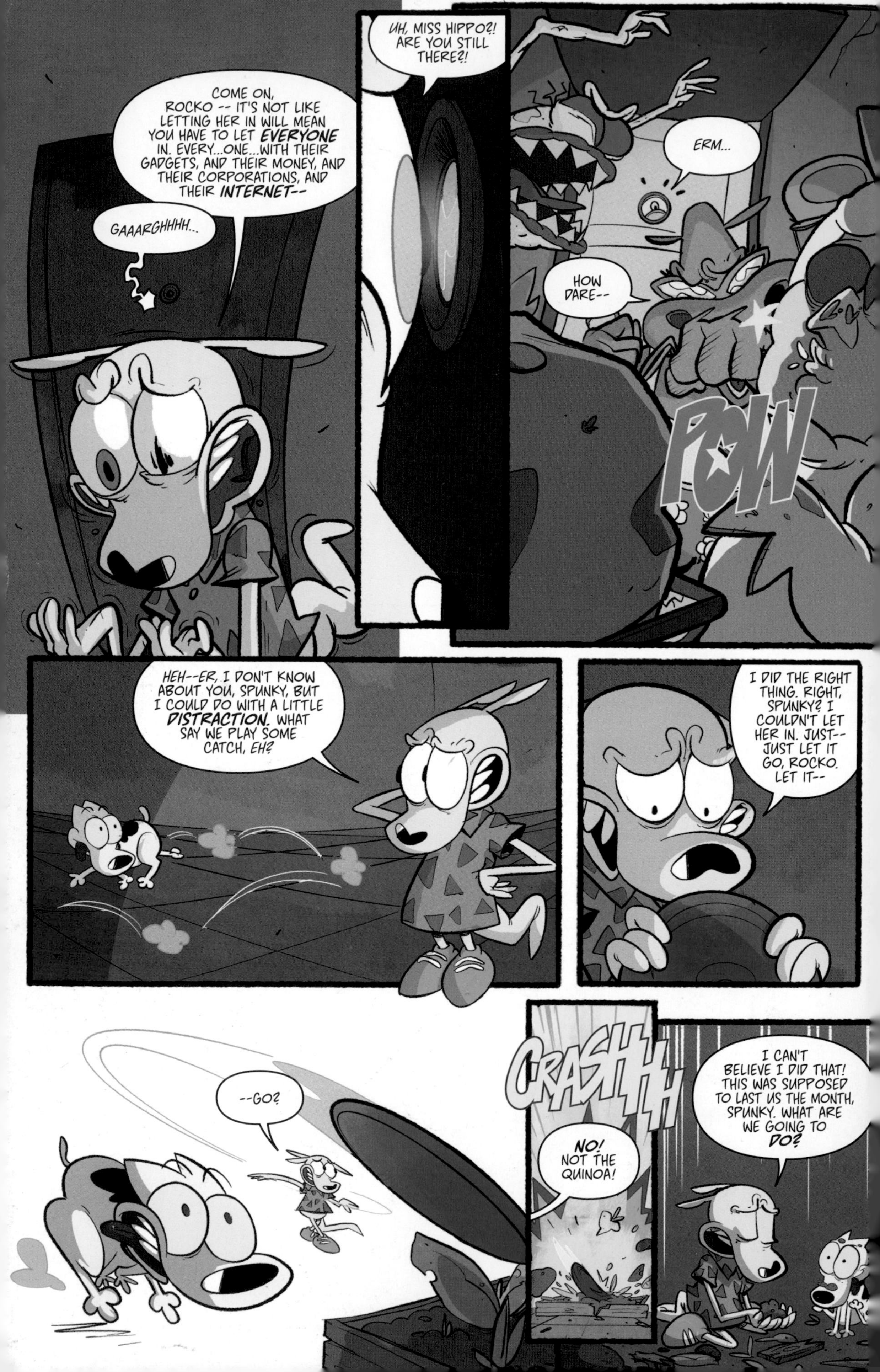
COME ON, ROCKO -- IT'S NOT LIKE LETTING HER IN WILL MEAN YOU HAVE TO LET EVERYONE IN. EVERY...ONE...WITH THEIR GADGETS, AND THEIR MONEY, AND THEIR CORPORATIONS, AND THEIR INTERNET--
GAAARGHHHH...
UH, MISS HIPPO?! ARE YOU STILL THERE?!
ERM...
HOW DARE--
POW
HEH--ER, I DON'T KNOW ABOUT YOU, SPUNKY, BUT I COULD DO WITH A LITTLE DISTRACTION. WHAT SAY WE PLAY SOME CATCH, EH?
I DID THE RIGHT THING. RIGHT, SPUNKY? I COULDN'T LET HER IN. JUST--JUST LET IT GO, ROCKO. LET IT--
--GO?
CRASHHH
NO! NOT THE QUINOA!
I CAN'T BELIEVE I DID THAT! THIS WAS SUPPOSED TO LAST US THE MONTH, SPUNKY. WHAT ARE WE GOING TO DO?

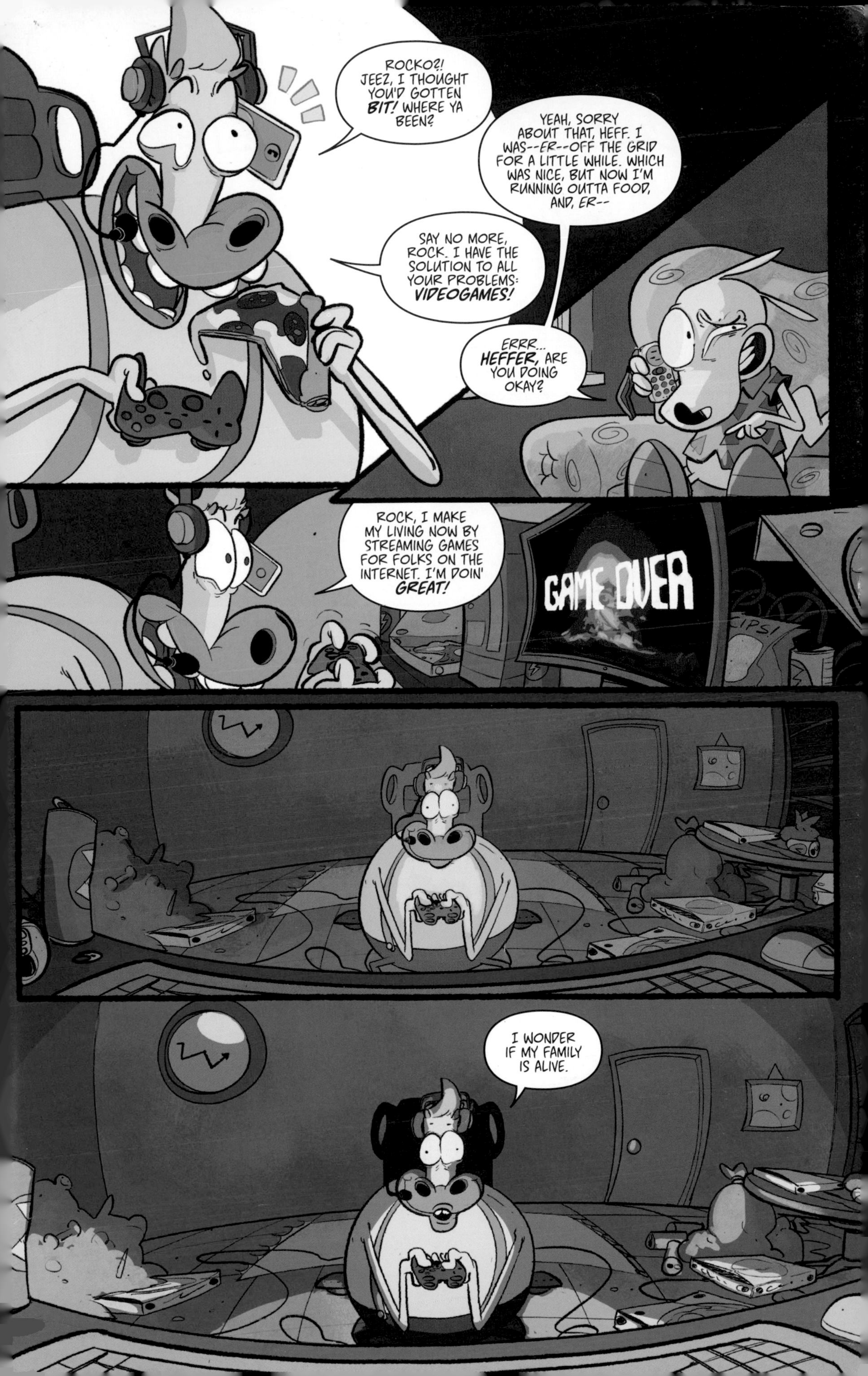
ROCKO?! JEEZ, I THOUGHT YOU'D GOTTEN **BIT!** WHERE YA BEEN?
YEAH, SORRY ABOUT THAT, HEFF. I WAS--*ER*--OFF THE GRID FOR A LITTLE WHILE. WHICH WAS NICE, BUT NOW I'M RUNNING OUTTA FOOD, AND, *ER*--
SAY NO MORE, ROCK. I HAVE THE SOLUTION TO ALL YOUR PROBLEMS: ***VIDEOGAMES!***
ERRR... **HEFFER,** ARE YOU DOING OKAY?
ROCK, I MAKE MY LIVING NOW BY STREAMING GAMES FOR FOLKS ON THE INTERNET. I'M DOIN' ***GREAT!***
GAME OVER
CHIPS!
I WONDER IF MY FAMILY IS ALIVE.

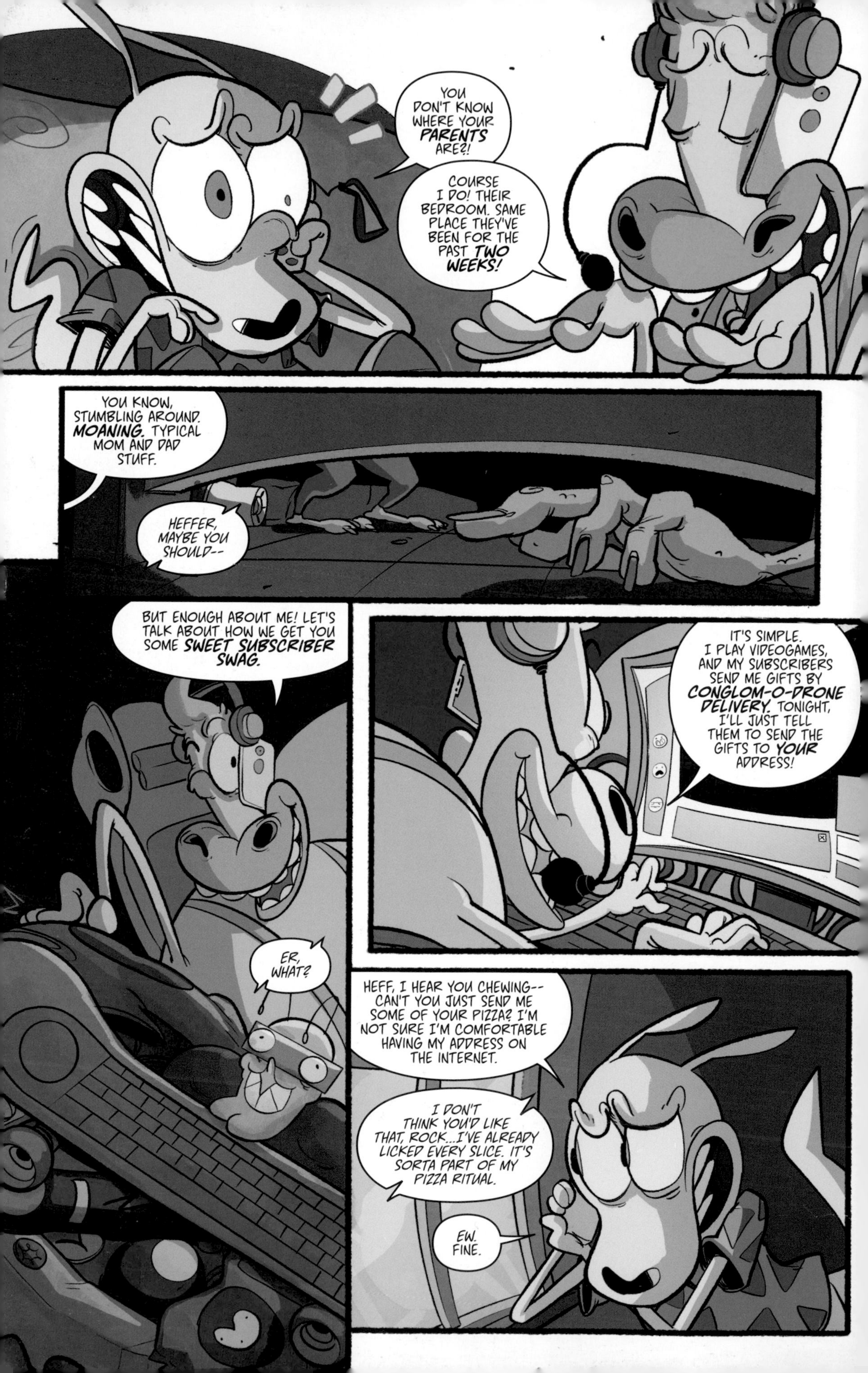

YOU DON'T KNOW WHERE YOUR PARENTS ARE?!
COURSE I DO! THEIR BEDROOM. SAME PLACE THEY'VE BEEN FOR THE PAST TWO WEEKS!
YOU KNOW, STUMBLING AROUND. MOANING. TYPICAL MOM AND DAD STUFF.
HEFFER, MAYBE YOU SHOULD--
BUT ENOUGH ABOUT ME! LET'S TALK ABOUT HOW WE GET YOU SOME SWEET SUBSCRIBER SWAG.
ER, WHAT?
IT'S SIMPLE. I PLAY VIDEOGAMES, AND MY SUBSCRIBERS SEND ME GIFTS BY CONGLOM-O-DRONE DELIVERY. TONIGHT, I'LL JUST TELL THEM TO SEND THE GIFTS TO YOUR ADDRESS!
HEFF, I HEAR YOU CHEWING-- CAN'T YOU JUST SEND ME SOME OF YOUR PIZZA? I'M NOT SURE I'M COMFORTABLE HAVING MY ADDRESS ON THE INTERNET.
I DON'T THINK YOU'D LIKE THAT, ROCK...I'VE ALREADY LICKED EVERY SLICE. IT'S SORTA PART OF MY PIZZA RITUAL.
EW. FINE.

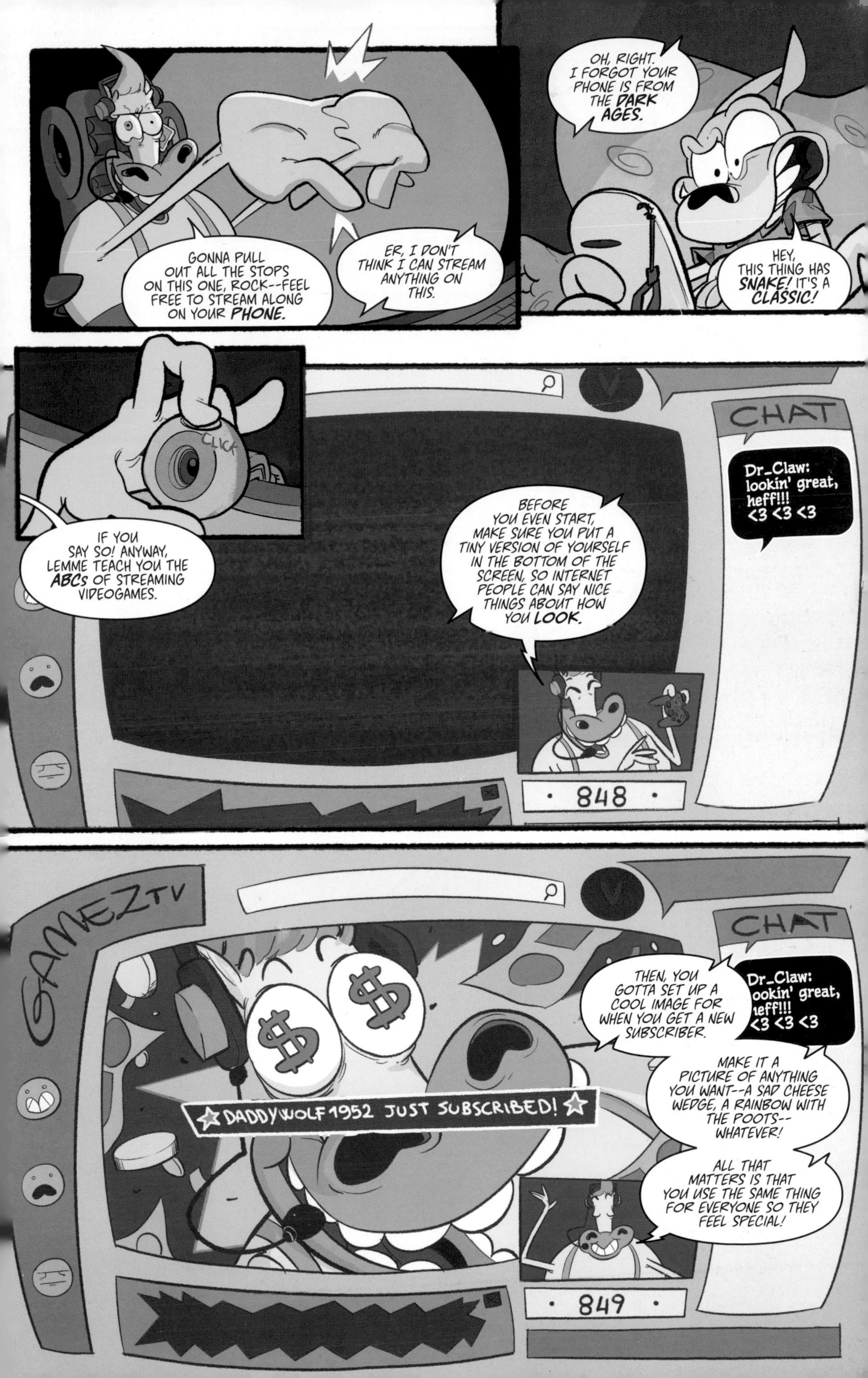
GONNA PULL OUT ALL THE STOPS ON THIS ONE, ROCK--FEEL FREE TO STREAM ALONG ON YOUR PHONE.
ER, I DON'T THINK I CAN STREAM ANYTHING ON THIS.
OH, RIGHT. I FORGOT YOUR PHONE IS FROM THE DARK AGES.
HEY, THIS THING HAS SNAKE! IT'S A CLASSIC!
CLICK
IF YOU SAY SO! ANYWAY, LEMME TEACH YOU THE ABCs OF STREAMING VIDEOGAMES.
BEFORE YOU EVEN START, MAKE SURE YOU PUT A TINY VERSION OF YOURSELF IN THE BOTTOM OF THE SCREEN, SO INTERNET PEOPLE CAN SAY NICE THINGS ABOUT HOW YOU LOOK.
CHAT
Dr_Claw: lookin' great, heff!!! <3 <3 <3
848
GAMEZ TV
CHAT
THEN, YOU GOTTA SET UP A COOL IMAGE FOR WHEN YOU GET A NEW SUBSCRIBER.
Dr_Claw: lookin' great, heff!!! <3 <3 <3
MAKE IT A PICTURE OF ANYTHING YOU WANT--A SAD CHEESE WEDGE, A RAINBOW WITH THE POOTS--WHATEVER!
DADDYWOLF1952 JUST SUBSCRIBED!
ALL THAT MATTERS IS THAT YOU USE THE SAME THING FOR EVERYONE SO THEY FEEL SPECIAL!
849

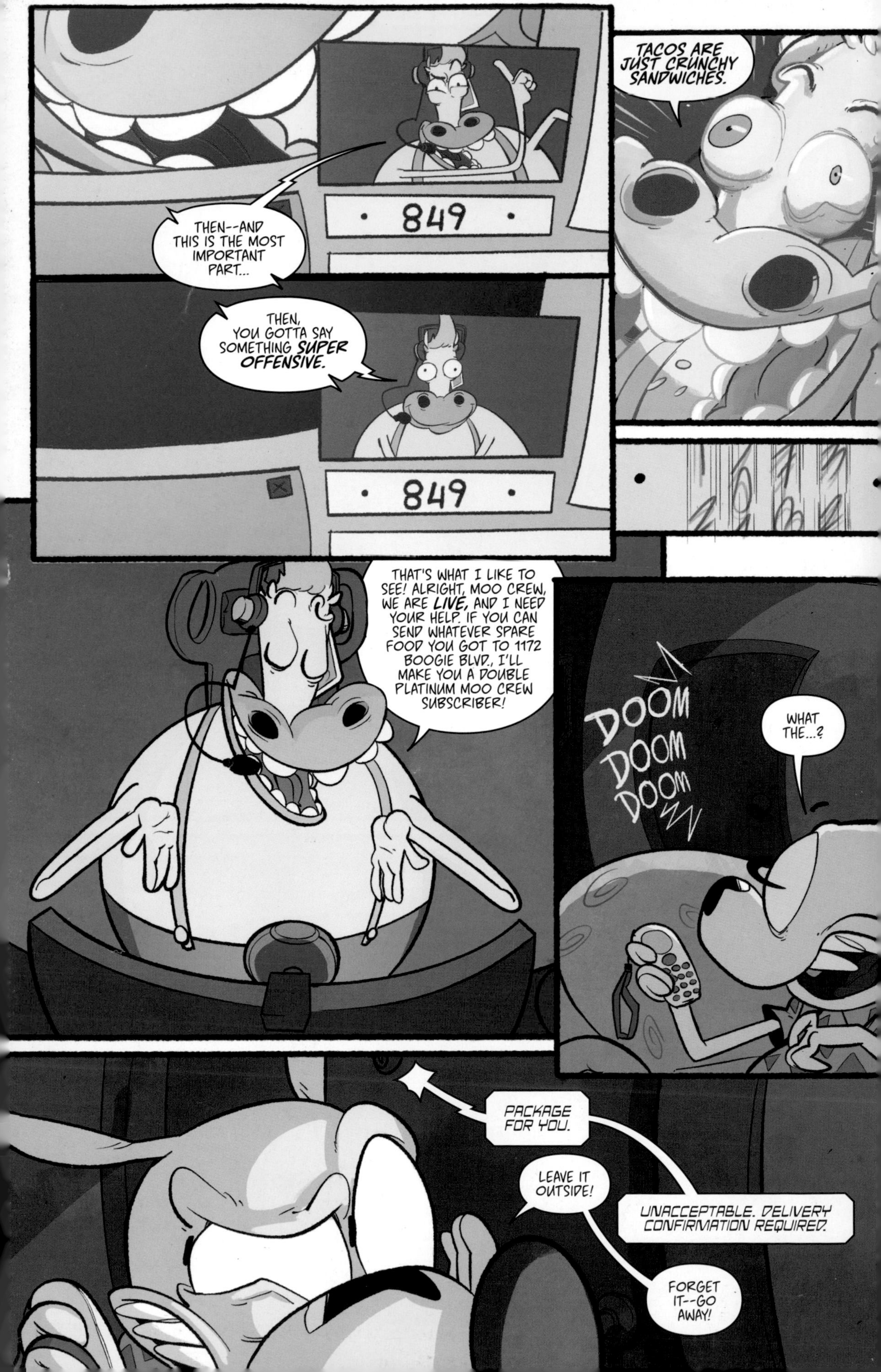
THEN--AND THIS IS THE MOST IMPORTANT PART...
849
TACOS ARE JUST CRUNCHY SANDWICHES.
THEN, YOU GOTTA SAY SOMETHING SUPER OFFENSIVE.
849
THAT'S WHAT I LIKE TO SEE! ALRIGHT, MOO CREW, WE ARE LIVE, AND I NEED YOUR HELP. IF YOU CAN SEND WHATEVER SPARE FOOD YOU GOT TO 1172 BOOGIE BLVD., I'LL MAKE YOU A DOUBLE PLATINUM MOO CREW SUBSCRIBER!
DOOM DOOM DOOM
WHAT THE...?
PACKAGE FOR YOU.
LEAVE IT OUTSIDE!
UNACCEPTABLE. DELIVERY CONFIRMATION REQUIRED.
FORGET IT--GO AWAY!

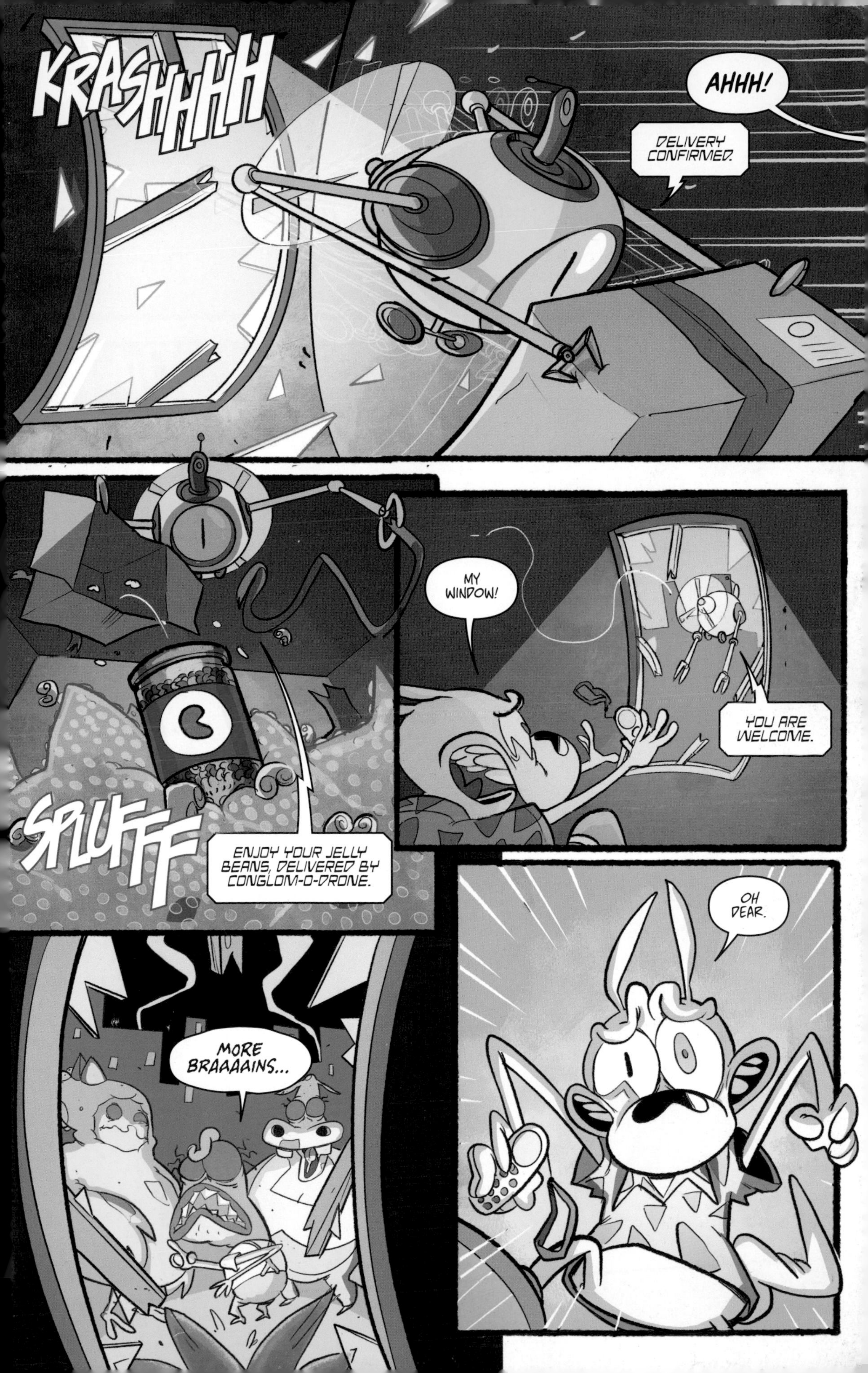
KRASHHHH
AHHH!
DELIVERY CONFIRMED.
SPLUFFF
ENJOY YOUR JELLY BEANS, DELIVERED BY CONGLOM-O-DRONE.
MY WINDOW!
YOU ARE WELCOME.
MORE BRAAAAINS...
OH DEAR.

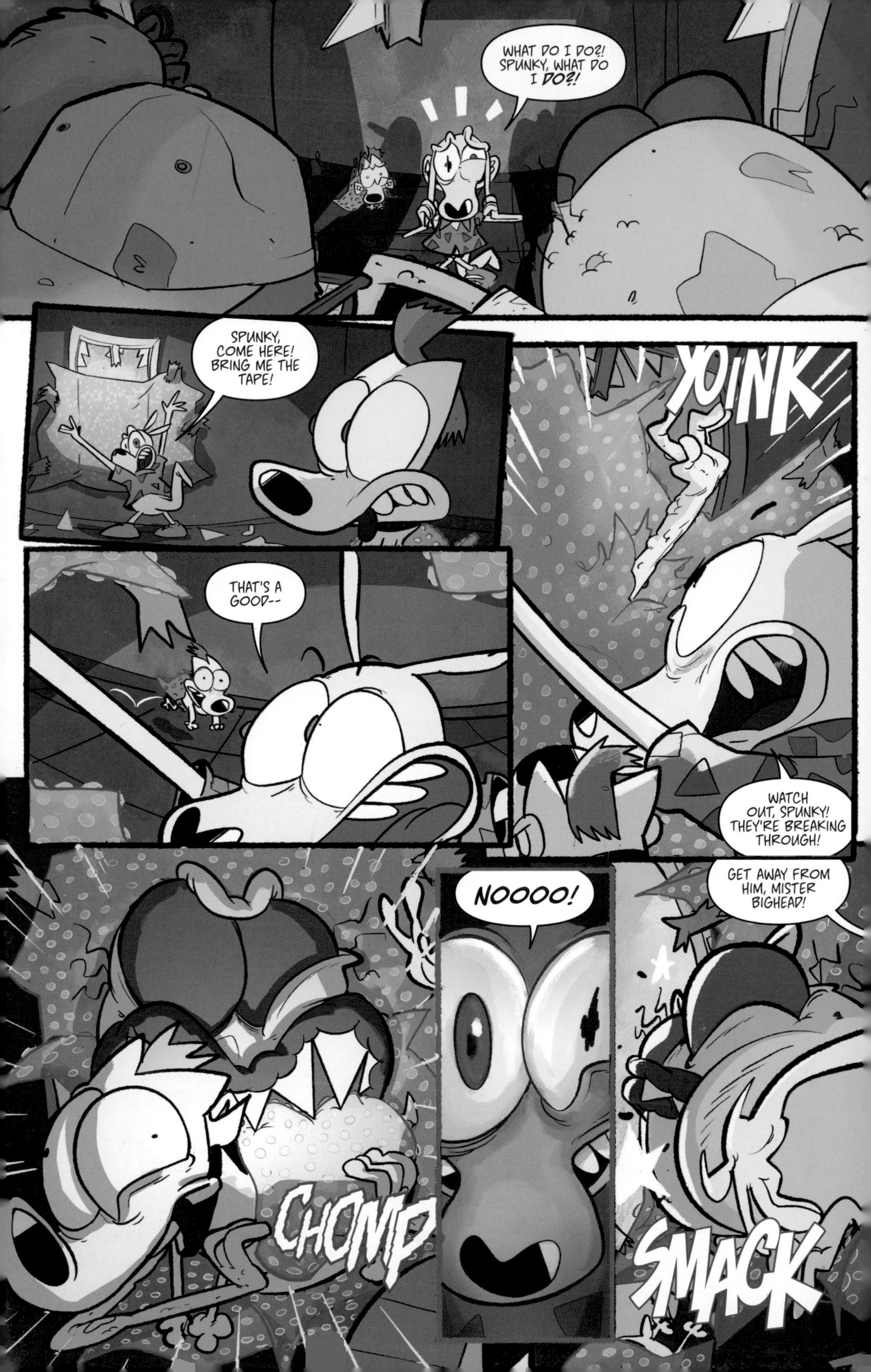
WHAT DO I DO?! SPUNKY, WHAT DO I DO?!
SPUNKY, COME HERE! BRING ME THE TAPE!
YOINK
THAT'S A GOOD--
WATCH OUT, SPUNKY! THEY'RE BREAKING THROUGH!
CHOMP
NOOOO!
GET AWAY FROM HIM, MISTER BIGHEAD!
SMACK

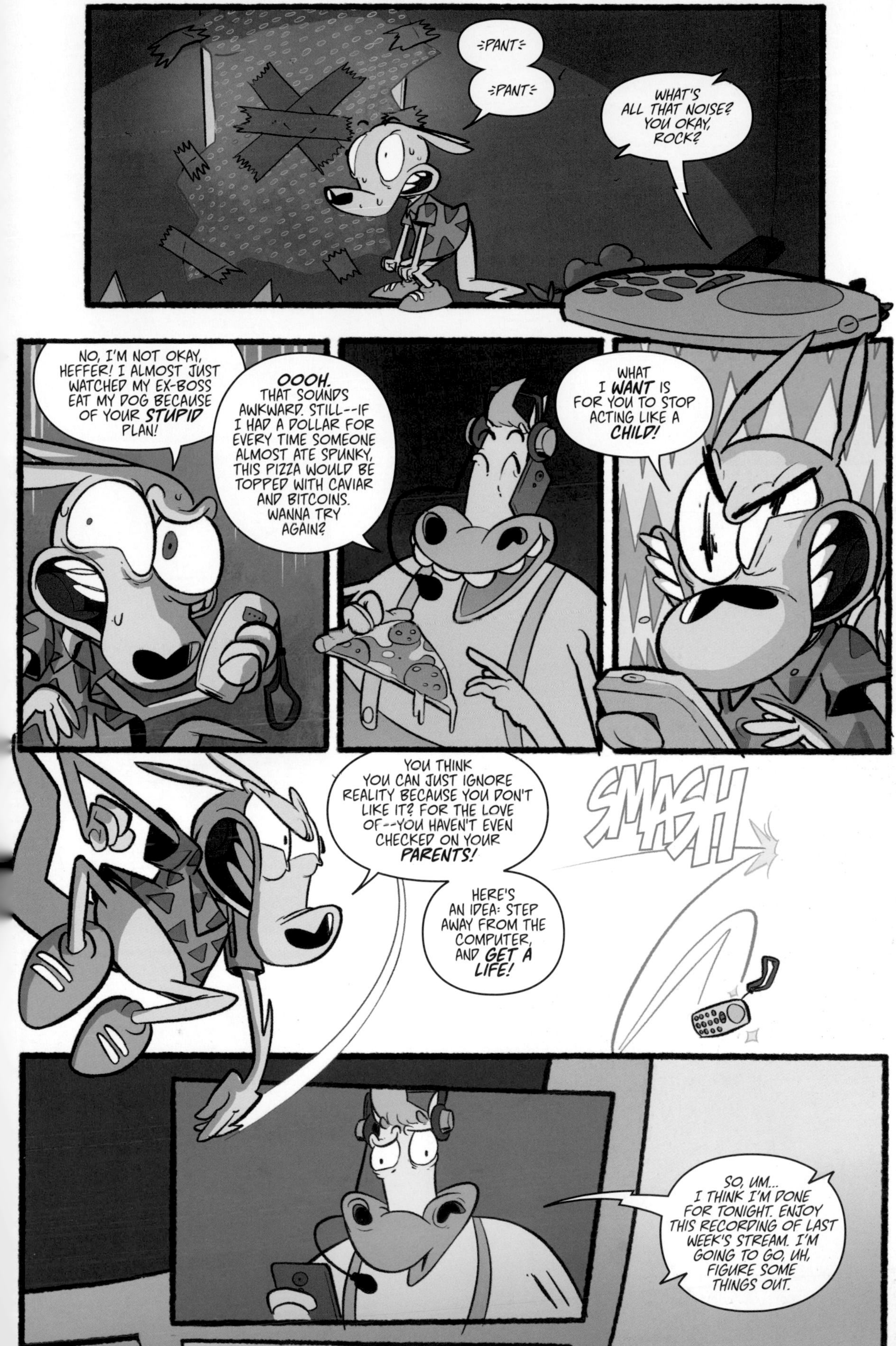

PANT
PANT
WHAT'S ALL THAT NOISE? YOU OKAY, ROCK?
NO, I'M NOT OKAY, HEFFER! I ALMOST JUST WATCHED MY EX-BOSS EAT MY DOG BECAUSE OF YOUR STUPID PLAN!
OOOH. THAT SOUNDS AWKWARD. STILL--IF I HAD A DOLLAR FOR EVERY TIME SOMEONE ALMOST ATE SPUNKY, THIS PIZZA WOULD BE TOPPED WITH CAVIAR AND BITCOINS. WANNA TRY AGAIN?
WHAT I WANT IS FOR YOU TO STOP ACTING LIKE A CHILD!
YOU THINK YOU CAN JUST IGNORE REALITY BECAUSE YOU DON'T LIKE IT? FOR THE LOVE OF--YOU HAVEN'T EVEN CHECKED ON YOUR PARENTS!
HERE'S AN IDEA: STEP AWAY FROM THE COMPUTER, AND GET A LIFE!
SMASH
SO, UM... I THINK I'M DONE FOR TONIGHT. ENJOY THIS RECORDING OF LAST WEEK'S STREAM. I'M GOING TO GO, UH, FIGURE SOME THINGS OUT.

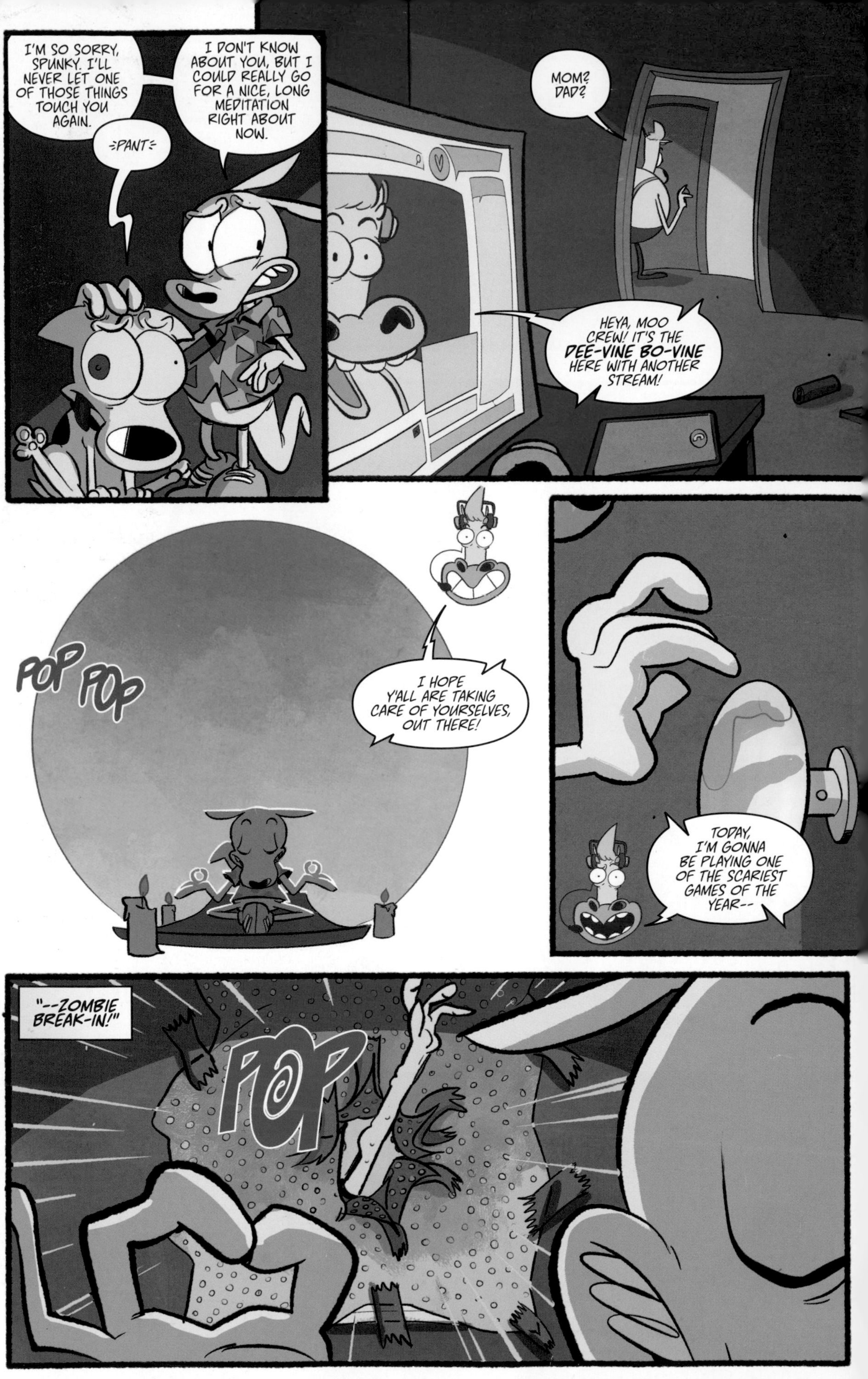
I'M SO SORRY, SPUNKY. I'LL NEVER LET ONE OF THOSE THINGS TOUCH YOU AGAIN.
I DON'T KNOW ABOUT YOU, BUT I COULD REALLY GO FOR A NICE, LONG MEDITATION RIGHT ABOUT NOW.
=PANT=
MOM? DAD?
HEYA, MOO CREW! IT'S THE DEE-VINE BO-VINE HERE WITH ANOTHER STREAM!
POP POP
I HOPE Y'ALL ARE TAKING CARE OF YOURSELVES, OUT THERE!
TODAY, I'M GONNA BE PLAYING ONE OF THE SCARIEST GAMES OF THE YEAR--
"--ZOMBIE BREAK-IN!"
POP

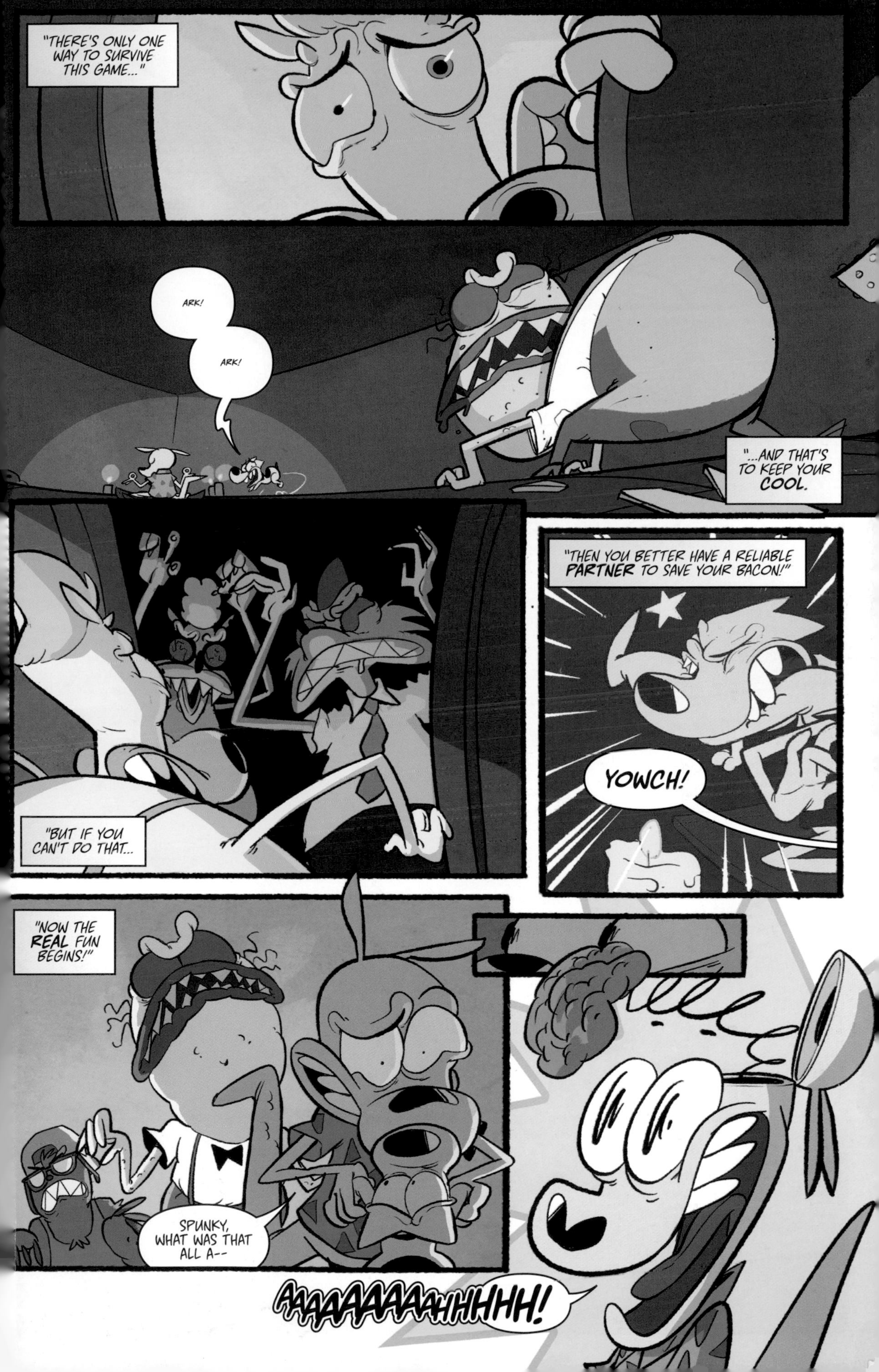
"THERE'S ONLY ONE WAY TO SURVIVE THIS GAME..."
ARK!
ARK!
"...AND THAT'S TO KEEP YOUR COOL.
"BUT IF YOU CAN'T DO THAT...
"THEN YOU BETTER HAVE A RELIABLE PARTNER TO SAVE YOUR BACON!"
YOWCH!
"NOW THE REAL FUN BEGINS!"
SPUNKY, WHAT WAS THAT ALL A--
AAAAAAAAAHHHHH!

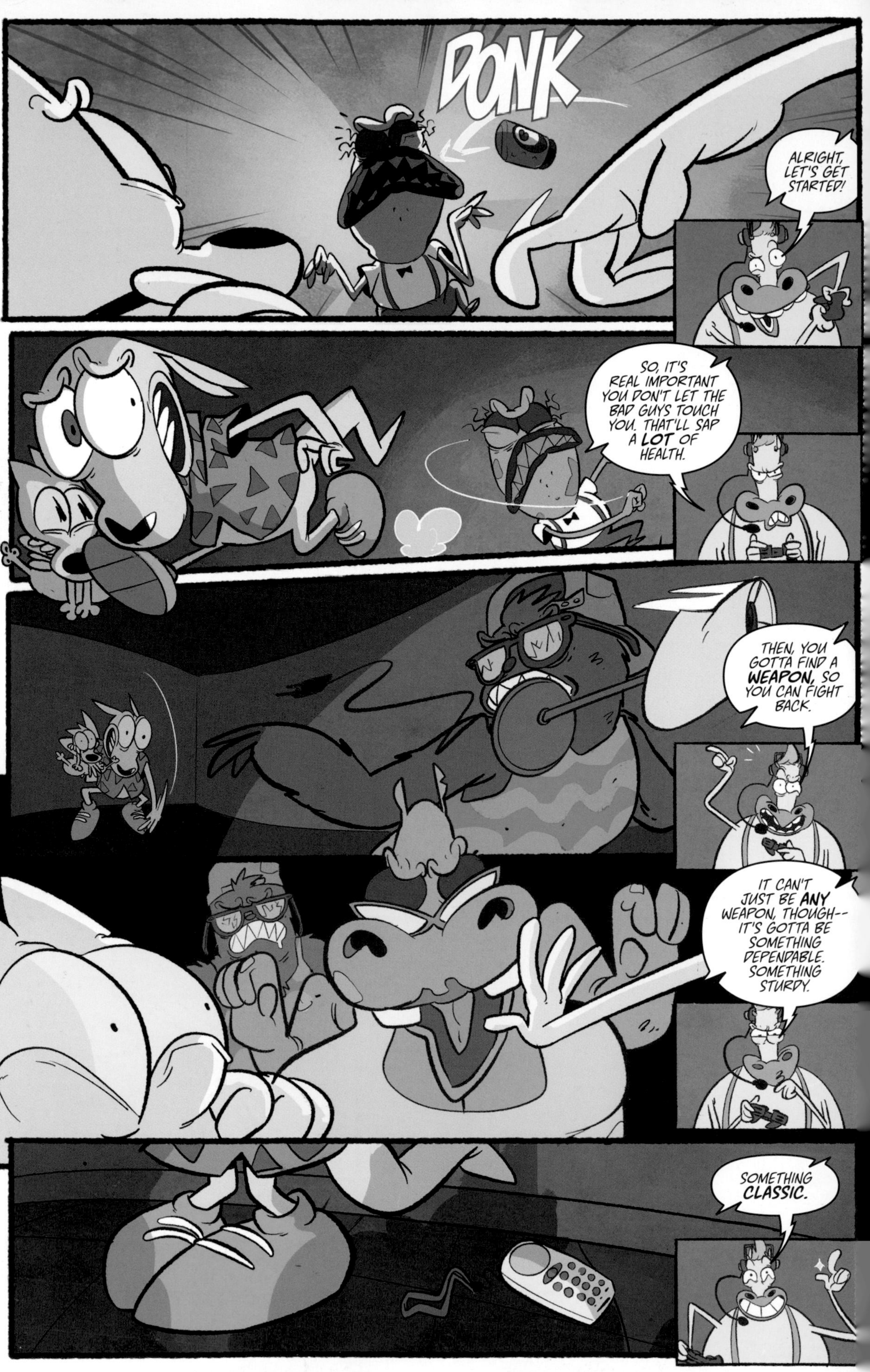
DONK
ALRIGHT, LET'S GET STARTED!
SO, IT'S REAL IMPORTANT YOU DON'T LET THE BAD GUYS TOUCH YOU. THAT'LL SAP A **LOT** OF HEALTH.
THEN, YOU GOTTA FIND A **WEAPON,** SO YOU CAN FIGHT BACK.
IT CAN'T JUST BE **ANY** WEAPON, THOUGH-- IT'S GOTTA BE SOMETHING DEPENDABLE. SOMETHING STURDY.
SOMETHING **CLASSIC.**

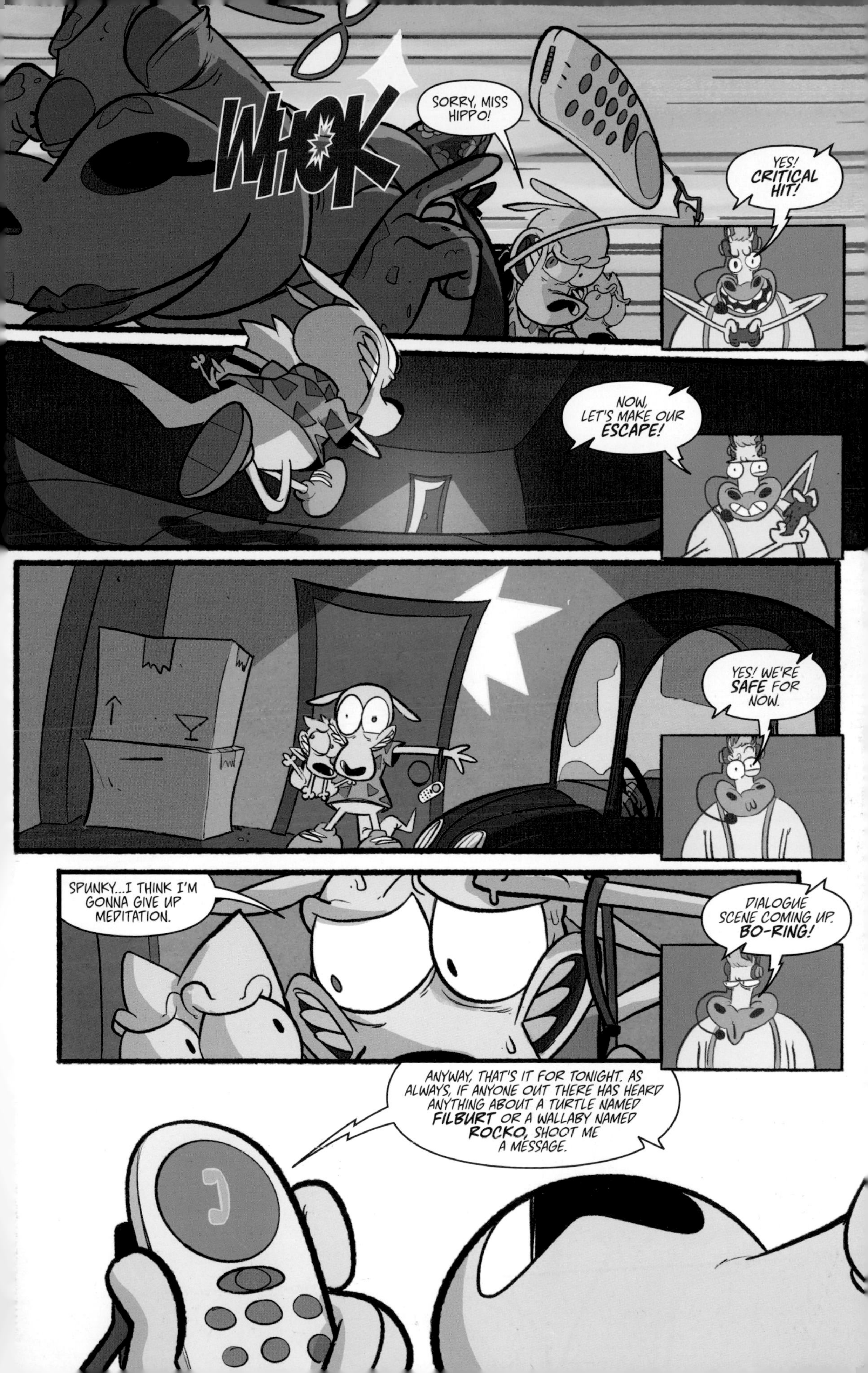
WHOK
SORRY, MISS HIPPO!
YES! CRITICAL HIT!
NOW, LET'S MAKE OUR ESCAPE!
YES! WE'RE SAFE FOR NOW.
SPUNKY...I THINK I'M GONNA GIVE UP MEDITATION.
DIALOGUE SCENE COMING UP. BO-RING!
ANYWAY, THAT'S IT FOR TONIGHT. AS ALWAYS, IF ANYONE OUT THERE HAS HEARD ANYTHING ABOUT A TURTLE NAMED FILBURT OR A WALLABY NAMED ROCKO, SHOOT ME A MESSAGE.

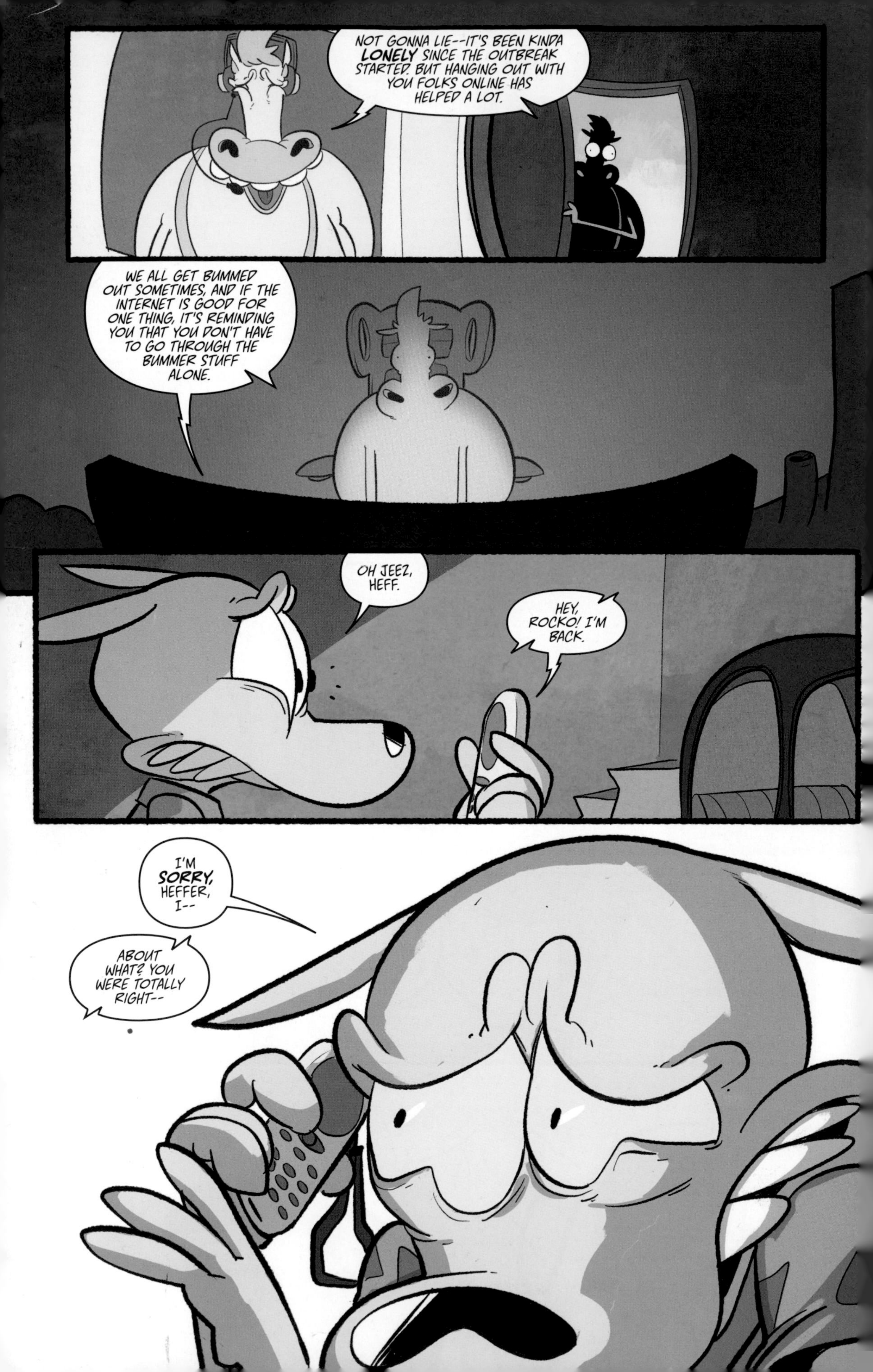
NOT GONNA LIE--IT'S BEEN KINDA LONELY SINCE THE OUTBREAK STARTED. BUT HANGING OUT WITH YOU FOLKS ONLINE HAS HELPED A LOT.
WE ALL GET BUMMED OUT SOMETIMES, AND IF THE INTERNET IS GOOD FOR ONE THING, IT'S REMINDING YOU THAT YOU DON'T HAVE TO GO THROUGH THE BUMMER STUFF ALONE.
OH JEEZ, HEFF.
HEY, ROCKO! I'M BACK.
I'M SORRY, HEFFER, I--
ABOUT WHAT? YOU WERE TOTALLY RIGHT--

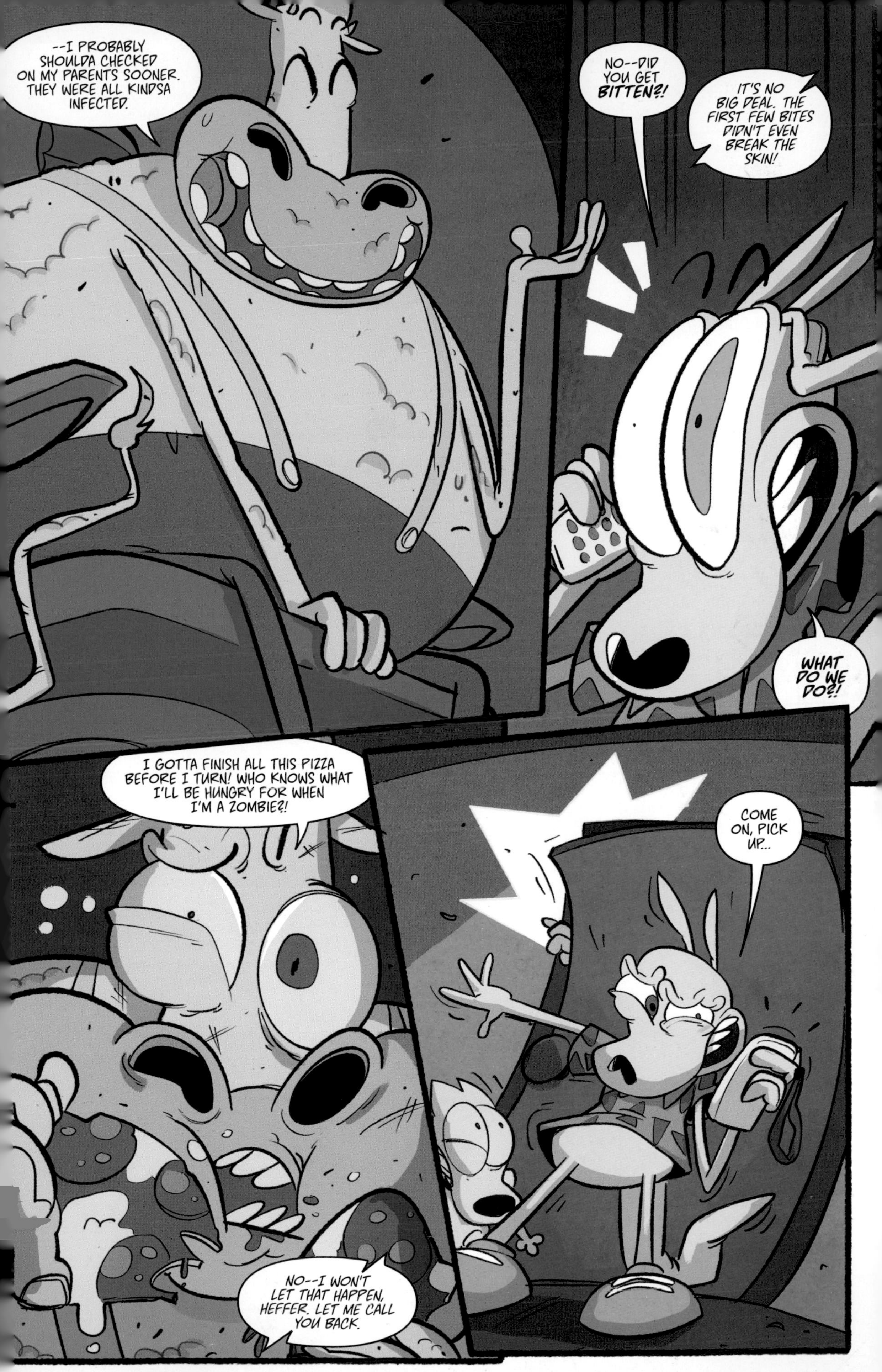
--I PROBABLY SHOULDA CHECKED ON MY PARENTS SOONER. THEY WERE ALL KINDSA INFECTED.
NO--DID YOU GET BITTEN?!
IT'S NO BIG DEAL. THE FIRST FEW BITES DIDN'T EVEN BREAK THE SKIN!
WHAT DO WE DO?!
I GOTTA FINISH ALL THIS PIZZA BEFORE I TURN! WHO KNOWS WHAT I'LL BE HUNGRY FOR WHEN I'M A ZOMBIE?!
NO--I WON'T LET THAT HAPPEN, HEFFER. LET ME CALL YOU BACK.
COME ON, PICK UP...

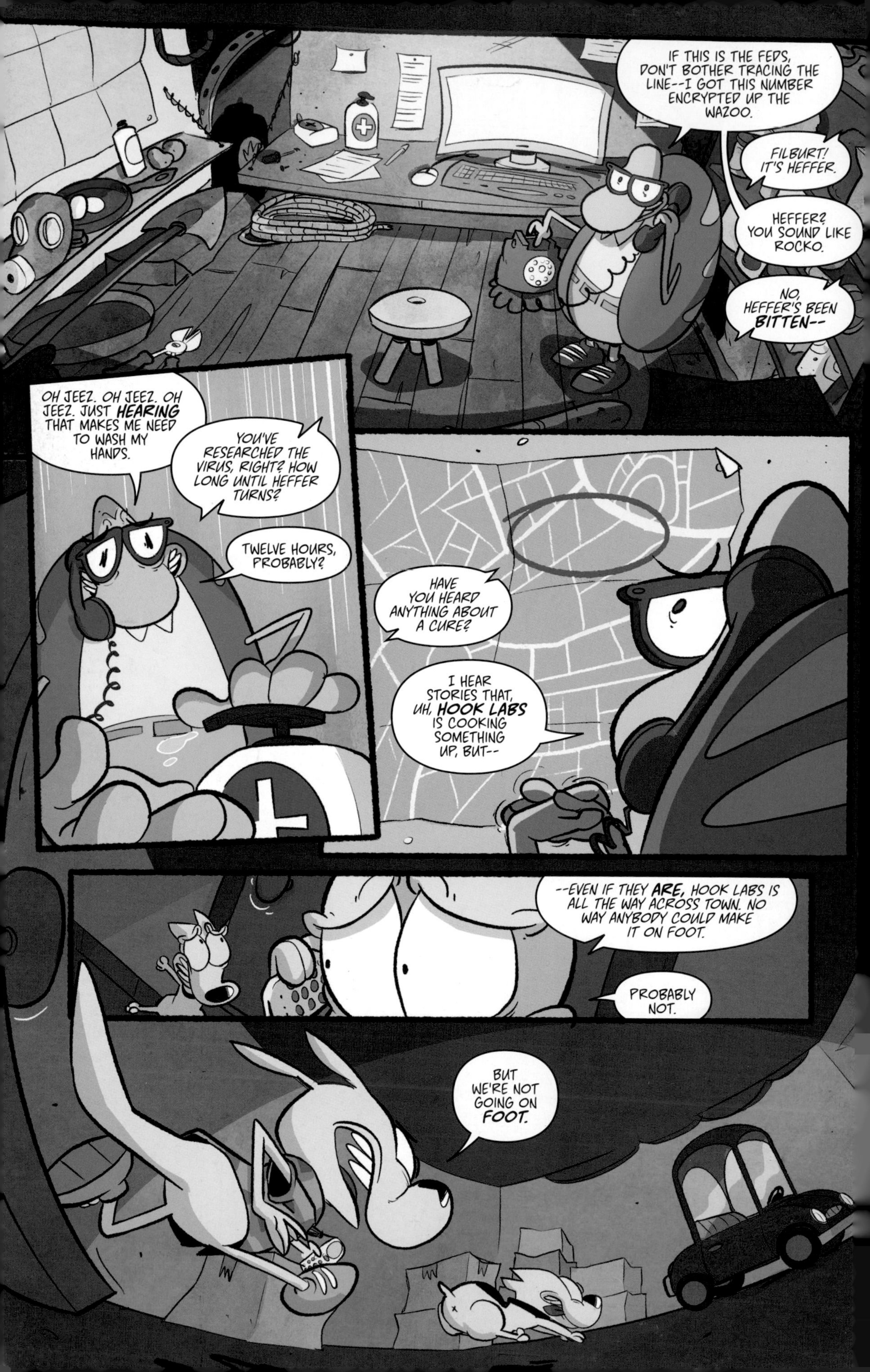
IF THIS IS THE FEDS, DON'T BOTHER TRACING THE LINE--I GOT THIS NUMBER ENCRYPTED UP THE WAZOO.
FILBURT! IT'S HEFFER.
HEFFER? YOU SOUND LIKE ROCKO.
NO, HEFFER'S BEEN BITTEN--
OH JEEZ. OH JEEZ. OH JEEZ. JUST HEARING THAT MAKES ME NEED TO WASH MY HANDS.
YOU'VE RESEARCHED THE VIRUS, RIGHT? HOW LONG UNTIL HEFFER TURNS?
TWELVE HOURS, PROBABLY?
HAVE YOU HEARD ANYTHING ABOUT A CURE?
I HEAR STORIES THAT, UH, HOOK LABS IS COOKING SOMETHING UP, BUT--
--EVEN IF THEY ARE, HOOK LABS IS ALL THE WAY ACROSS TOWN. NO WAY ANYBODY COULD MAKE IT ON FOOT.
PROBABLY NOT.
BUT WE'RE NOT GOING ON FOOT.

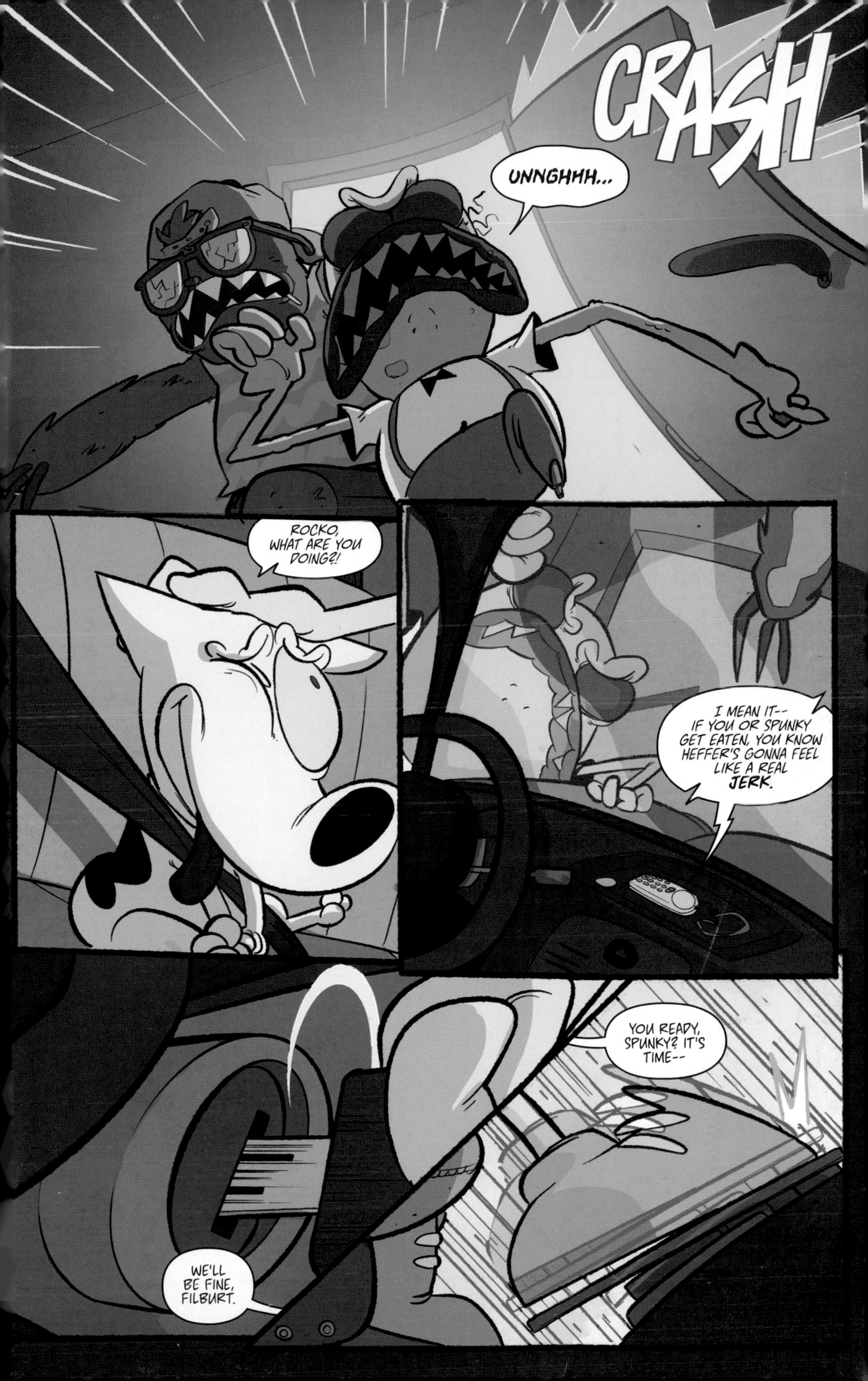
CRASH
UNNGHHH...
ROCKO, WHAT ARE YOU DOING?!
I MEAN IT-- IF YOU OR SPUNKY GET EATEN, YOU KNOW HEFFER'S GONNA FEEL LIKE A REAL JERK.
YOU READY, SPUNKY? IT'S TIME--
WE'LL BE FINE, FILBURT.

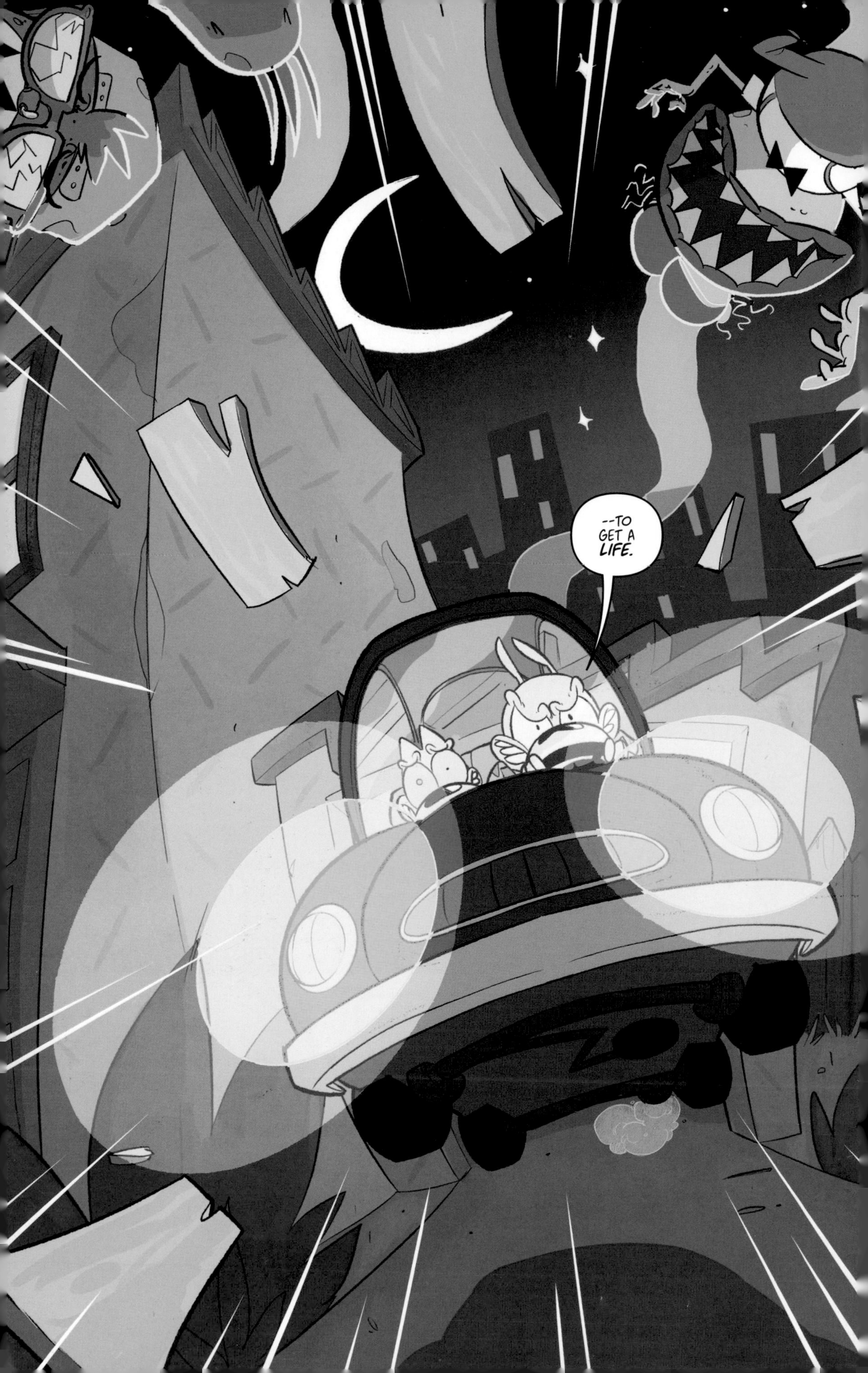
--TO GET A LIFE.

CHAPTER
TWO

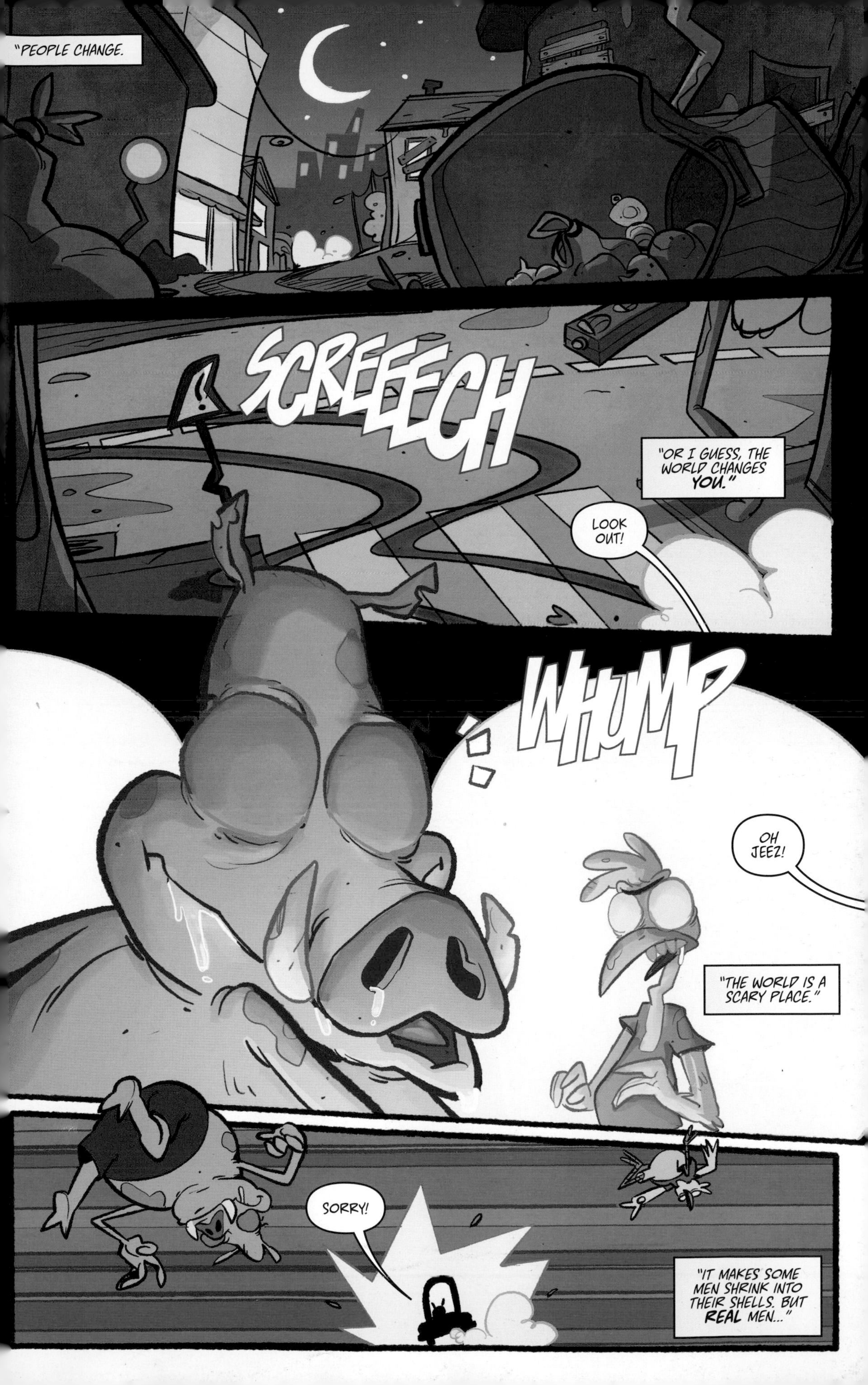
"PEOPLE CHANGE.
SCREEECH
"OR I GUESS, THE WORLD CHANGES YOU."
LOOK OUT!
WHUMP
OH JEEZ!
"THE WORLD IS A SCARY PLACE."
SORRY!
"IT MAKES SOME MEN SHRINK INTO THEIR SHELLS. BUT REAL MEN..."

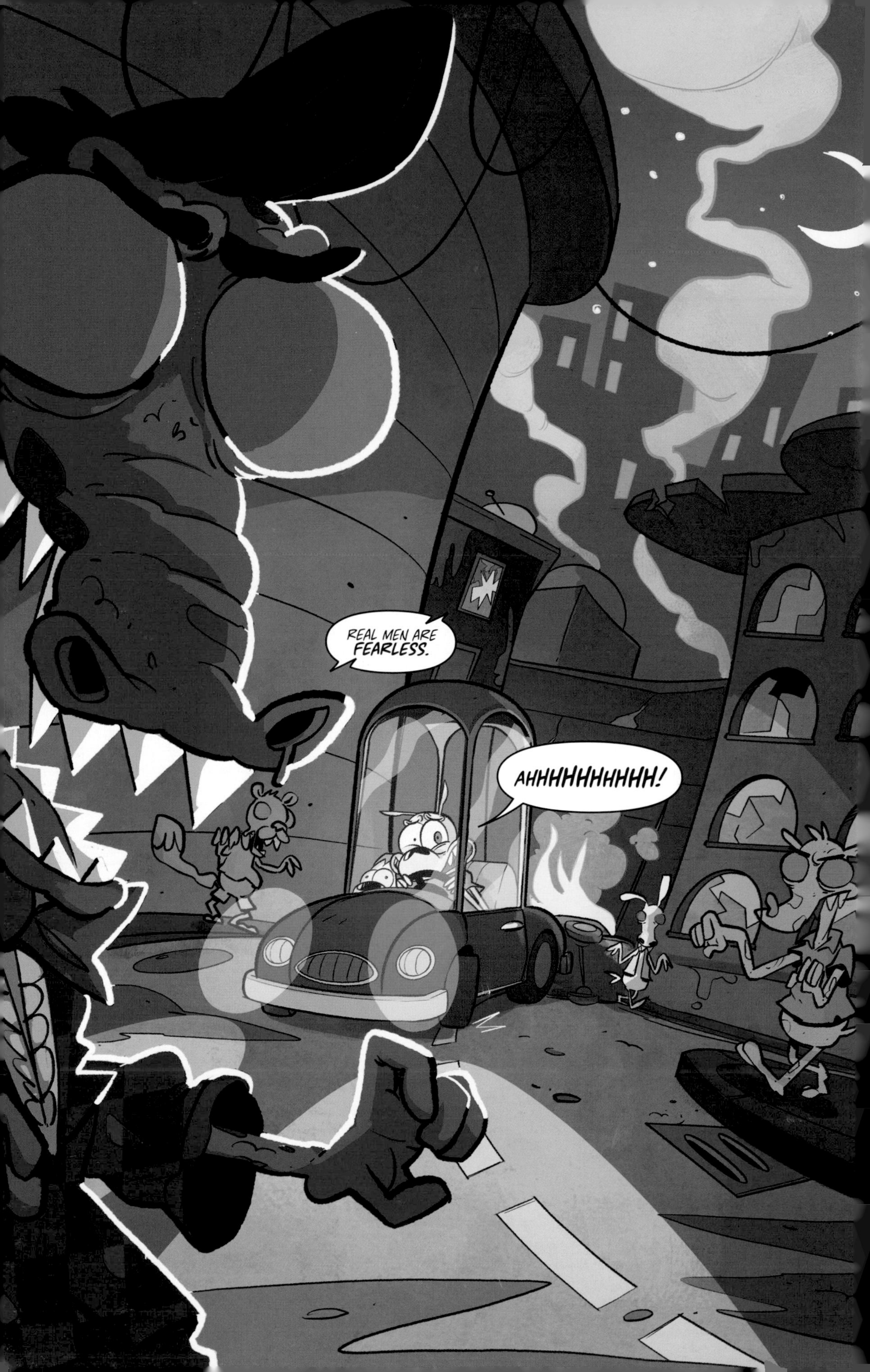
REAL MEN ARE FEARLESS.
AHHHHHHHHHH!

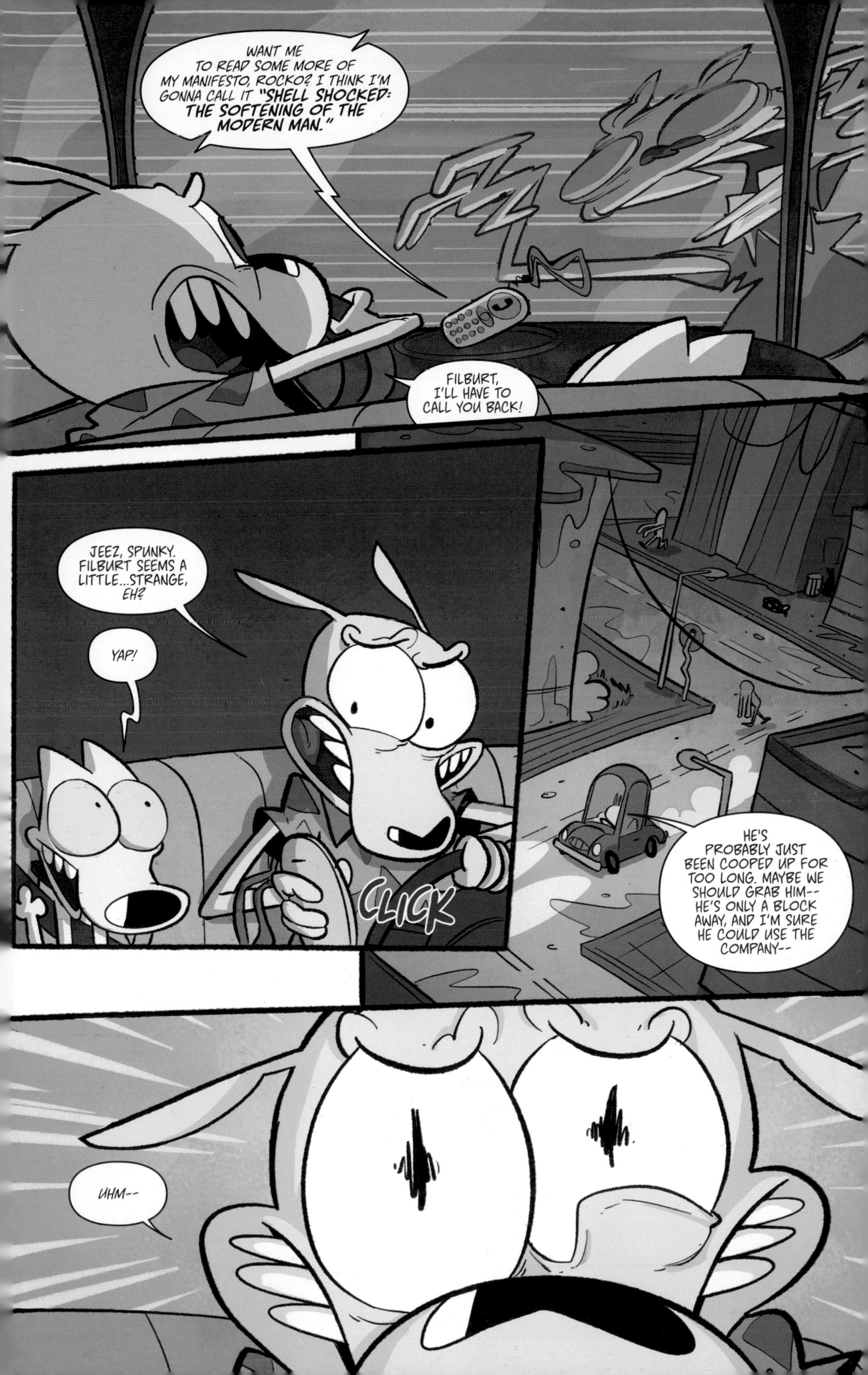
WANT ME TO READ SOME MORE OF MY MANIFESTO, ROCKO? I THINK I'M GONNA CALL IT "SHELL SHOCKED: THE SOFTENING OF THE MODERN MAN."
FILBURT, I'LL HAVE TO CALL YOU BACK!
JEEZ, SPUNKY. FILBURT SEEMS A LITTLE...STRANGE, EH?
YAP!
CLICK
HE'S PROBABLY JUST BEEN COOPED UP FOR TOO LONG. MAYBE WE SHOULD GRAB HIM--HE'S ONLY A BLOCK AWAY, AND I'M SURE HE COULD USE THE COMPANY--
UHM--

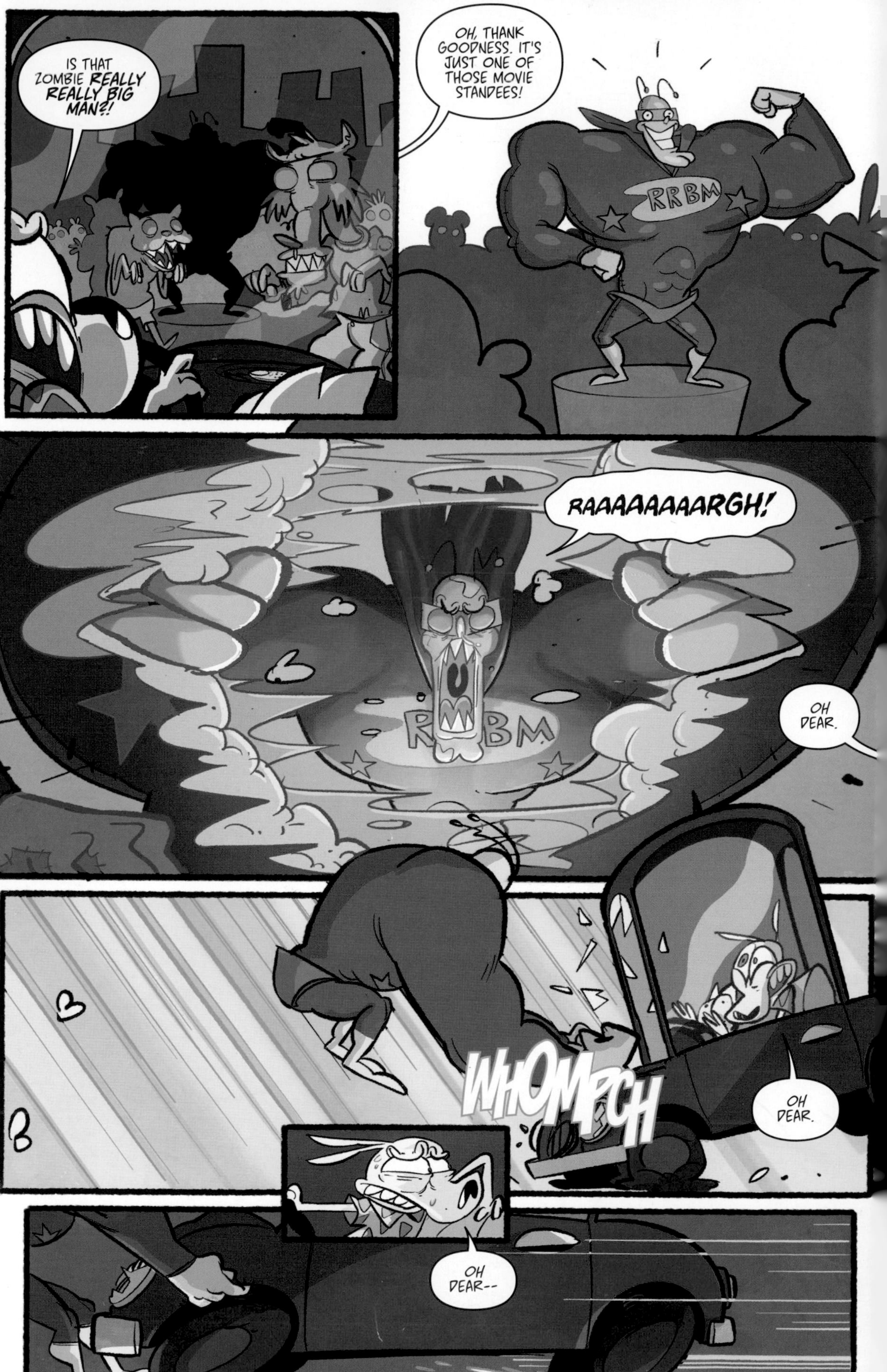
IS THAT ZOMBIE REALLY REALLY BIG MAN?!
OH, THANK GOODNESS. IT'S JUST ONE OF THOSE MOVIE STANDEES!
RRBM
RAAAAAAAARGH!
RRBM
OH DEAR.
WHOMPCH
OH DEAR.
OH DEAR--

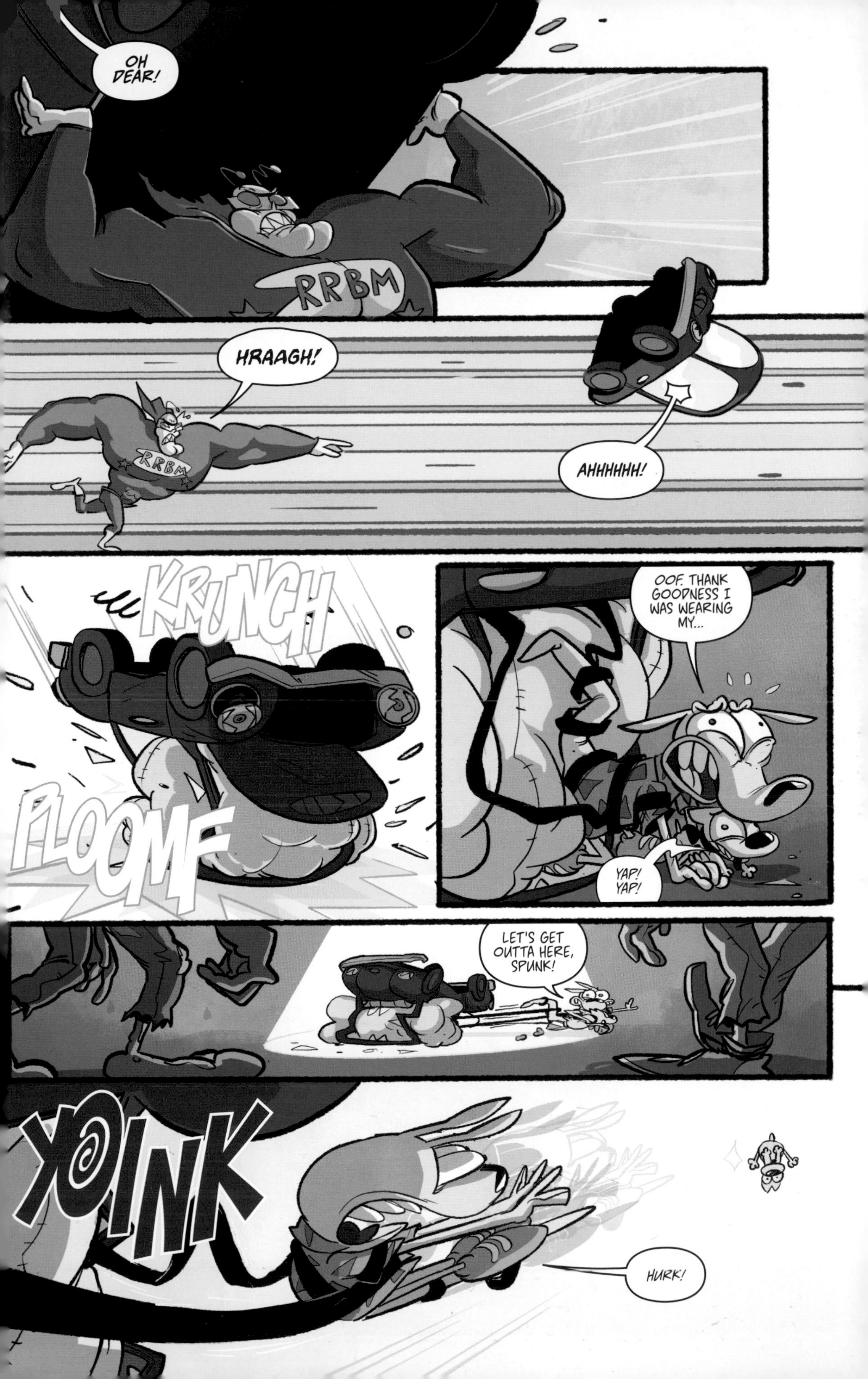
OH DEAR!
RRBM
HRAAGH!
RRBM
AHHHHHH!
KRUNCH
PLOOMF
OOF. THANK GOODNESS I WAS WEARING MY...
YAP! YAP!
LET'S GET OUTTA HERE, SPUNK!
YOINK
HURK!

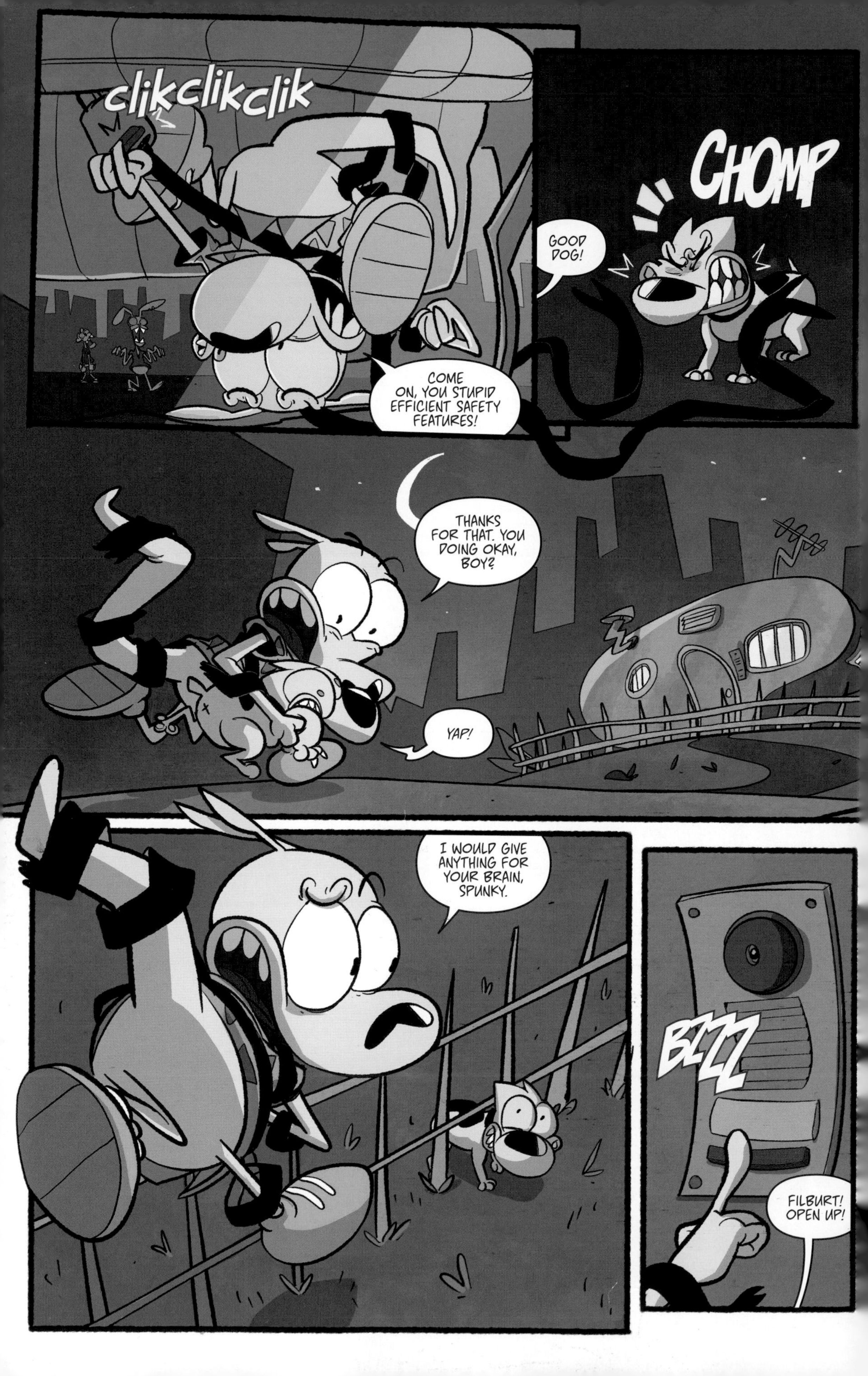
clikclikclik
COME ON, YOU STUPID EFFICIENT SAFETY FEATURES!
CHOMP
GOOD DOG!
THANKS FOR THAT. YOU DOING OKAY, BOY?
YAP!
I WOULD GIVE ANYTHING FOR YOUR BRAIN, SPUNKY.
BZZZ
FILBURT! OPEN UP!

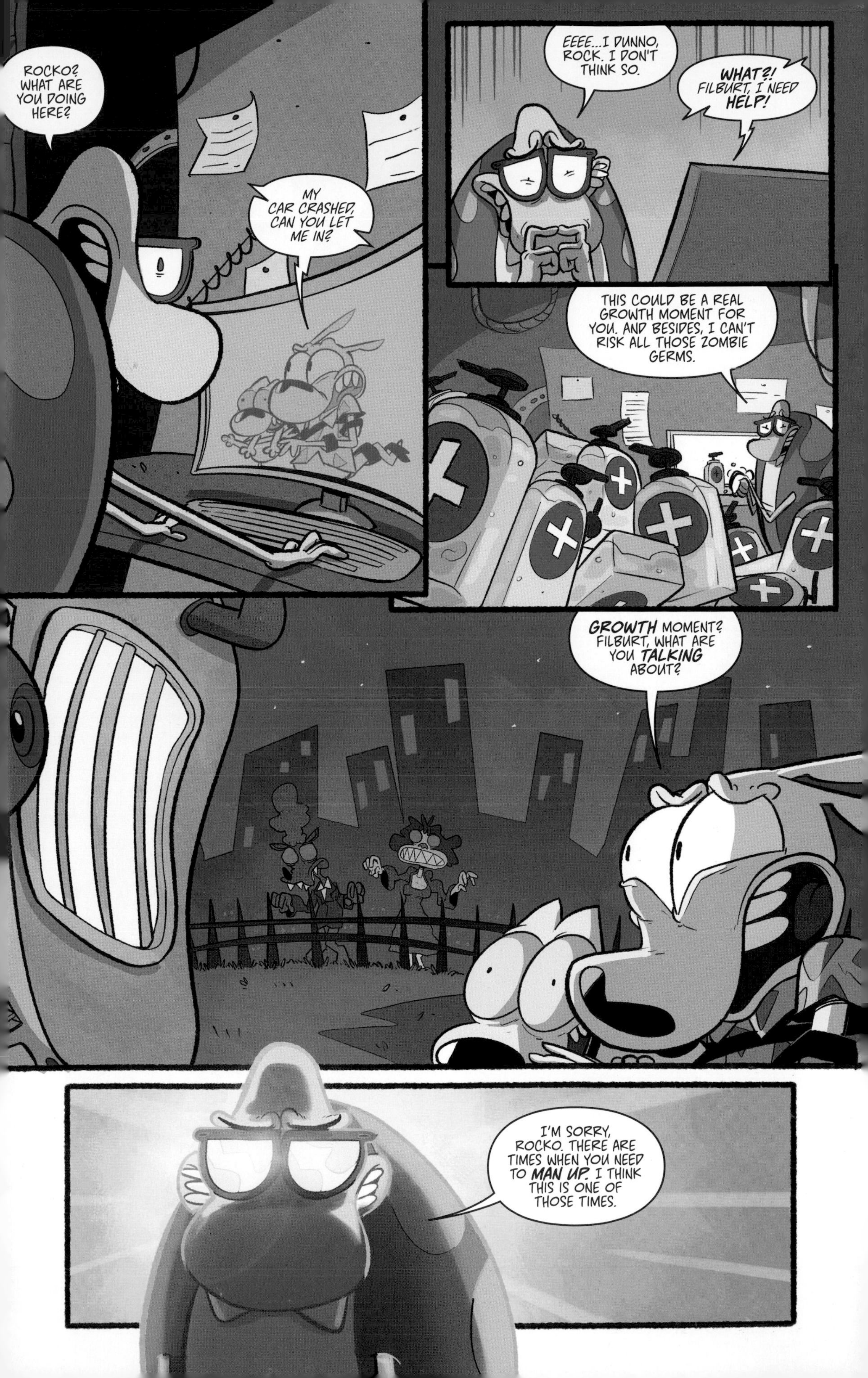
ROCKO? WHAT ARE YOU DOING HERE?
MY CAR CRASHED. CAN YOU LET ME IN?
EEEE...I DUNNO, ROCK. I DON'T THINK SO.
WHAT?! FILBURT, I NEED HELP!
THIS COULD BE A REAL GROWTH MOMENT FOR YOU. AND BESIDES, I CAN'T RISK ALL THOSE ZOMBIE GERMS.
GROWTH MOMENT? FILBURT, WHAT ARE YOU TALKING ABOUT?
I'M SORRY, ROCKO. THERE ARE TIMES WHEN YOU NEED TO MAN UP. I THINK THIS IS ONE OF THOSE TIMES.

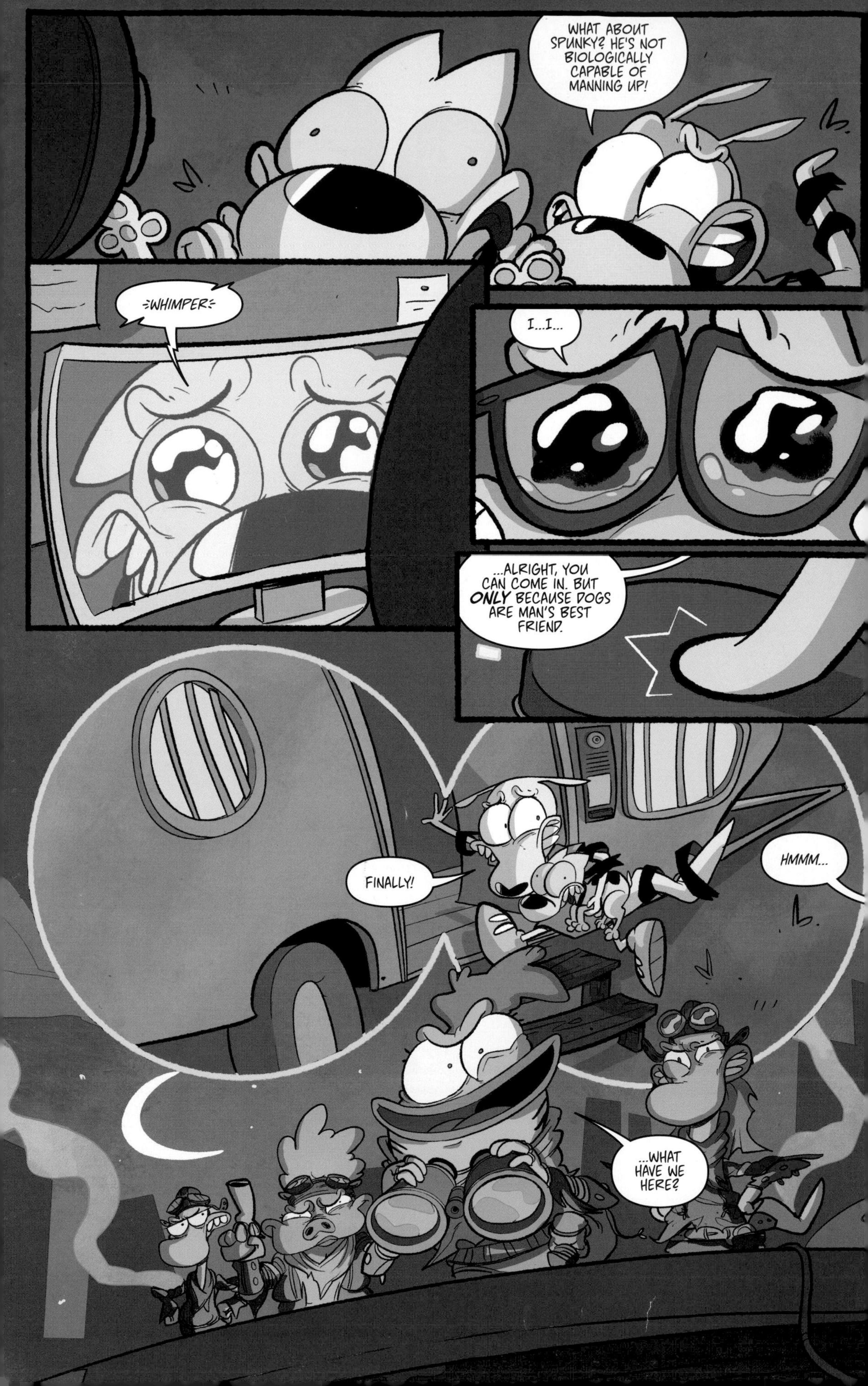
WHAT ABOUT SPUNKY? HE'S NOT BIOLOGICALLY CAPABLE OF MANNING UP!
=WHIMPER=
I...I...
...ALRIGHT, YOU CAN COME IN. BUT ONLY BECAUSE DOGS ARE MAN'S BEST FRIEND.
FINALLY!
HMMM...
...WHAT HAVE WE HERE?

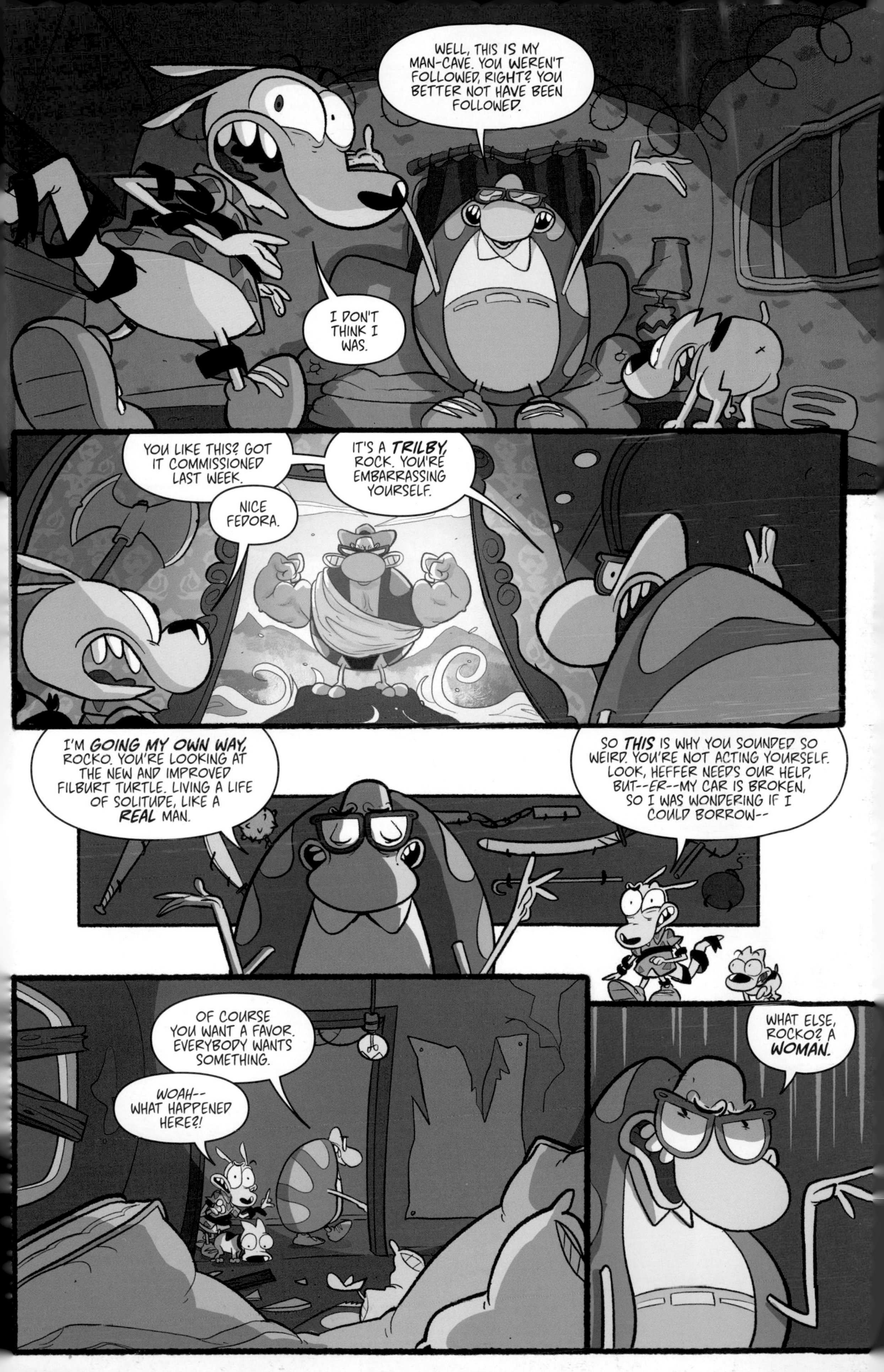
WELL, THIS IS MY MAN-CAVE. YOU WEREN'T FOLLOWED, RIGHT? YOU BETTER NOT HAVE BEEN FOLLOWED.
I DON'T THINK I WAS.
YOU LIKE THIS? GOT IT COMMISSIONED LAST WEEK.
NICE FEDORA.
IT'S A **TRILBY,** ROCK. YOU'RE EMBARRASSING YOURSELF.
I'M **GOING MY OWN WAY,** ROCKO. YOU'RE LOOKING AT THE NEW AND IMPROVED FILBURT TURTLE. LIVING A LIFE OF SOLITUDE, LIKE A **REAL** MAN.
SO **THIS** IS WHY YOU SOUNDED SO WEIRD. YOU'RE NOT ACTING YOURSELF. LOOK, HEFFER NEEDS OUR HELP, BUT--*ER*--MY CAR IS BROKEN, SO I WAS WONDERING IF I COULD BORROW--
OF COURSE YOU WANT A FAVOR. EVERYBODY WANTS SOMETHING.
WOAH-- WHAT HAPPENED HERE?!
WHAT ELSE, ROCKO? A **WOMAN.**

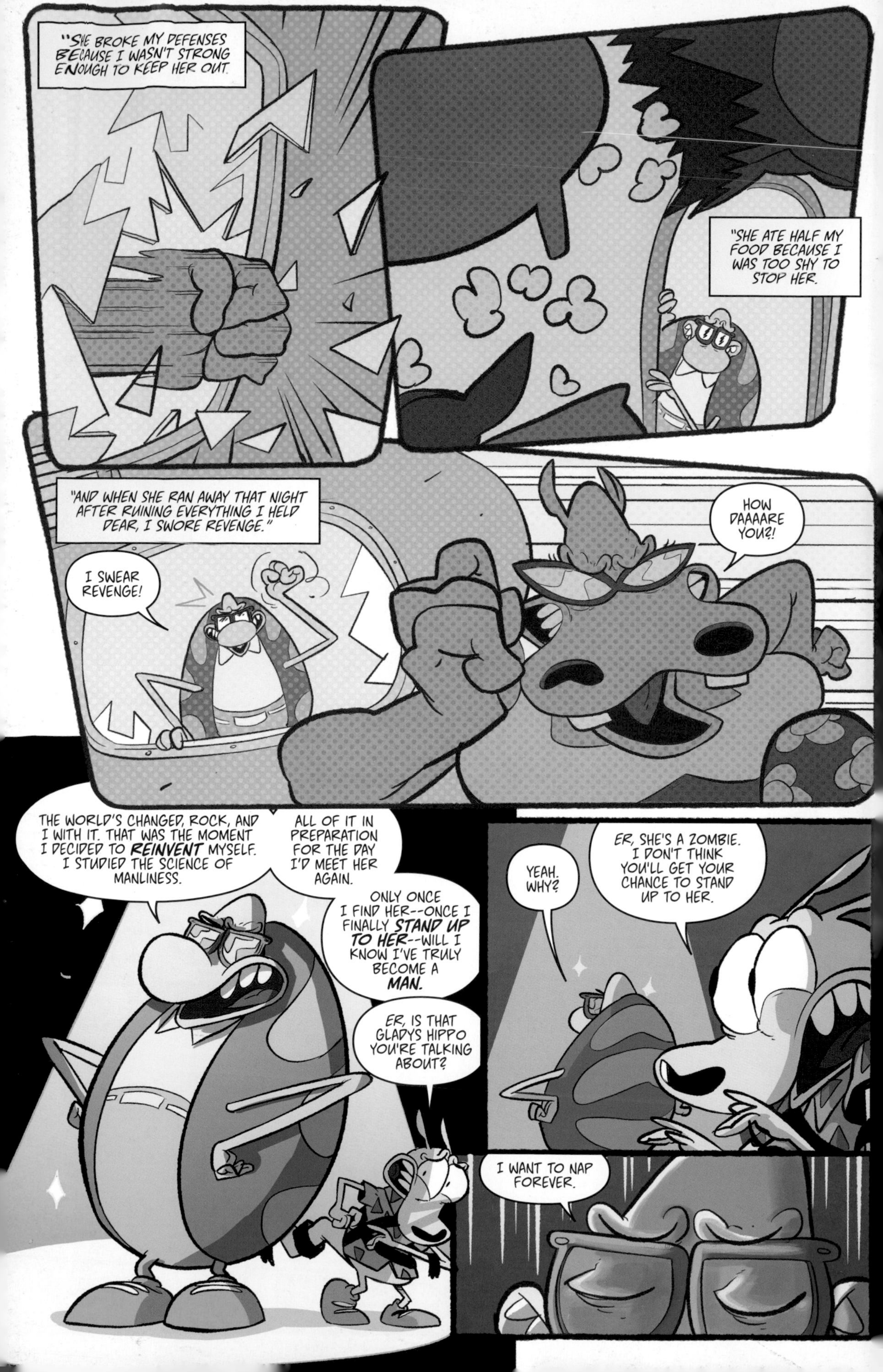
"SHE BROKE MY DEFENSES BECAUSE I WASN'T STRONG ENOUGH TO KEEP HER OUT.
"SHE ATE HALF MY FOOD BECAUSE I WAS TOO SHY TO STOP HER.
"AND WHEN SHE RAN AWAY THAT NIGHT AFTER RUINING EVERYTHING I HELD DEAR, I SWORE REVENGE."
I SWEAR REVENGE!
HOW DAAAARE YOU?!
THE WORLD'S CHANGED, ROCK, AND I WITH IT. THAT WAS THE MOMENT I DECIDED TO REINVENT MYSELF. I STUDIED THE SCIENCE OF MANLINESS.
ALL OF IT IN PREPARATION FOR THE DAY I'D MEET HER AGAIN.
ONLY ONCE I FIND HER--ONCE I FINALLY STAND UP TO HER--WILL I KNOW I'VE TRULY BECOME A MAN.
ER, IS THAT GLADYS HIPPO YOU'RE TALKING ABOUT?
YEAH. WHY?
ER, SHE'S A ZOMBIE. I DON'T THINK YOU'LL GET YOUR CHANCE TO STAND UP TO HER.
I WANT TO NAP FOREVER.

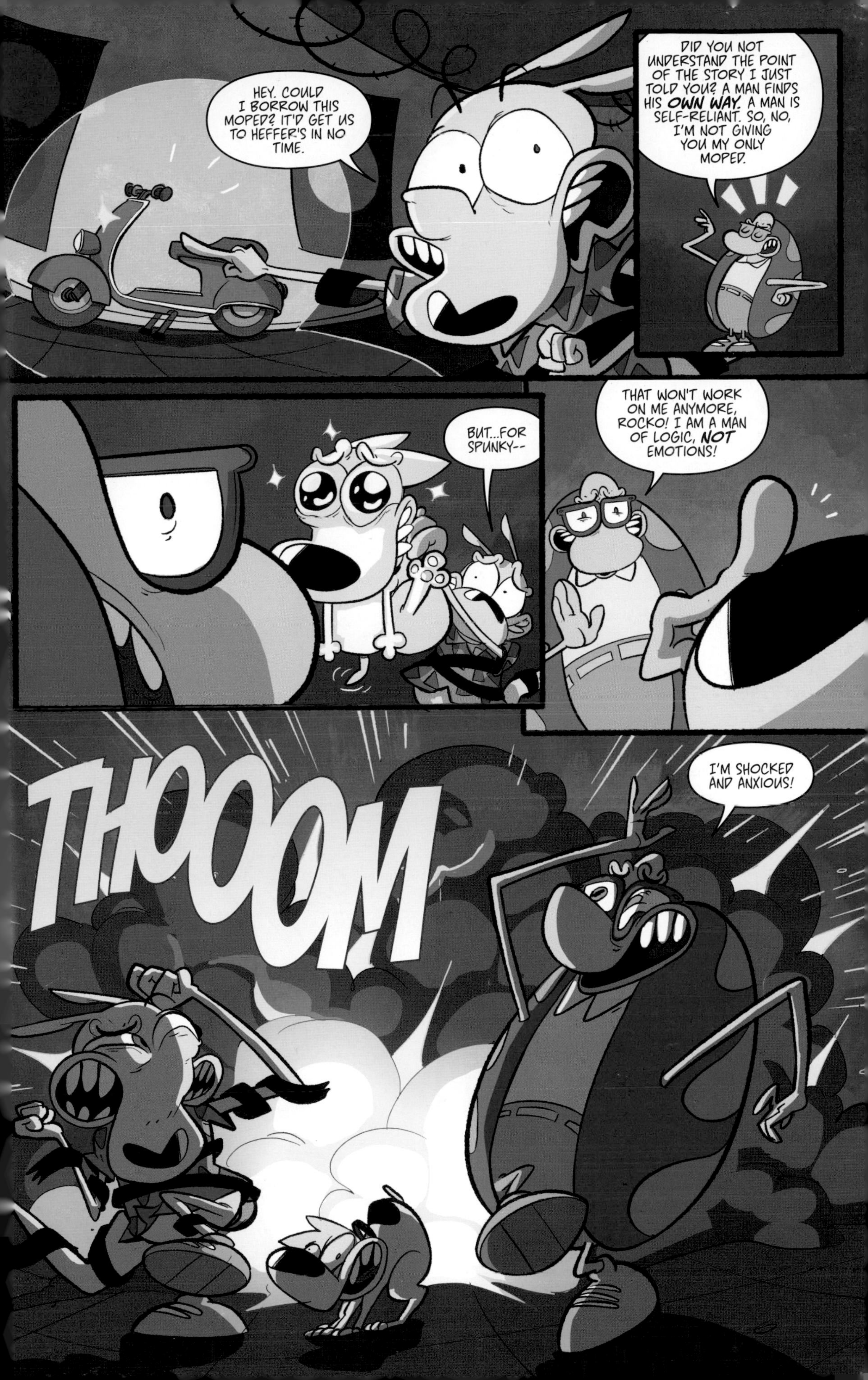
HEY. COULD I BORROW THIS MOPED? IT'D GET US TO HEFFER'S IN NO TIME.
DID YOU NOT UNDERSTAND THE POINT OF THE STORY I JUST TOLD YOU? A MAN FINDS HIS **OWN WAY.** A MAN IS SELF-RELIANT. SO, NO, I'M NOT GIVING YOU MY ONLY MOPED.
BUT...FOR SPUNKY--
THAT WON'T WORK ON ME ANYMORE, ROCKO! I AM A MAN OF LOGIC, **NOT** EMOTIONS!
THOOOM
I'M SHOCKED AND ANXIOUS!

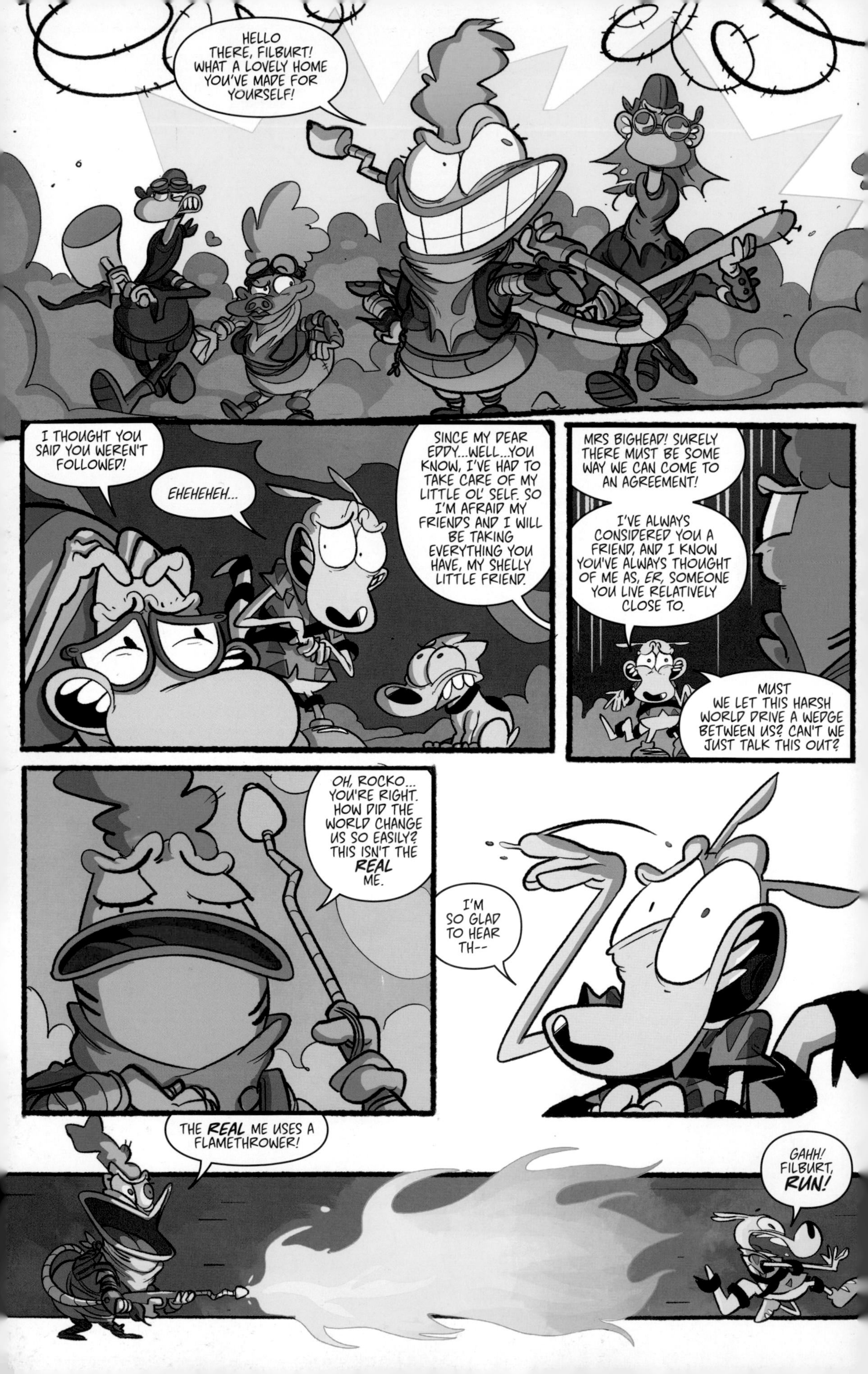
HELLO THERE, FILBURT! WHAT A LOVELY HOME YOU'VE MADE FOR YOURSELF!
I THOUGHT YOU SAID YOU WEREN'T FOLLOWED!
EHEHEHEH...
SINCE MY DEAR EDDY...WELL...YOU KNOW, I'VE HAD TO TAKE CARE OF MY LITTLE OL' SELF. SO I'M AFRAID MY FRIENDS AND I WILL BE TAKING EVERYTHING YOU HAVE, MY SHELLY LITTLE FRIEND.
MRS BIGHEAD! SURELY THERE MUST BE SOME WAY WE CAN COME TO AN AGREEMENT!
I'VE ALWAYS CONSIDERED YOU A FRIEND, AND I KNOW YOU'VE ALWAYS THOUGHT OF ME AS, ER, SOMEONE YOU LIVE RELATIVELY CLOSE TO.
MUST WE LET THIS HARSH WORLD DRIVE A WEDGE BETWEEN US? CAN'T WE JUST TALK THIS OUT?
OH, ROCKO... YOU'RE RIGHT. HOW DID THE WORLD CHANGE US SO EASILY? THIS ISN'T THE REAL ME.
I'M SO GLAD TO HEAR TH--
THE REAL ME USES A FLAMETHROWER!
GAHH! FILBURT, RUN!

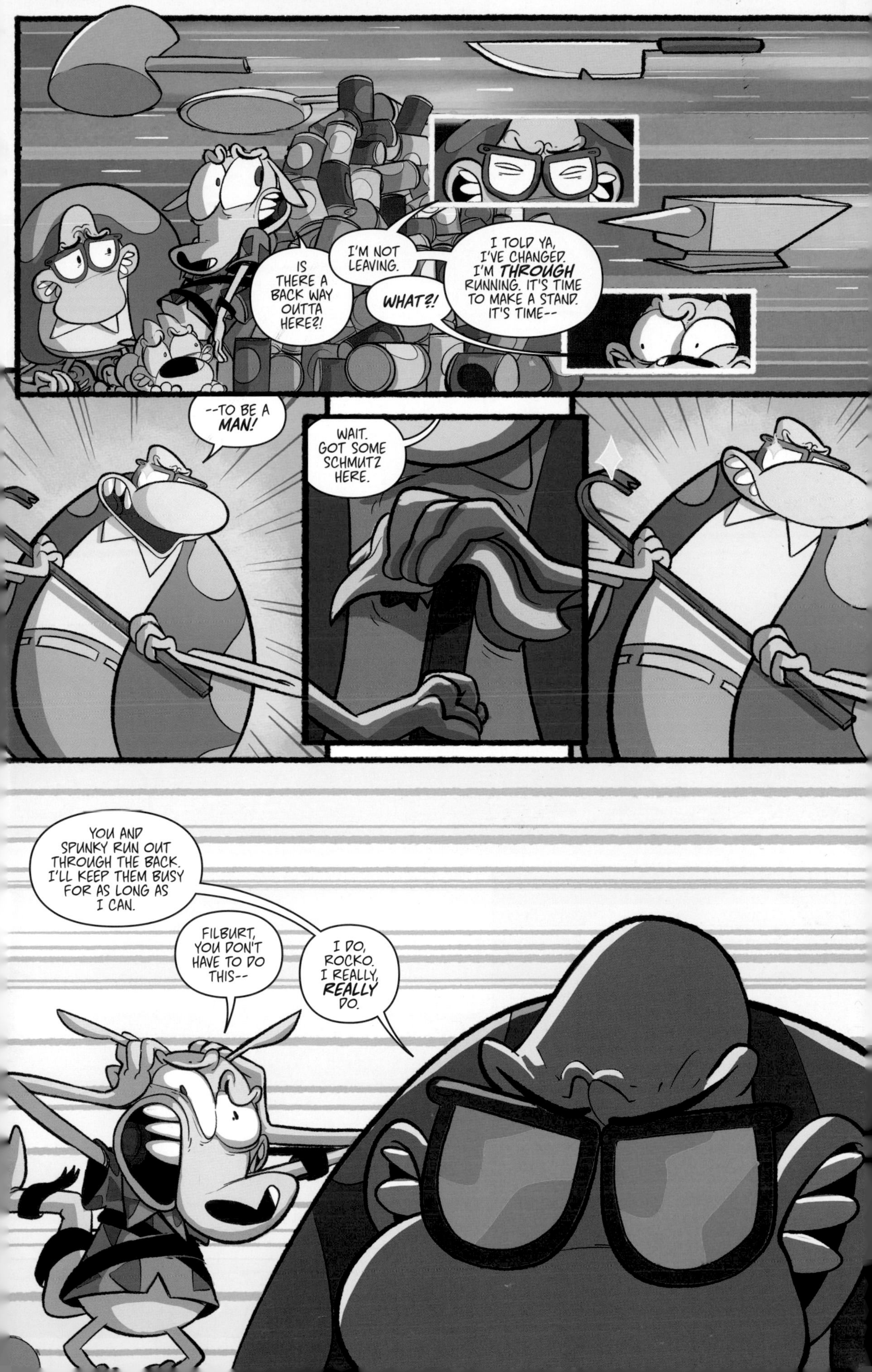
IS THERE A BACK WAY OUTTA HERE?!
I'M NOT LEAVING.
WHAT?!
I TOLD YA, I'VE CHANGED. I'M THROUGH RUNNING. IT'S TIME TO MAKE A STAND. IT'S TIME--
--TO BE A MAN!
WAIT. GOT SOME SCHMUTZ HERE.
YOU AND SPUNKY RUN OUT THROUGH THE BACK. I'LL KEEP THEM BUSY FOR AS LONG AS I CAN.
FILBURT, YOU DON'T HAVE TO DO THIS--
I DO, ROCKO. I REALLY, REALLY DO.

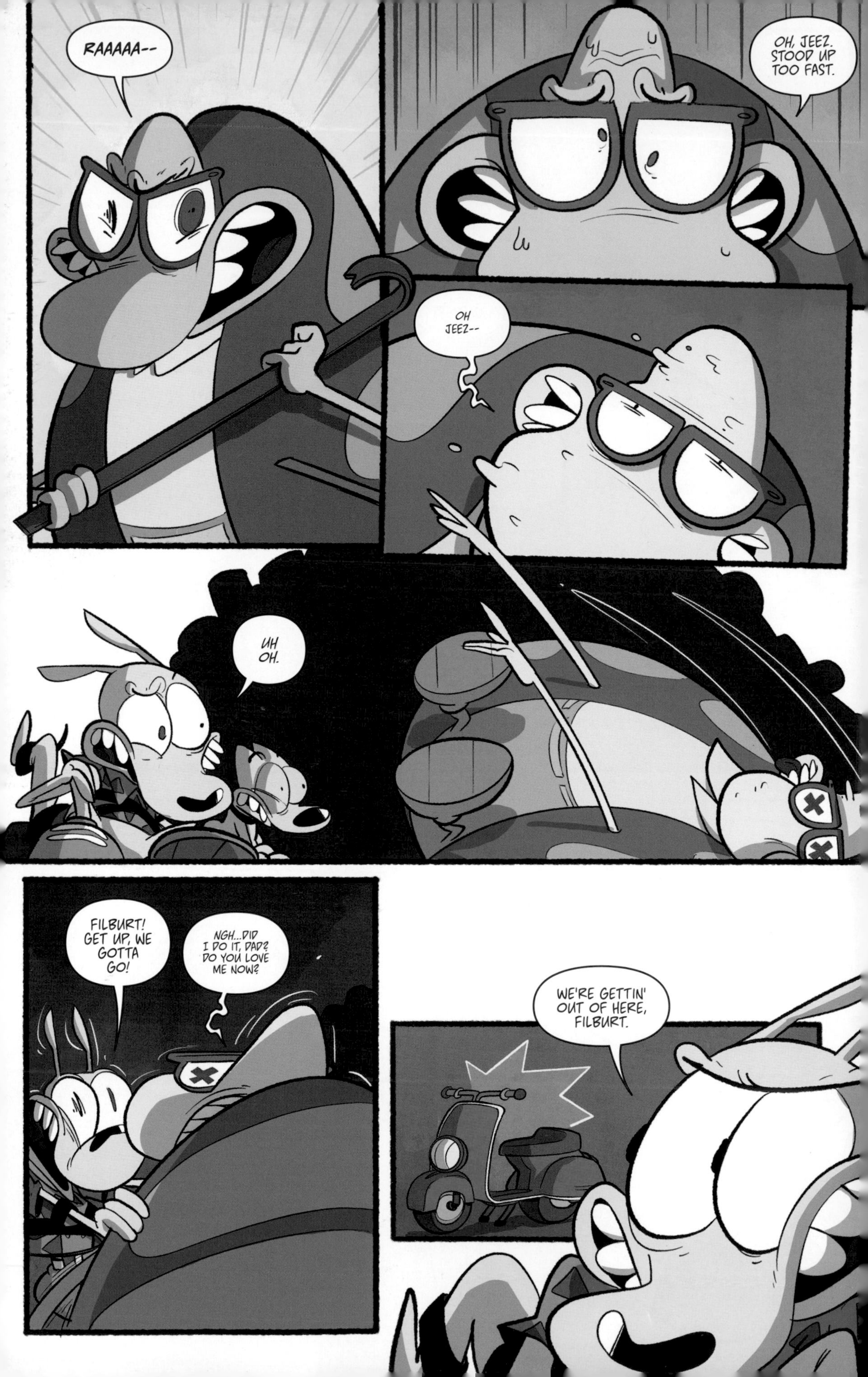
RAAAAA--
OH, JEEZ. STOOD UP TOO FAST.
OH JEEZ--
UH OH.
FILBURT! GET UP, WE GOTTA GO!
NGH...DID I DO IT, DAD? DO YOU LOVE ME NOW?
WE'RE GETTIN' OUT OF HERE, FILBURT.

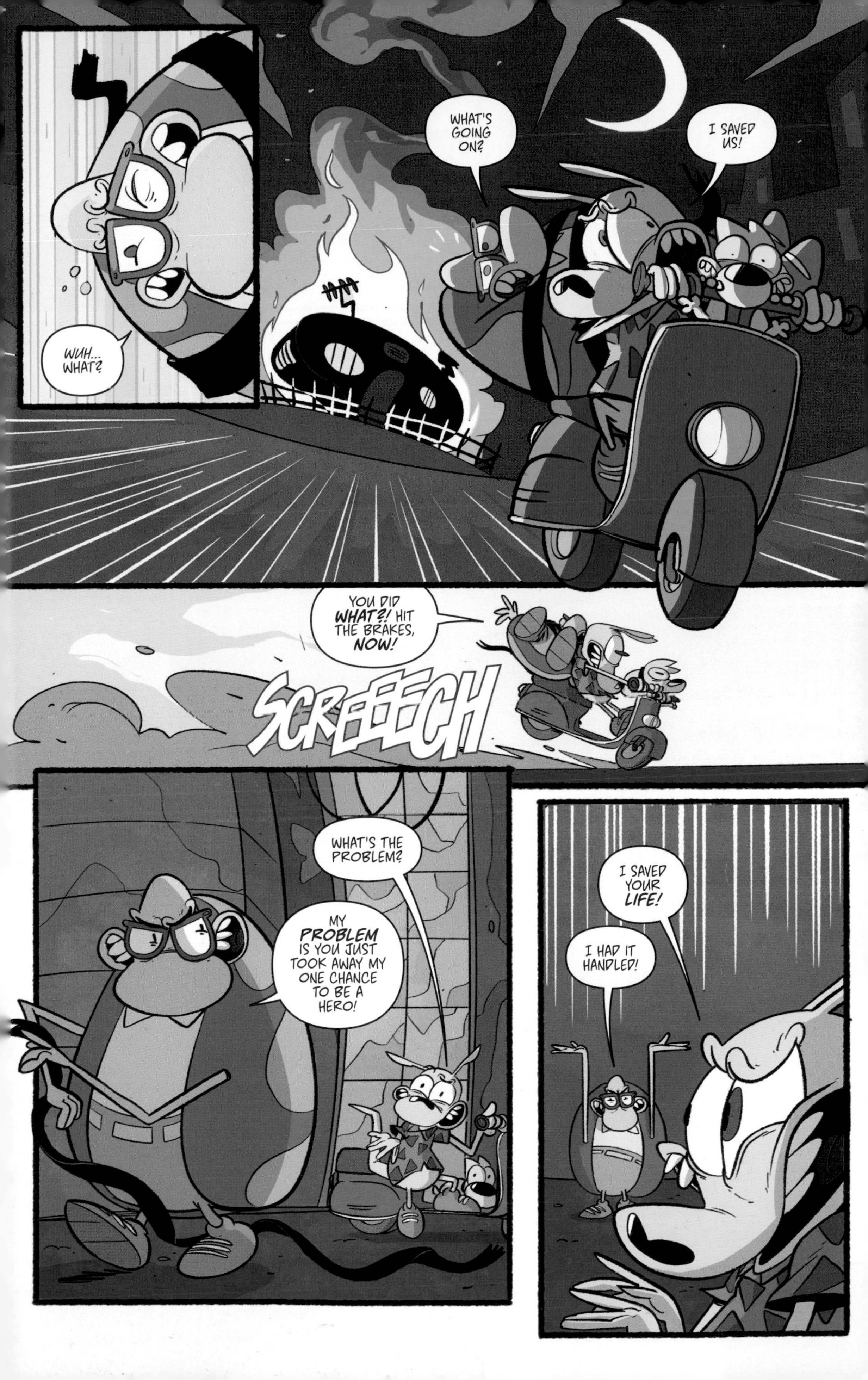
WUH... WHAT?
WHAT'S GOING ON?
I SAVED US!
YOU DID WHAT?! HIT THE BRAKES, NOW!
SCREEECH
WHAT'S THE PROBLEM?
MY PROBLEM IS YOU JUST TOOK AWAY MY ONE CHANCE TO BE A HERO!
I SAVED YOUR LIFE!
I HAD IT HANDLED!

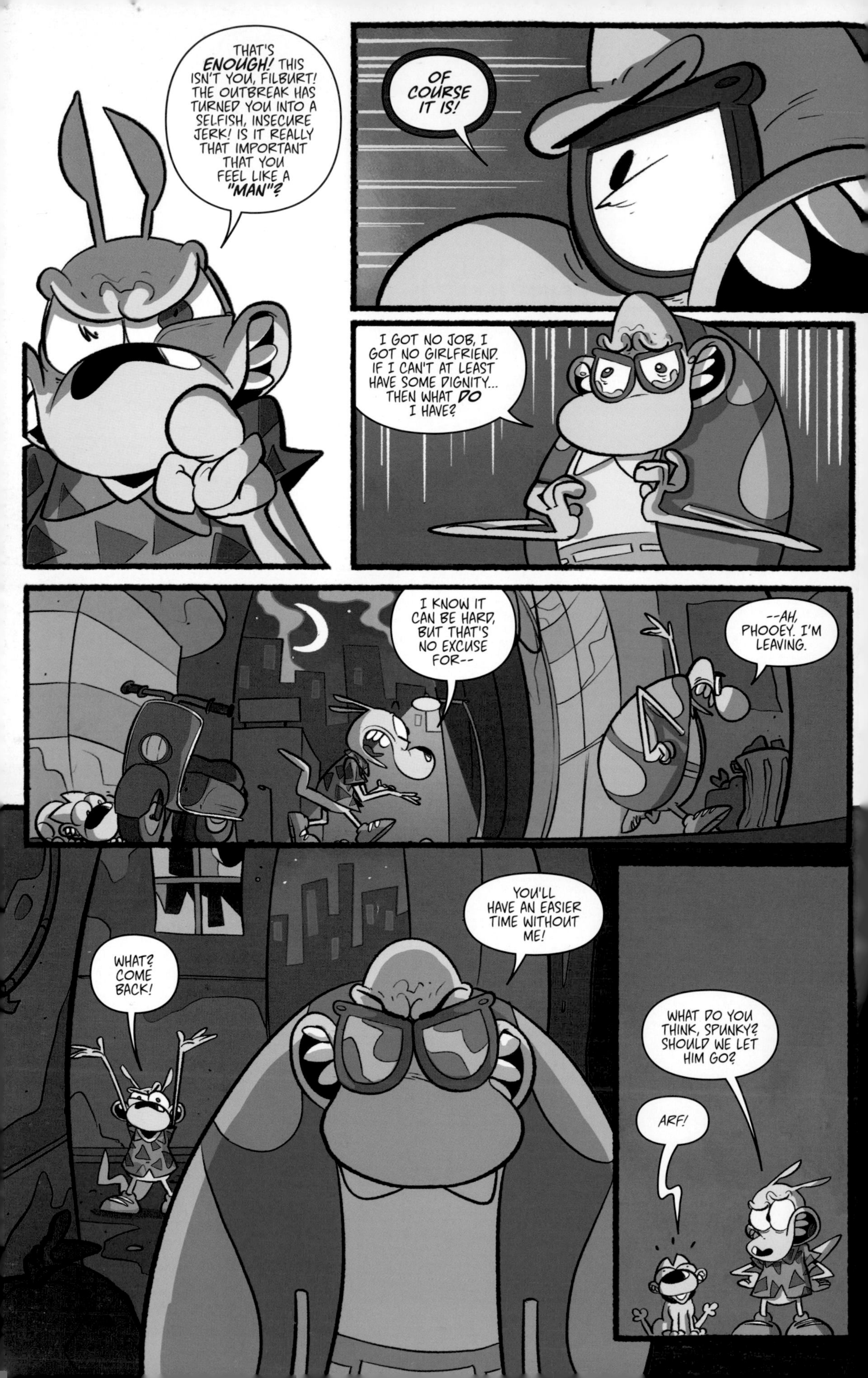
THAT'S ENOUGH! THIS ISN'T YOU, FILBURT! THE OUTBREAK HAS TURNED YOU INTO A SELFISH, INSECURE JERK! IS IT REALLY THAT IMPORTANT THAT YOU FEEL LIKE A "MAN"?
OF COURSE IT IS!
I GOT NO JOB, I GOT NO GIRLFRIEND. IF I CAN'T AT LEAST HAVE SOME DIGNITY... THEN WHAT DO I HAVE?
I KNOW IT CAN BE HARD, BUT THAT'S NO EXCUSE FOR--
--AH, PHOOEY. I'M LEAVING.
WHAT? COME BACK!
YOU'LL HAVE AN EASIER TIME WITHOUT ME!
WHAT DO YOU THINK, SPUNKY? SHOULD WE LET HIM GO?
ARF!

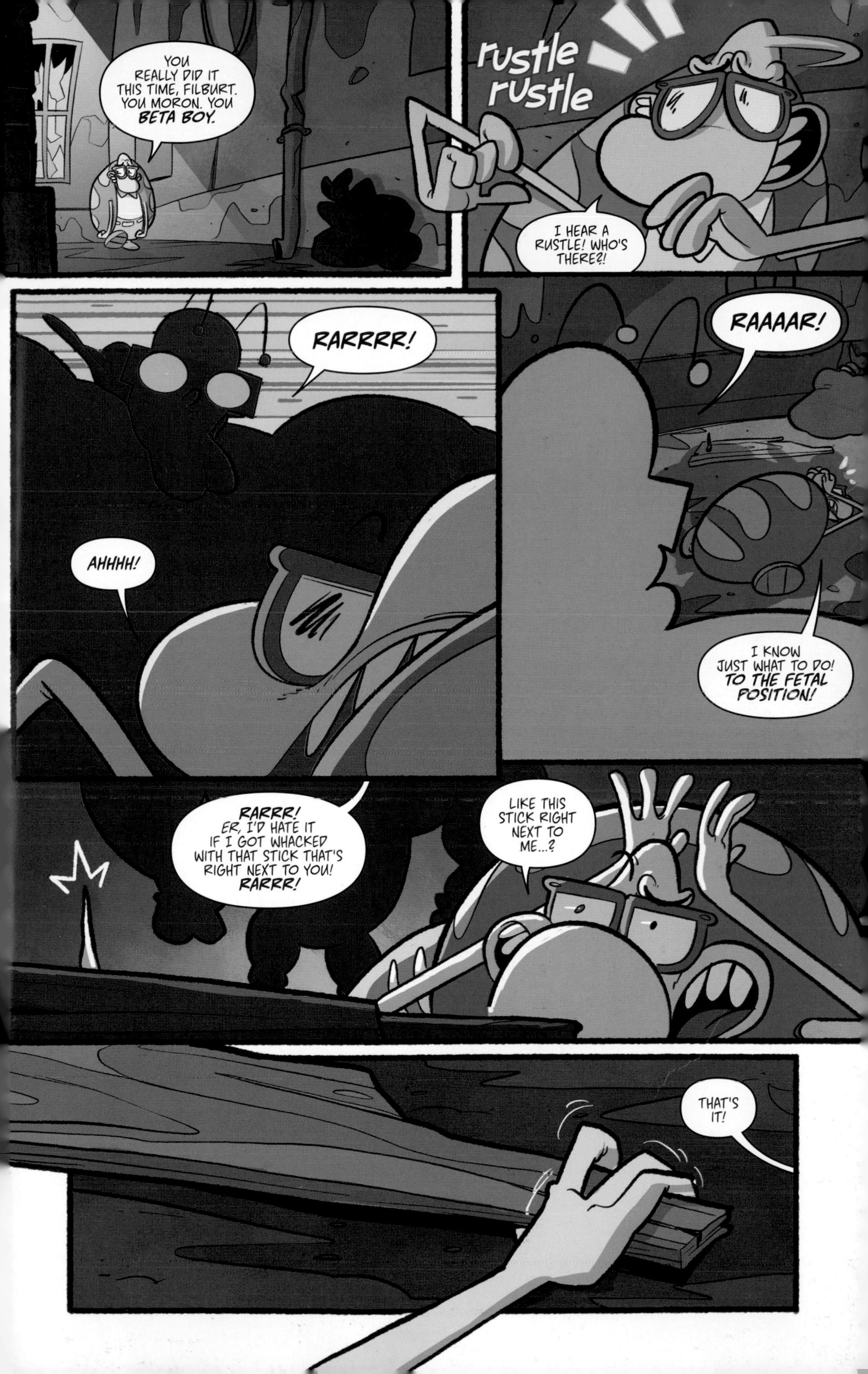
YOU REALLY DID IT THIS TIME, FILBURT. YOU MORON. YOU **BETA BOY.**
rustle rustle
I HEAR A RUSTLE! WHO'S THERE?!
RARRRR!
AHHHH!
RAAAAR!
I KNOW JUST WHAT TO DO! **TO THE FETAL POSITION!**
RARRR! ER, I'D HATE IT IF I GOT WHACKED WITH THAT STICK THAT'S RIGHT NEXT TO YOU! **RARRR!**
LIKE THIS STICK RIGHT NEXT TO ME...?
THAT'S IT!

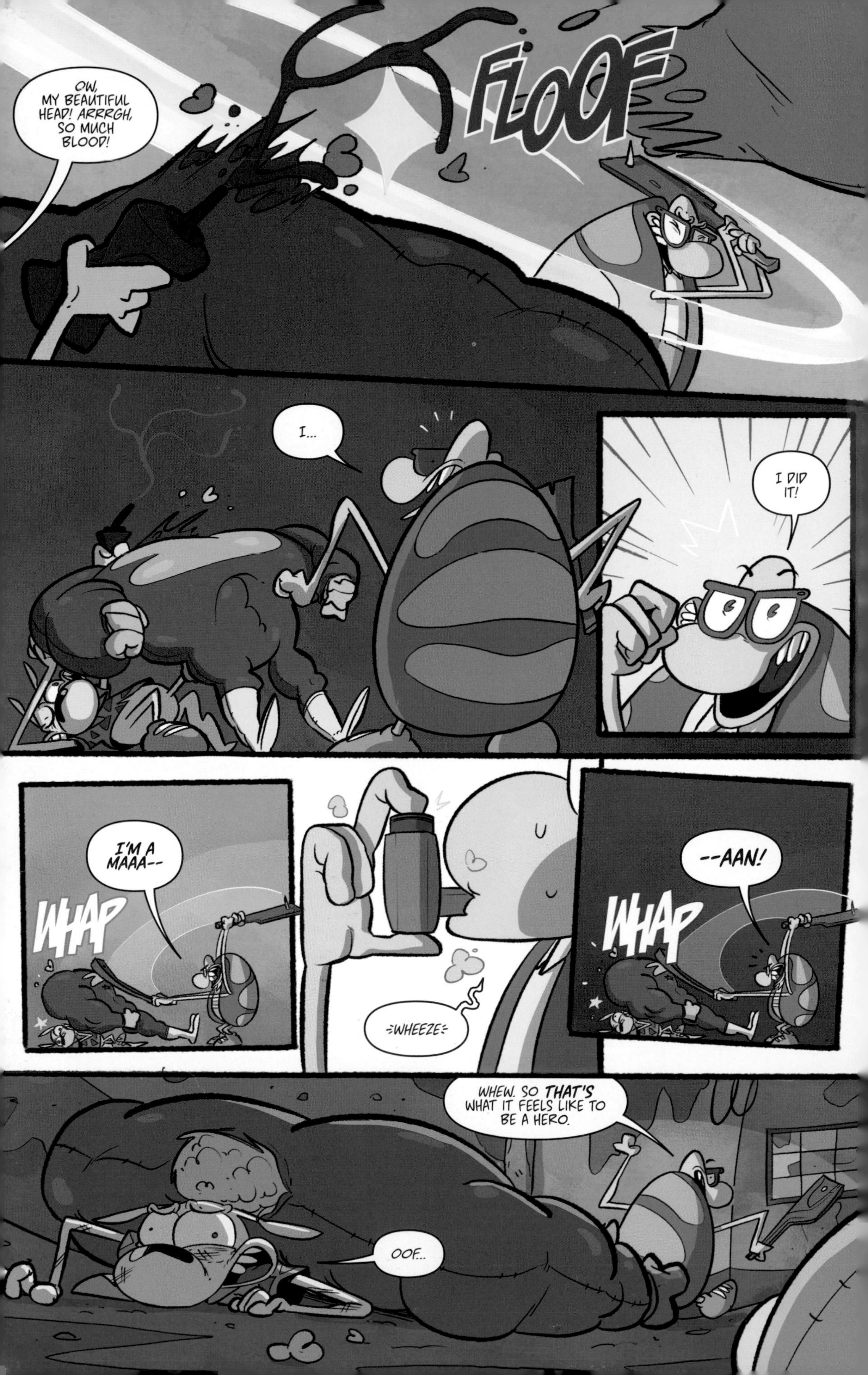
OW, MY BEAUTIFUL HEAD! ARRRGH, SO MUCH BLOOD!
FLOOF
I...
I DID IT!
I'M A MAAA--
WHAP
=WHEEZE=
--AAN!
WHAP
WHEW. SO THAT'S WHAT IT FEELS LIKE TO BE A HERO.
OOF...

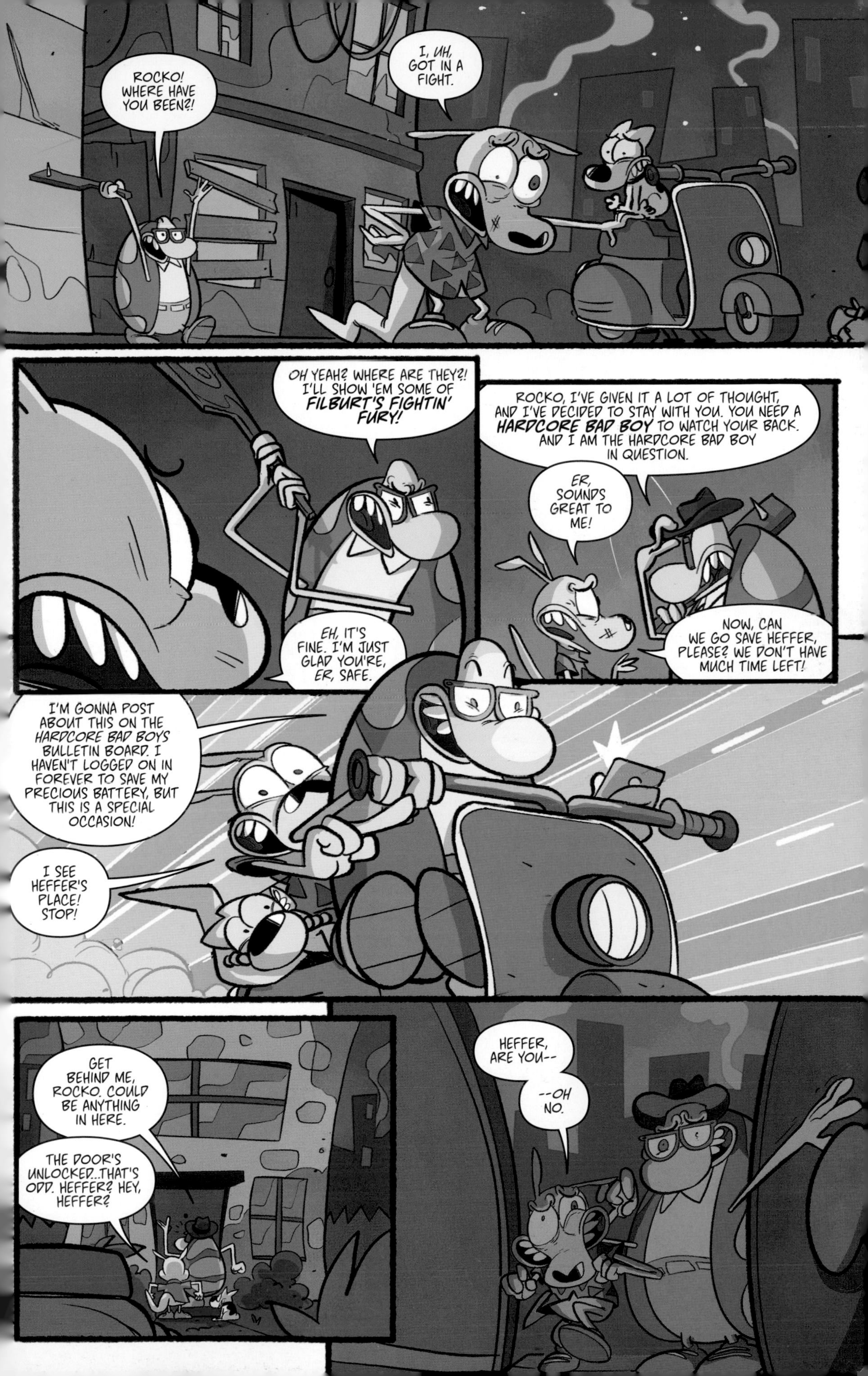
ROCKO! WHERE HAVE YOU BEEN?!
I, UH, GOT IN A FIGHT.
OH YEAH? WHERE ARE THEY?! I'LL SHOW 'EM SOME OF FILBURT'S FIGHTIN' FURY!
EH, IT'S FINE. I'M JUST GLAD YOU'RE, ER, SAFE.
ROCKO, I'VE GIVEN IT A LOT OF THOUGHT, AND I'VE DECIDED TO STAY WITH YOU. YOU NEED A HARDCORE BAD BOY TO WATCH YOUR BACK. AND I AM THE HARDCORE BAD BOY IN QUESTION.
ER, SOUNDS GREAT TO ME!
NOW, CAN WE GO SAVE HEFFER, PLEASE? WE DON'T HAVE MUCH TIME LEFT!
I'M GONNA POST ABOUT THIS ON THE HARDCORE BAD BOYS BULLETIN BOARD. I HAVEN'T LOGGED ON IN FOREVER TO SAVE MY PRECIOUS BATTERY, BUT THIS IS A SPECIAL OCCASION!
I SEE HEFFER'S PLACE! STOP!
GET BEHIND ME, ROCKO. COULD BE ANYTHING IN HERE.
THE DOOR'S UNLOCKED...THAT'S ODD. HEFFER? HEY, HEFFER?
HEFFER, ARE YOU--
--OH NO.

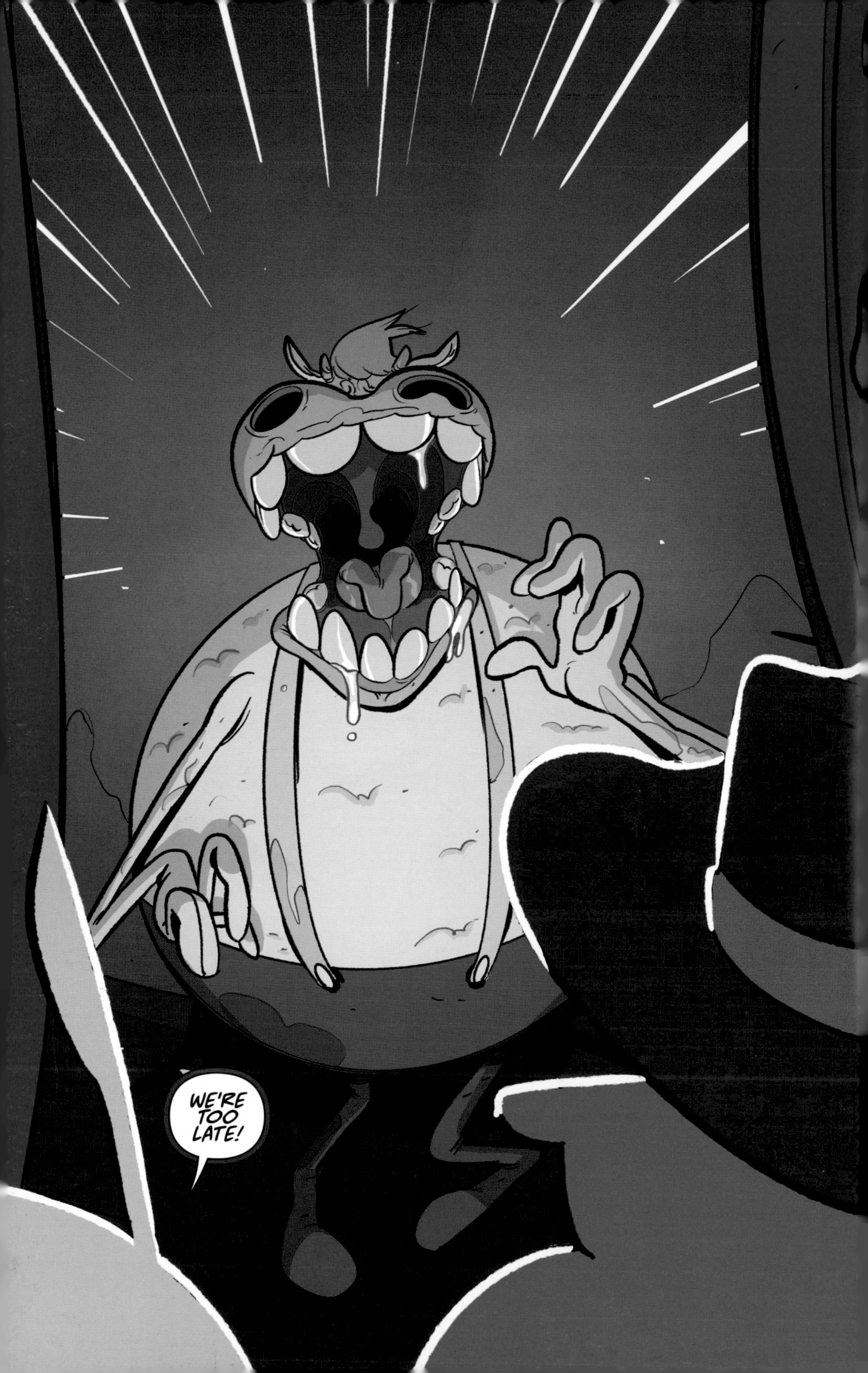
WE'RE TOO LATE!

CHAPTER
THREE

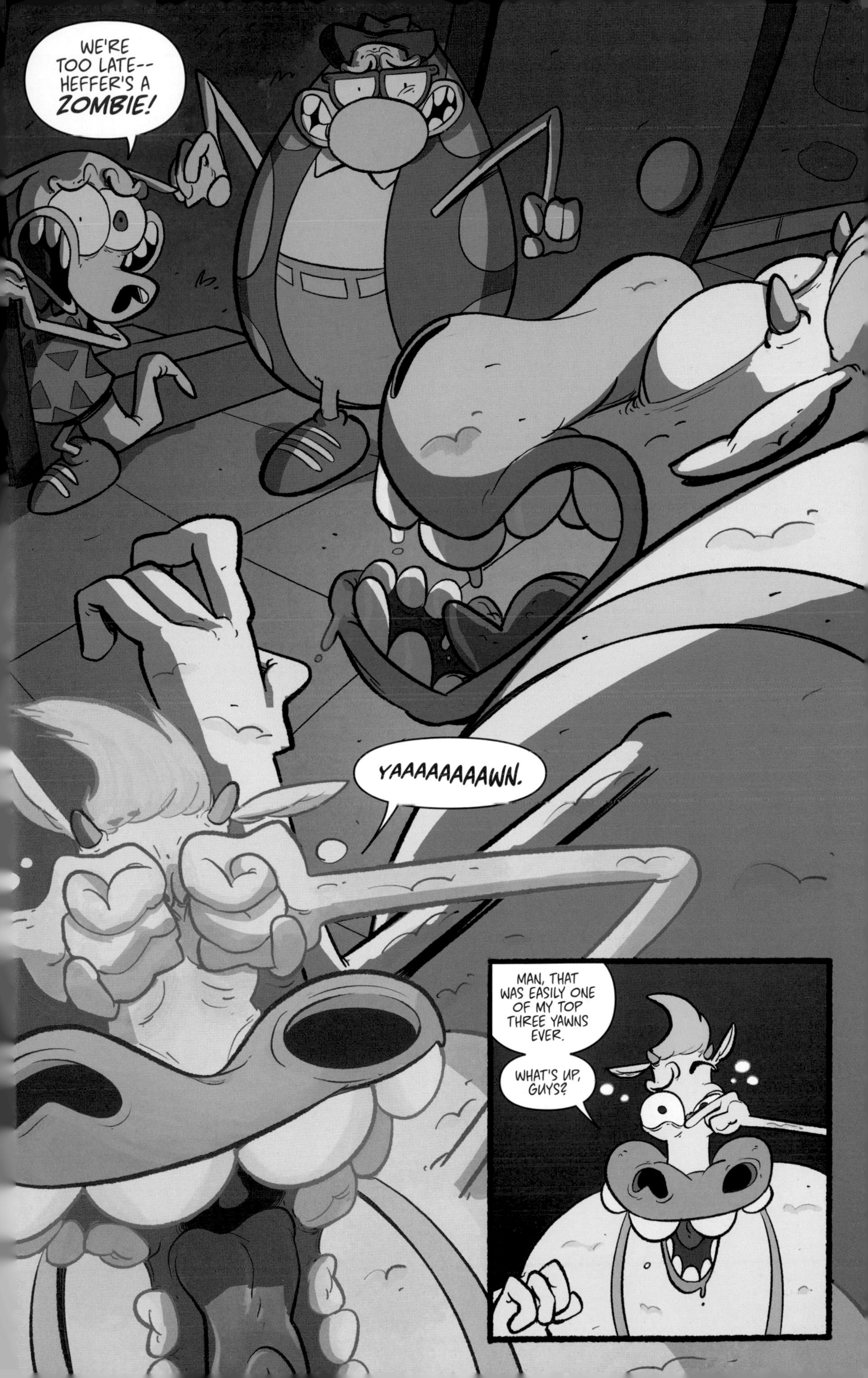
WE'RE TOO LATE-- HEFFER'S A ZOMBIE!
YAAAAAAAAWN.
MAN, THAT WAS EASILY ONE OF MY TOP THREE YAWNS EVER.
WHAT'S UP, GUYS?

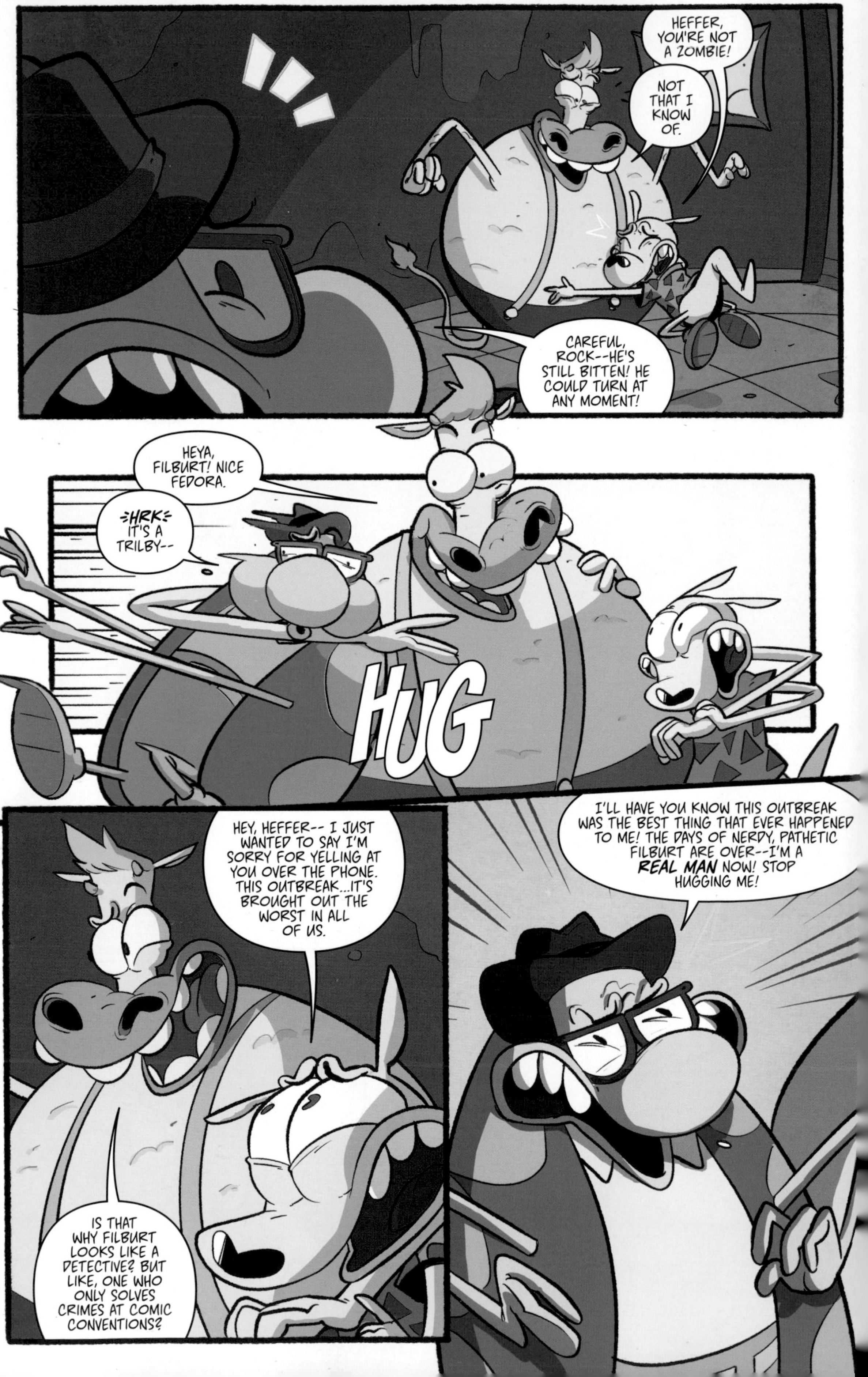
HEFFER, YOU'RE NOT A ZOMBIE!
NOT THAT I KNOW OF.
CAREFUL, ROCK--HE'S STILL BITTEN! HE COULD TURN AT ANY MOMENT!
HEYA, FILBURT! NICE FEDORA.
HRK IT'S A TRILBY--
HUG
HEY, HEFFER-- I JUST WANTED TO SAY I'M SORRY FOR YELLING AT YOU OVER THE PHONE. THIS OUTBREAK...IT'S BROUGHT OUT THE WORST IN ALL OF US.
IS THAT WHY FILBURT LOOKS LIKE A DETECTIVE? BUT LIKE, ONE WHO ONLY SOLVES CRIMES AT COMIC CONVENTIONS?
I'LL HAVE YOU KNOW THIS OUTBREAK WAS THE BEST THING THAT EVER HAPPENED TO ME! THE DAYS OF NERDY, PATHETIC FILBURT ARE OVER--I'M A REAL MAN NOW! STOP HUGGING ME!

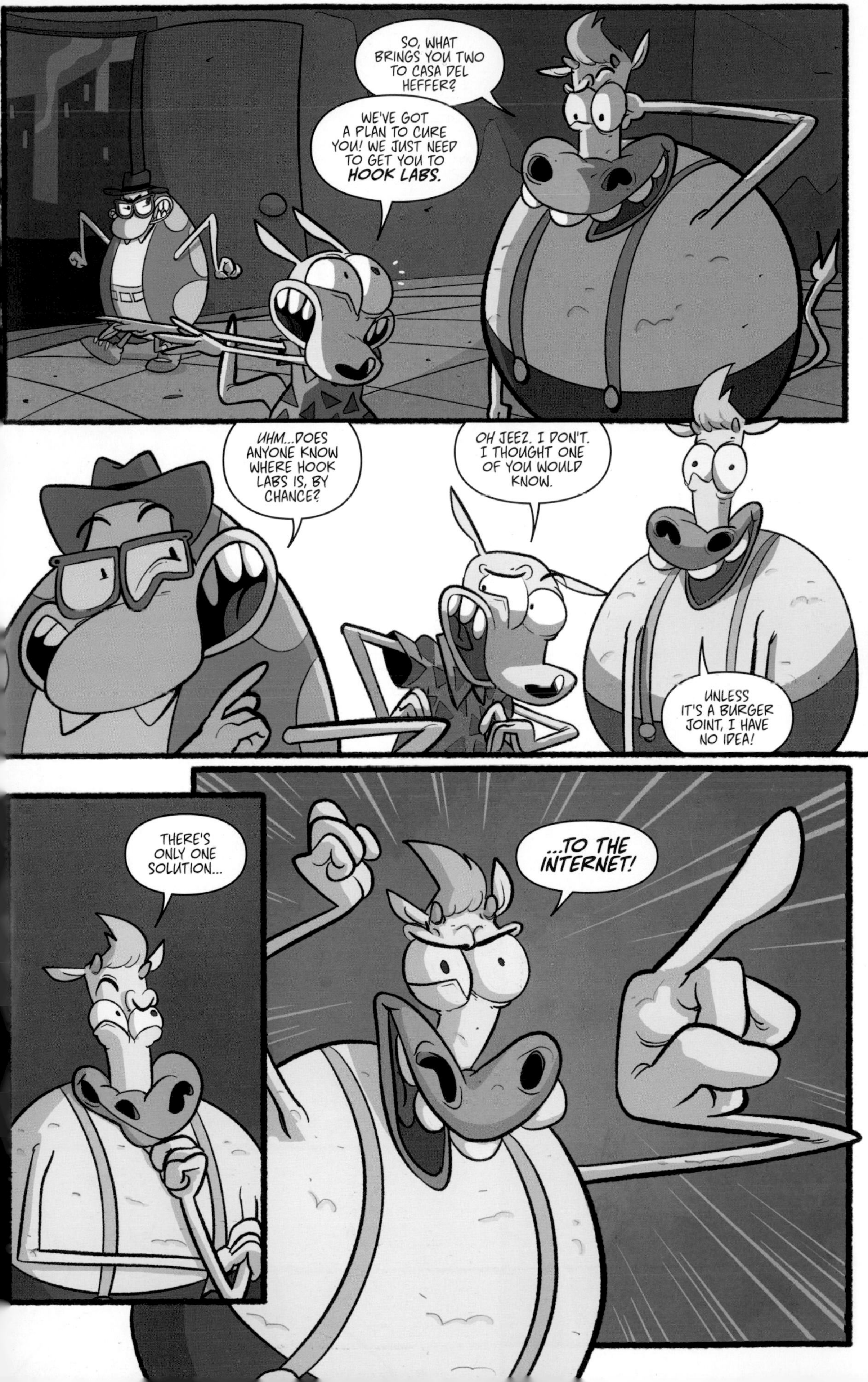

SO, WHAT BRINGS YOU TWO TO CASA DEL HEFFER?
WE'VE GOT A PLAN TO CURE YOU! WE JUST NEED TO GET YOU TO HOOK LABS.
UHM...DOES ANYONE KNOW WHERE HOOK LABS IS, BY CHANCE?
OH JEEZ. I DON'T. I THOUGHT ONE OF YOU WOULD KNOW.
UNLESS IT'S A BURGER JOINT, I HAVE NO IDEA!
THERE'S ONLY ONE SOLUTION...
...TO THE INTERNET!

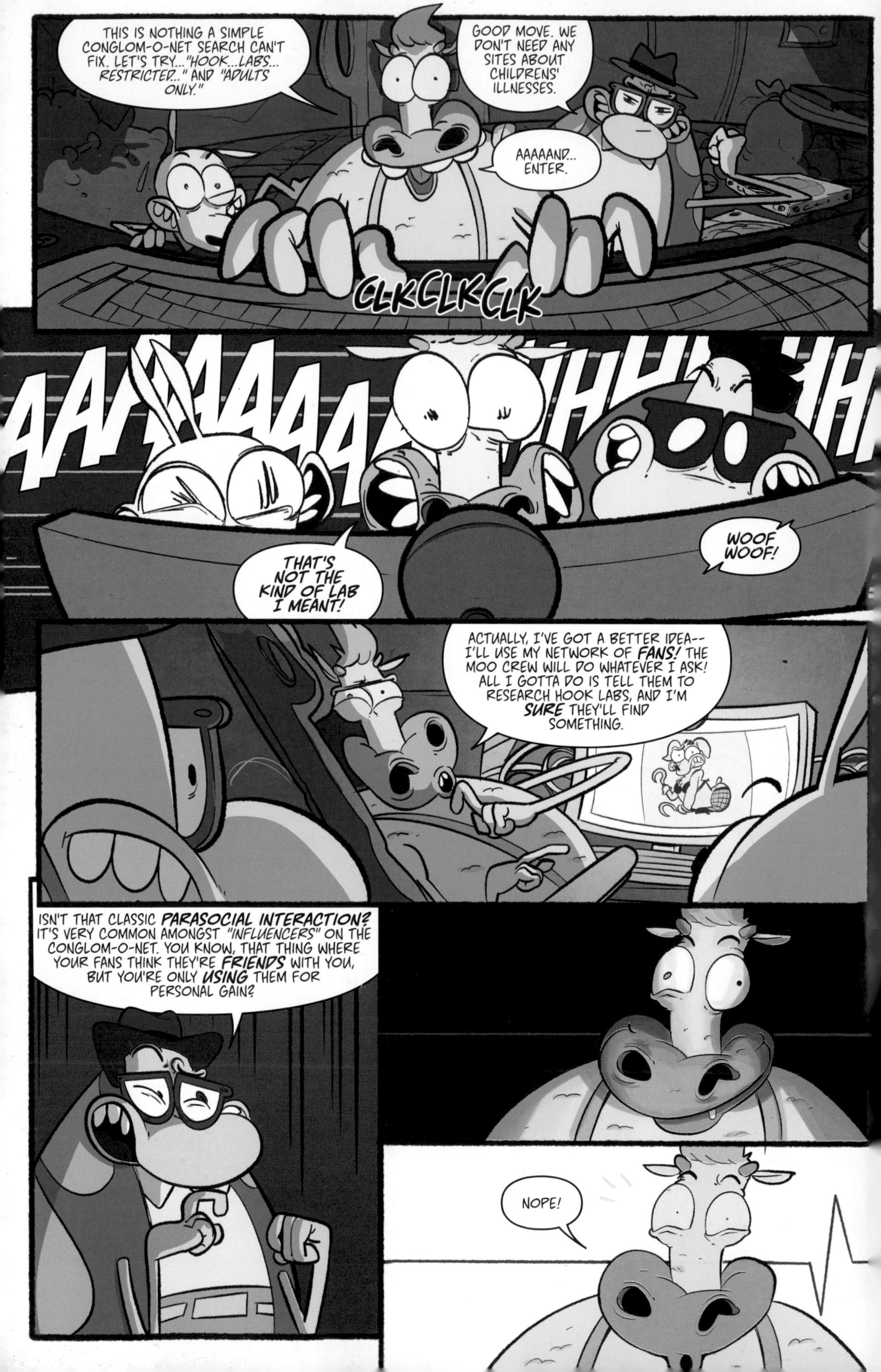
THIS IS NOTHING A SIMPLE CONGLOM-O-NET SEARCH CAN'T FIX. LET'S TRY..."HOOK...LABS... RESTRICTED..." AND "ADULTS ONLY."
GOOD MOVE. WE DON'T NEED ANY SITES ABOUT CHILDRENS' ILLNESSES.
AAAAAND... ENTER.
CLKCLKCLK
THAT'S NOT THE KIND OF LAB I MEANT!
WOOF WOOF!
ACTUALLY, I'VE GOT A BETTER IDEA-- I'LL USE MY NETWORK OF FANS! THE MOO CREW WILL DO WHATEVER I ASK! ALL I GOTTA DO IS TELL THEM TO RESEARCH HOOK LABS, AND I'M SURE THEY'LL FIND SOMETHING.
ISN'T THAT CLASSIC PARASOCIAL INTERACTION? IT'S VERY COMMON AMONGST "INFLUENCERS" ON THE CONGLOM-O-NET. YOU KNOW, THAT THING WHERE YOUR FANS THINK THEY'RE FRIENDS WITH YOU, BUT YOU'RE ONLY USING THEM FOR PERSONAL GAIN?
NOPE!

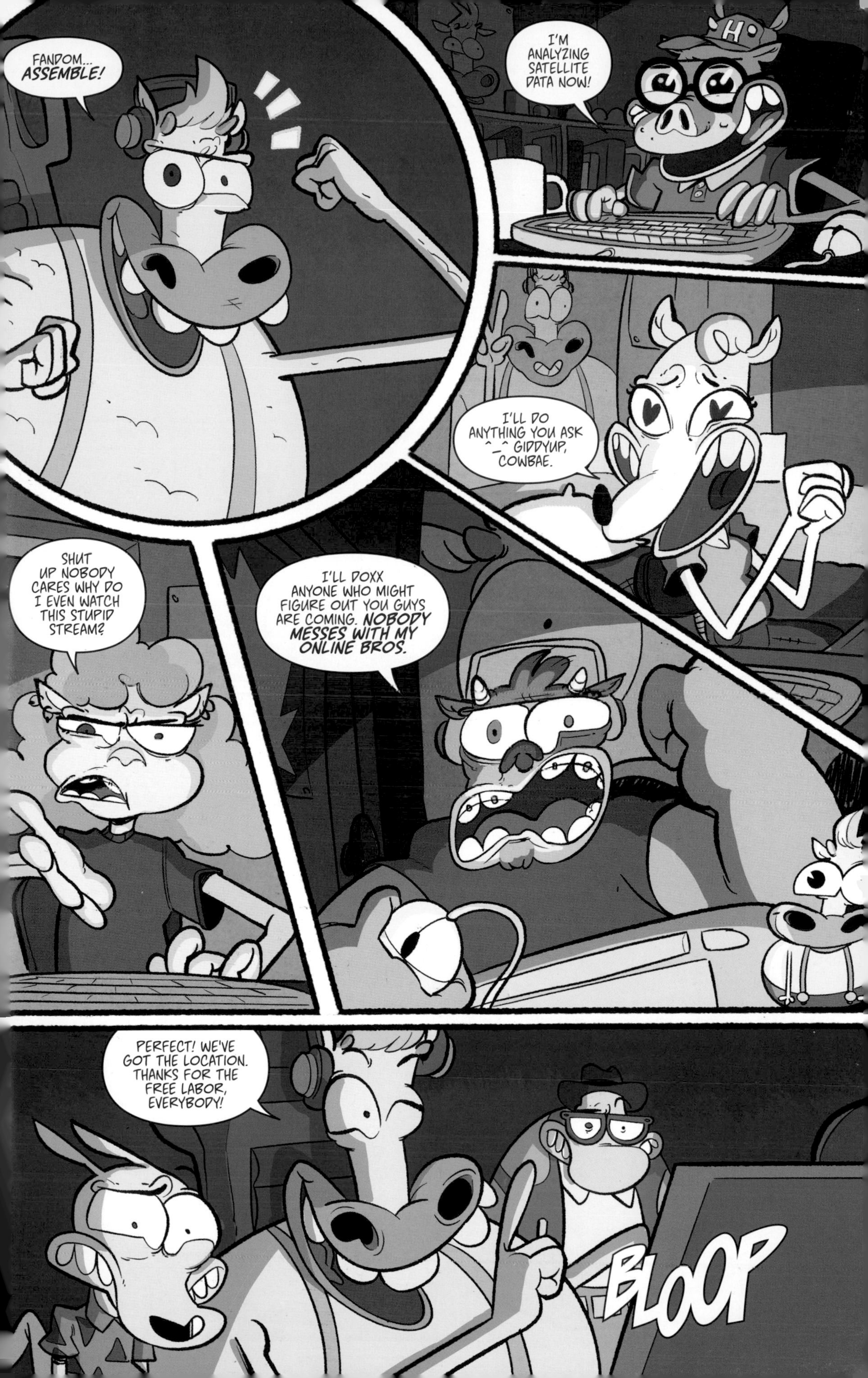
FANDOM... ASSEMBLE!
I'M ANALYZING SATELLITE DATA NOW!
I'LL DO ANYTHING YOU ASK ^_^ GIDDYUP, COWBAE.
SHUT UP NOBODY CARES WHY DO I EVEN WATCH THIS STUPID STREAM?
I'LL DOXX ANYONE WHO MIGHT FIGURE OUT YOU GUYS ARE COMING. NOBODY MESSES WITH MY ONLINE BROS.
PERFECT! WE'VE GOT THE LOCATION. THANKS FOR THE FREE LABOR, EVERYBODY!
BLOOP

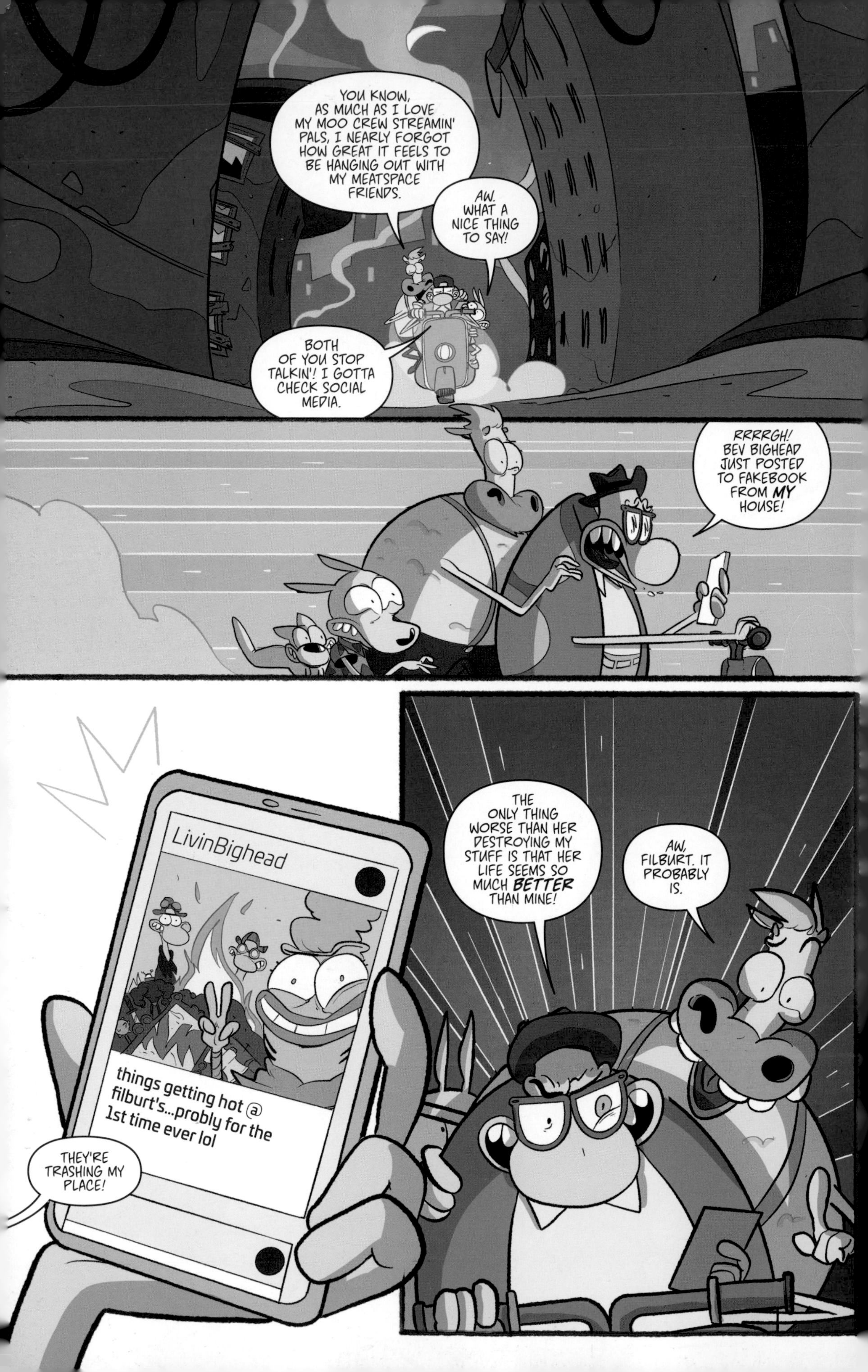
YOU KNOW, AS MUCH AS I LOVE MY MOO CREW STREAMIN' PALS, I NEARLY FORGOT HOW GREAT IT FEELS TO BE HANGING OUT WITH MY MEATSPACE FRIENDS.
AW. WHAT A NICE THING TO SAY!
BOTH OF YOU STOP TALKIN'! I GOTTA CHECK SOCIAL MEDIA.
RRRRGH! BEV BIGHEAD JUST POSTED TO FAKEBOOK FROM MY HOUSE!
LivinBighead
things getting hot @ filburt's...probly for the 1st time ever lol
THEY'RE TRASHING MY PLACE!
THE ONLY THING WORSE THAN HER DESTROYING MY STUFF IS THAT HER LIFE SEEMS SO MUCH BETTER THAN MINE!
AW, FILBURT. IT PROBABLY IS.

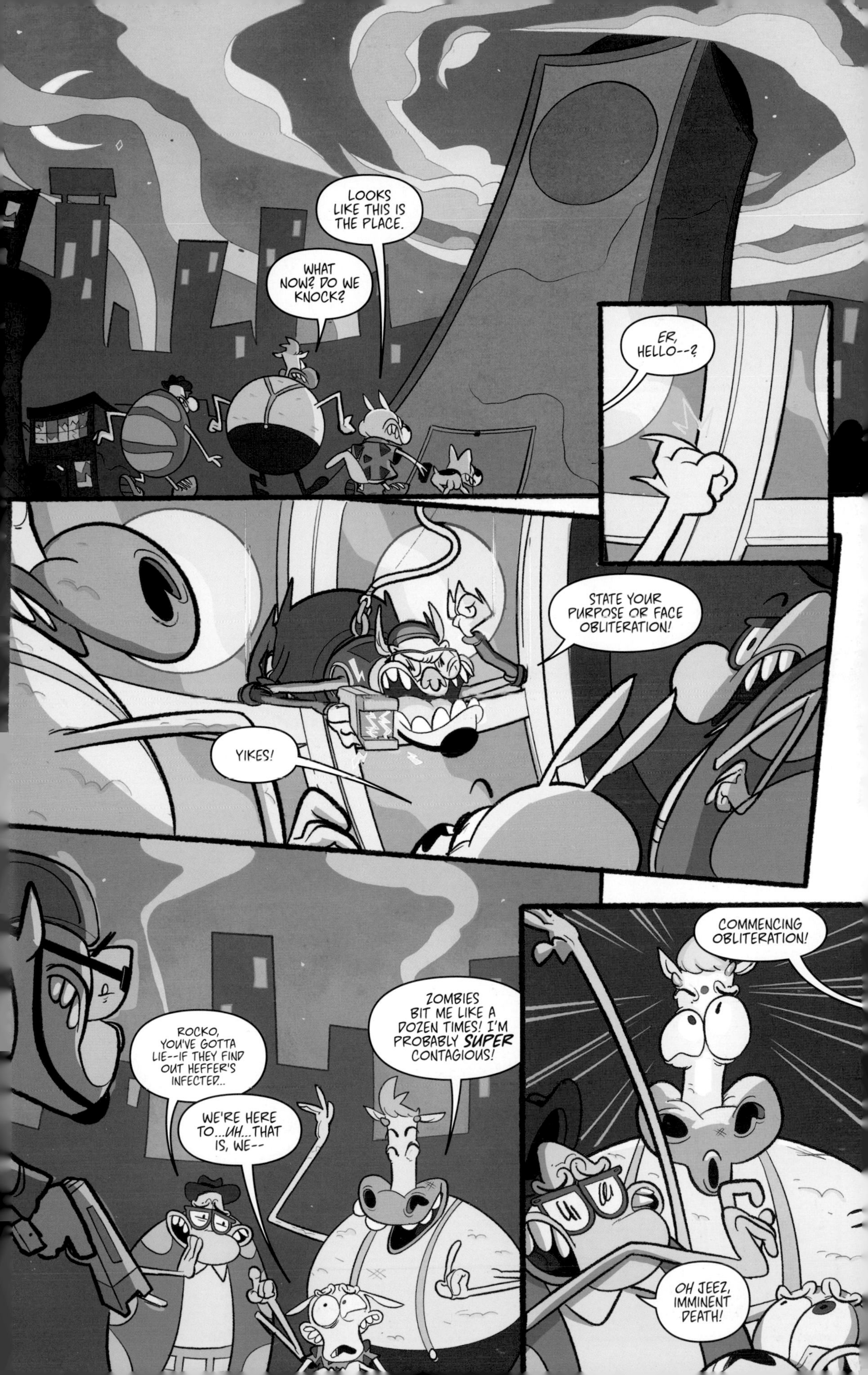
LOOKS LIKE THIS IS THE PLACE.
WHAT NOW? DO WE KNOCK?
ER, HELLO--?
STATE YOUR PURPOSE OR FACE OBLITERATION!
YIKES!
ROCKO, YOU'VE GOTTA LIE--IF THEY FIND OUT HEFFER'S INFECTED...
WE'RE HERE TO...UH...THAT IS, WE--
ZOMBIES BIT ME LIKE A DOZEN TIMES! I'M PROBABLY SUPER CONTAGIOUS!
COMMENCING OBLITERATION!
OH JEEZ, IMMINENT DEATH!

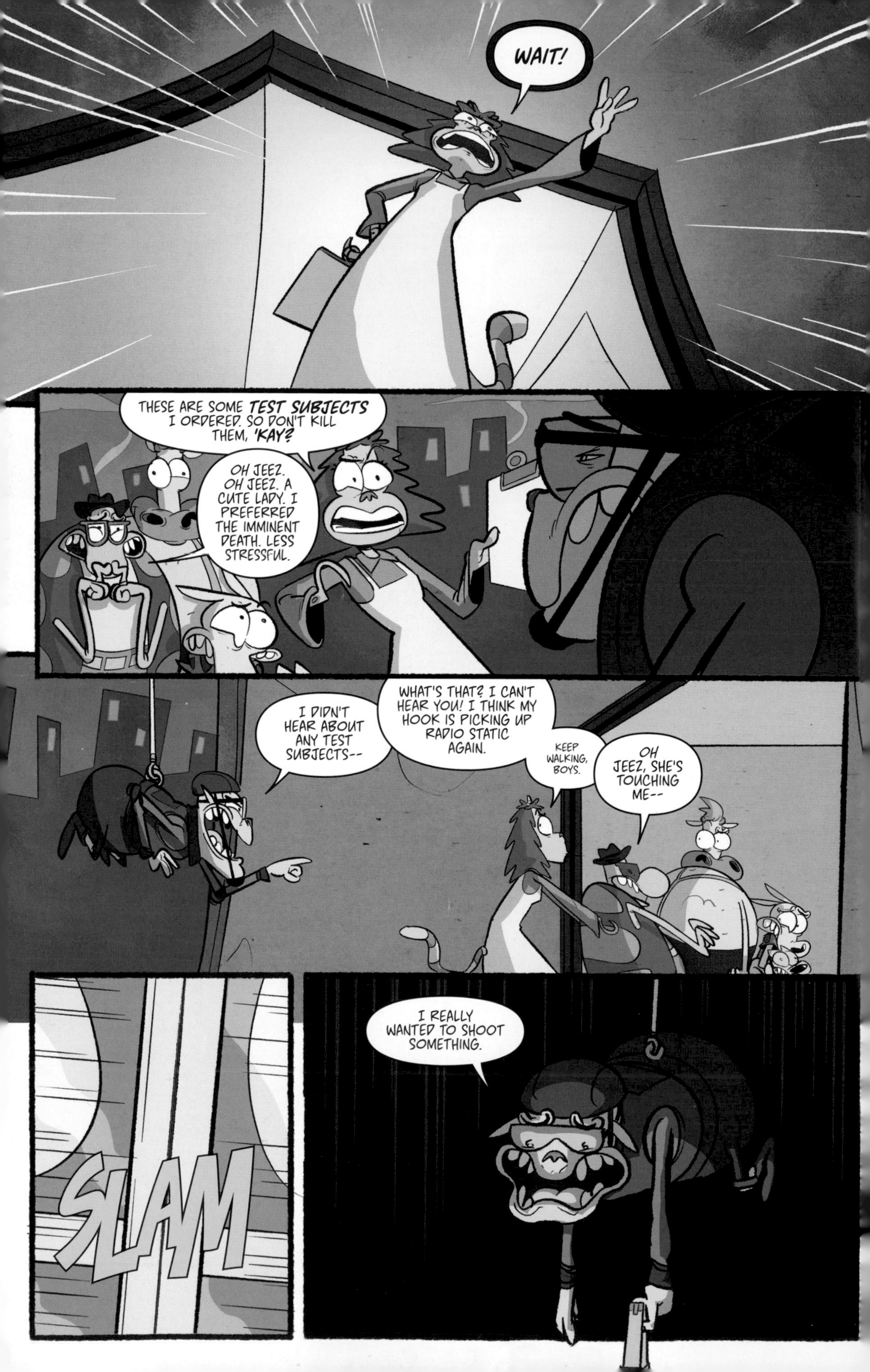
WAIT!
THESE ARE SOME TEST SUBJECTS I ORDERED. SO DON'T KILL THEM, 'KAY?
OH JEEZ. OH JEEZ. A CUTE LADY. I PREFERRED THE IMMINENT DEATH. LESS STRESSFUL.
I DIDN'T HEAR ABOUT ANY TEST SUBJECTS--
WHAT'S THAT? I CAN'T HEAR YOU! I THINK MY HOOK IS PICKING UP RADIO STATIC AGAIN.
KEEP WALKING, BOYS.
OH JEEZ, SHE'S TOUCHING ME--
SLAM
I REALLY WANTED TO SHOOT SOMETHING.

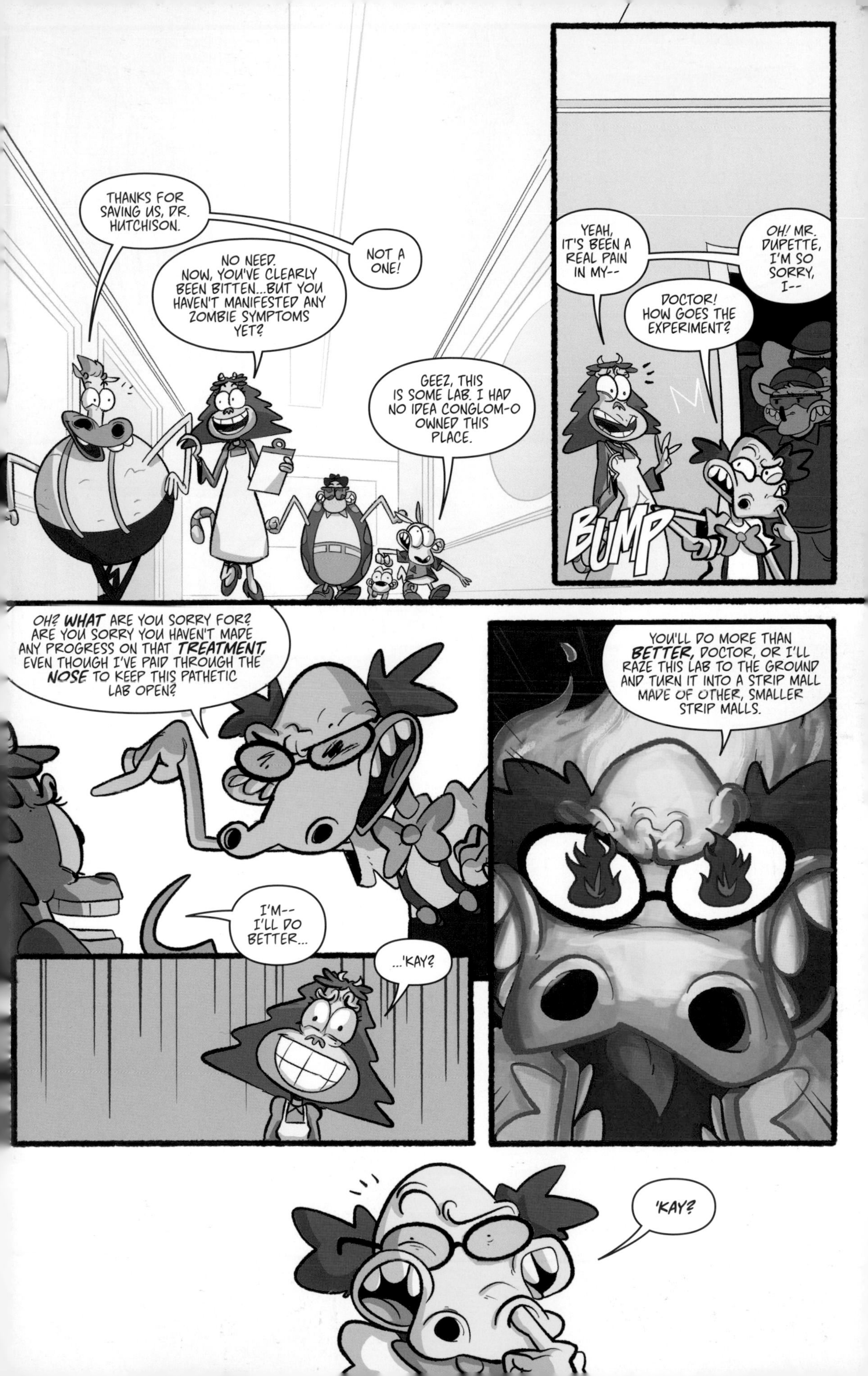
THANKS FOR SAVING US, DR. HUTCHISON.
NOT A ONE!
NO NEED. NOW, YOU'VE CLEARLY BEEN BITTEN...BUT YOU HAVEN'T MANIFESTED ANY ZOMBIE SYMPTOMS YET?
GEEZ, THIS IS SOME LAB. I HAD NO IDEA CONGLOM-O OWNED THIS PLACE.
YEAH, IT'S BEEN A REAL PAIN IN MY--
OH! MR. DUPETTE, I'M SO SORRY, I--
DOCTOR! HOW GOES THE EXPERIMENT?
BUMP
OH? WHAT ARE YOU SORRY FOR? ARE YOU SORRY YOU HAVEN'T MADE ANY PROGRESS ON THAT TREATMENT, EVEN THOUGH I'VE PAID THROUGH THE NOSE TO KEEP THIS PATHETIC LAB OPEN?
I'M-- I'LL DO BETTER...
YOU'LL DO MORE THAN BETTER, DOCTOR, OR I'LL RAZE THIS LAB TO THE GROUND AND TURN IT INTO A STRIP MALL MADE OF OTHER, SMALLER STRIP MALLS.
...'KAY?
'KAY?

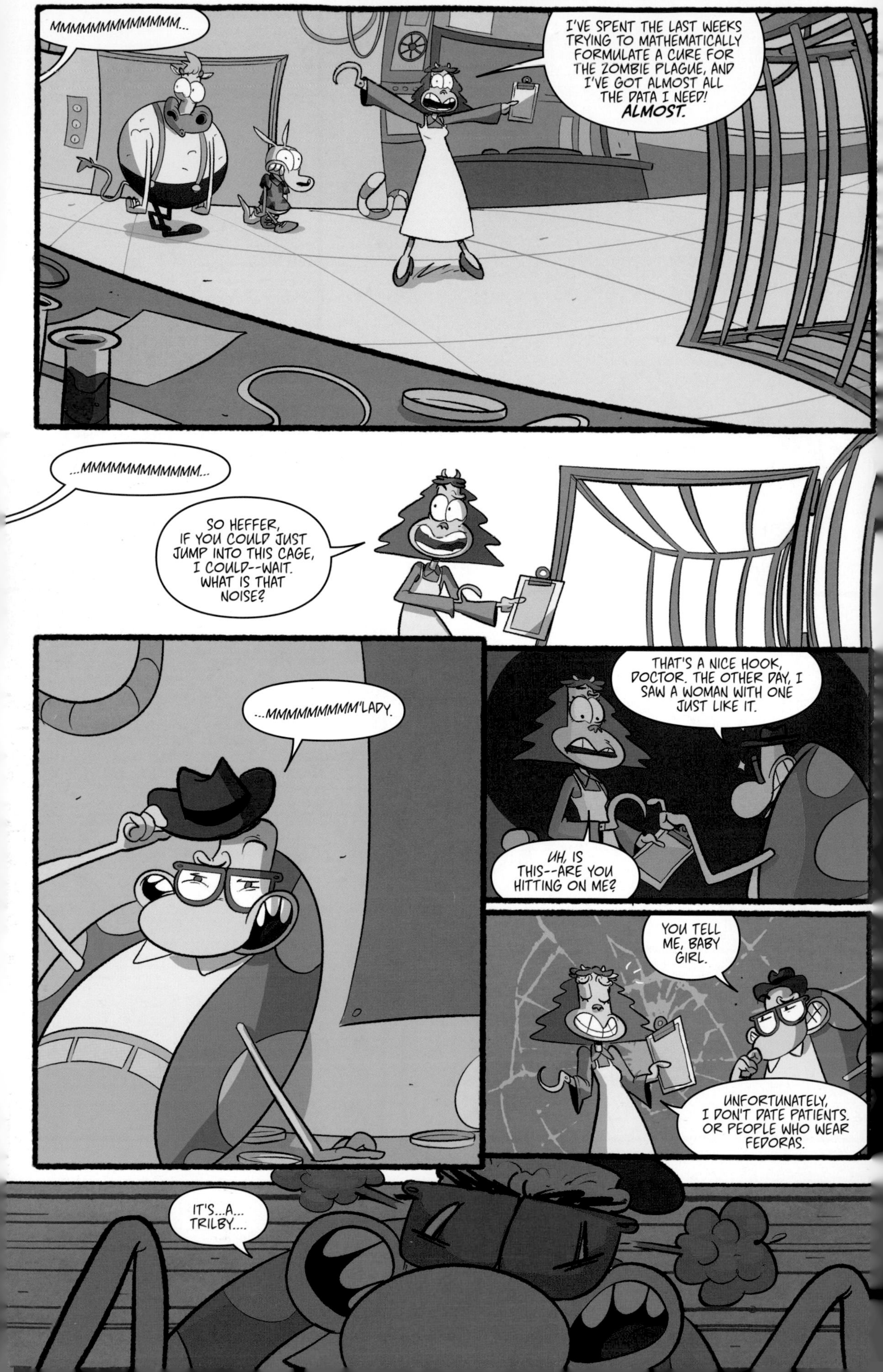
MMMMMMMMMMMMMM...
I'VE SPENT THE LAST WEEKS TRYING TO MATHEMATICALLY FORMULATE A CURE FOR THE ZOMBIE PLAGUE, AND I'VE GOT ALMOST ALL THE DATA I NEED! ALMOST.
...MMMMMMMMMMMM...
SO HEFFER, IF YOU COULD JUST JUMP INTO THIS CAGE, I COULD--WAIT. WHAT IS THAT NOISE?
...MMMMMMMMM'LADY.
THAT'S A NICE HOOK, DOCTOR. THE OTHER DAY, I SAW A WOMAN WITH ONE JUST LIKE IT.
UH, IS THIS--ARE YOU HITTING ON ME?
YOU TELL ME, BABY GIRL.
UNFORTUNATELY, I DON'T DATE PATIENTS. OR PEOPLE WHO WEAR FEDORAS.
IT'S...A... TRILBY....

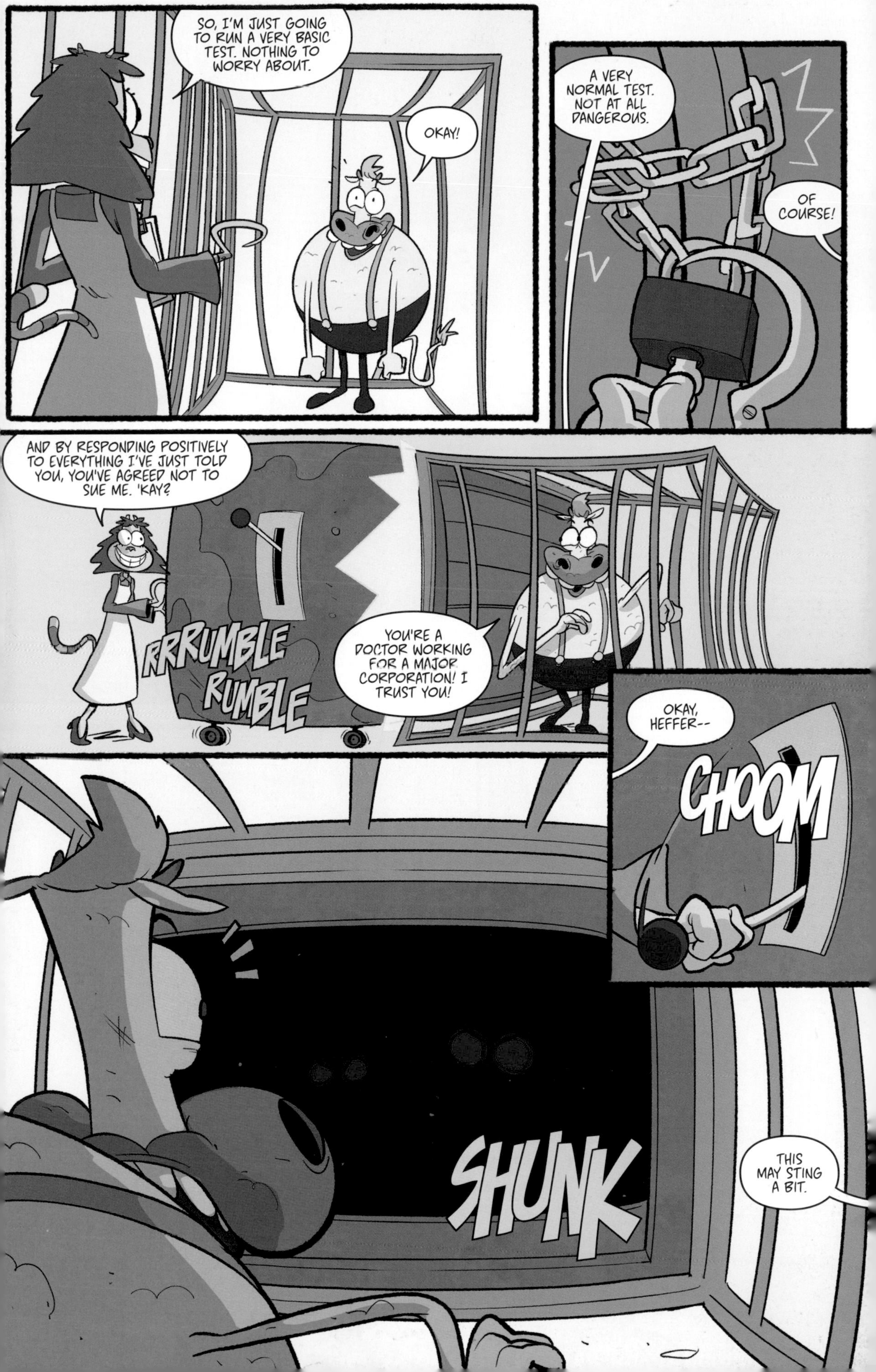
SO, I'M JUST GOING TO RUN A VERY BASIC TEST. NOTHING TO WORRY ABOUT.
OKAY!
A VERY NORMAL TEST. NOT AT ALL DANGEROUS.
OF COURSE!
AND BY RESPONDING POSITIVELY TO EVERYTHING I'VE JUST TOLD YOU, YOU'VE AGREED NOT TO SUE ME. 'KAY?
RRRUMBLE RUMBLE
YOU'RE A DOCTOR WORKING FOR A MAJOR CORPORATION! I TRUST YOU!
OKAY, HEFFER--
CHOOM
SHUNK
THIS MAY STING A BIT.

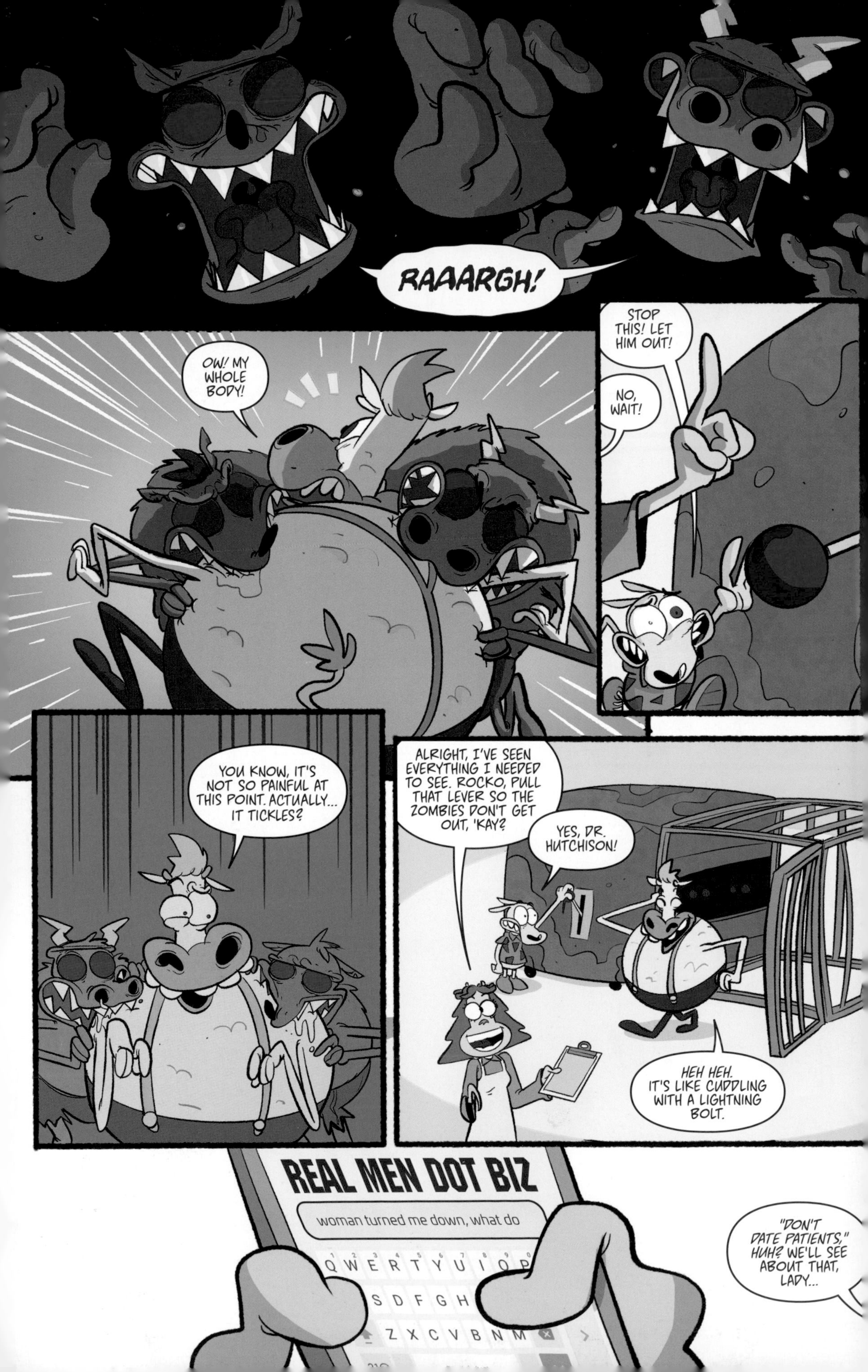
RAAARGH!
OW! MY WHOLE BODY!
STOP THIS! LET HIM OUT!
NO, WAIT!
YOU KNOW, IT'S NOT SO PAINFUL AT THIS POINT. ACTUALLY... IT TICKLES?
ALRIGHT, I'VE SEEN EVERYTHING I NEEDED TO SEE. ROCKO, PULL THAT LEVER SO THE ZOMBIES DON'T GET OUT, 'KAY?
YES, DR. HUTCHISON!
HEH HEH. IT'S LIKE CUDDLING WITH A LIGHTNING BOLT.
REAL MEN DOT BIZ
woman turned me down, what do
"DON'T DATE PATIENTS," HUH? WE'LL SEE ABOUT THAT, LADY...

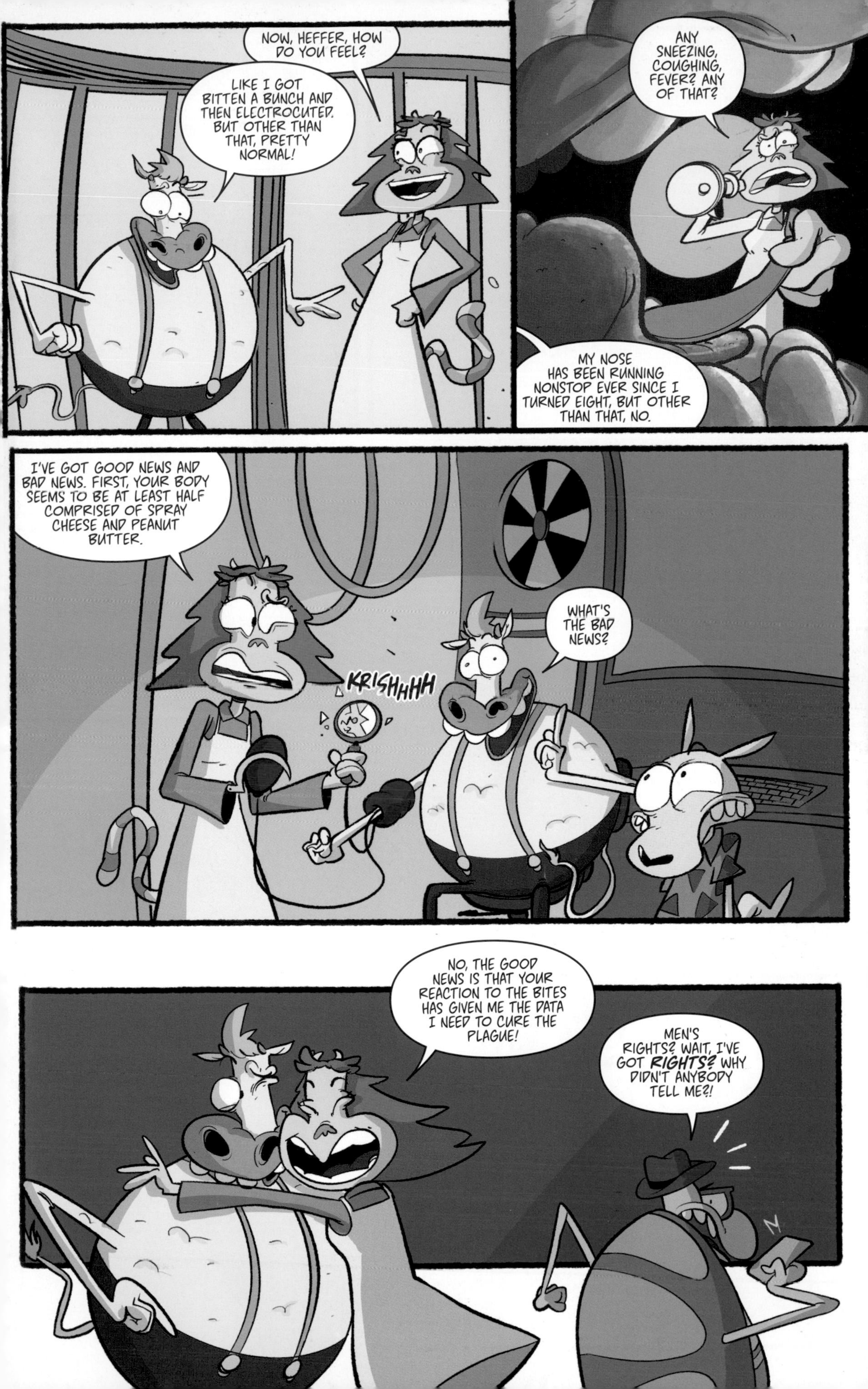
NOW, HEFFER, HOW DO YOU FEEL?
LIKE I GOT BITTEN A BUNCH AND THEN ELECTROCUTED. BUT OTHER THAN THAT, PRETTY NORMAL!
ANY SNEEZING, COUGHING, FEVER? ANY OF THAT?
MY NOSE HAS BEEN RUNNING NONSTOP EVER SINCE I TURNED EIGHT, BUT OTHER THAN THAT, NO.
I'VE GOT GOOD NEWS AND BAD NEWS. FIRST, YOUR BODY SEEMS TO BE AT LEAST HALF COMPRISED OF SPRAY CHEESE AND PEANUT BUTTER.
KRISHHHH
WHAT'S THE BAD NEWS?
NO, THE GOOD NEWS IS THAT YOUR REACTION TO THE BITES HAS GIVEN ME THE DATA I NEED TO CURE THE PLAGUE!
MEN'S RIGHTS? WAIT, I'VE GOT RIGHTS? WHY DIDN'T ANYBODY TELL ME?!

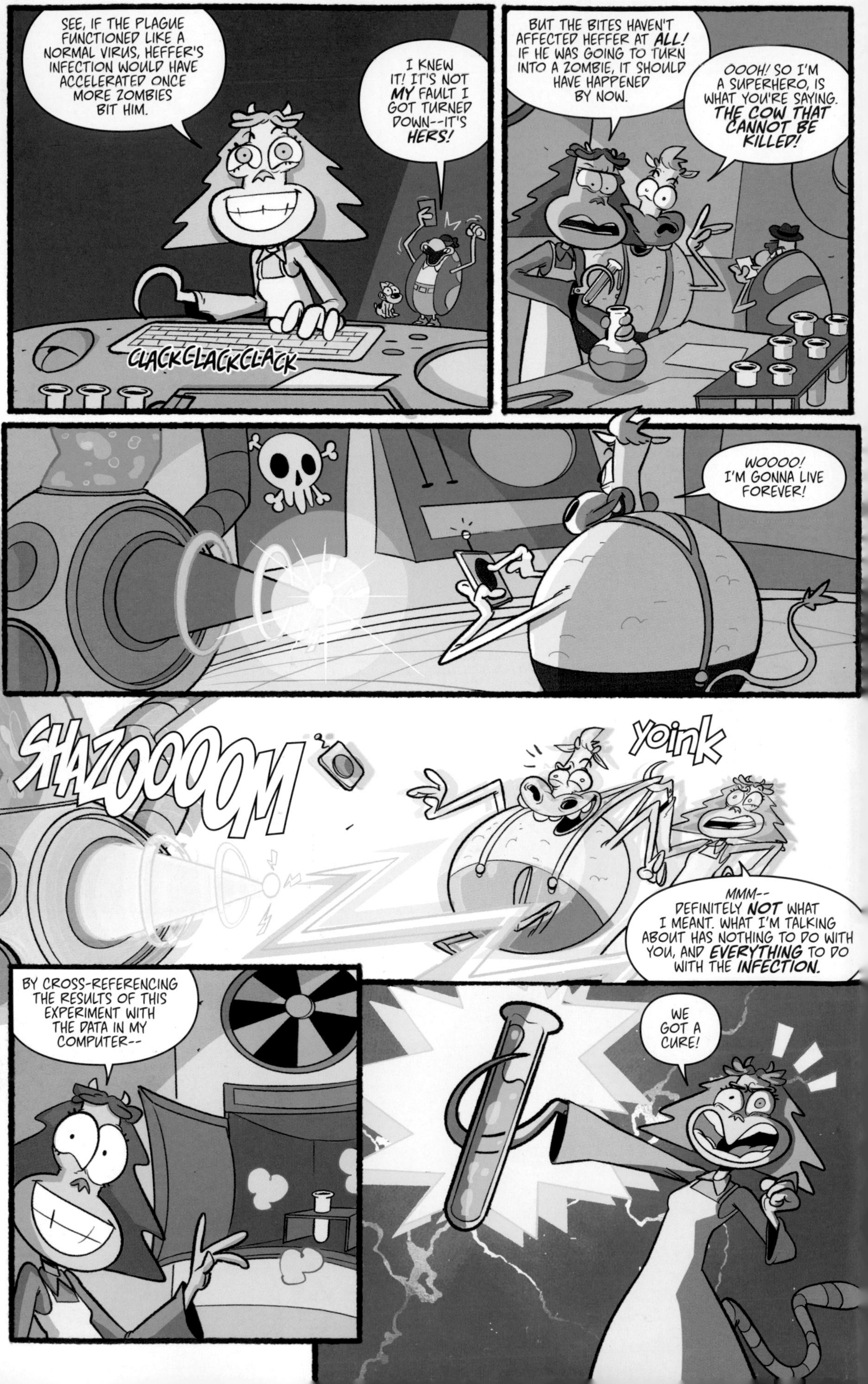
SEE, IF THE PLAGUE FUNCTIONED LIKE A NORMAL VIRUS, HEFFER'S INFECTION WOULD HAVE ACCELERATED ONCE MORE ZOMBIES BIT HIM.
I KNEW IT! IT'S NOT MY FAULT I GOT TURNED DOWN--IT'S HERS!
CLACKCLACKCLACK
BUT THE BITES HAVEN'T AFFECTED HEFFER AT ALL! IF HE WAS GOING TO TURN INTO A ZOMBIE, IT SHOULD HAVE HAPPENED BY NOW.
OOOH! SO I'M A SUPERHERO, IS WHAT YOU'RE SAYING. THE COW THAT CANNOT BE KILLED!
WOOOO! I'M GONNA LIVE FOREVER!
SHAZOOOOOM
YOINK
MMM-- DEFINITELY NOT WHAT I MEANT. WHAT I'M TALKING ABOUT HAS NOTHING TO DO WITH YOU, AND EVERYTHING TO DO WITH THE INFECTION.
BY CROSS-REFERENCING THE RESULTS OF THIS EXPERIMENT WITH THE DATA IN MY COMPUTER--
WE GOT A CURE!

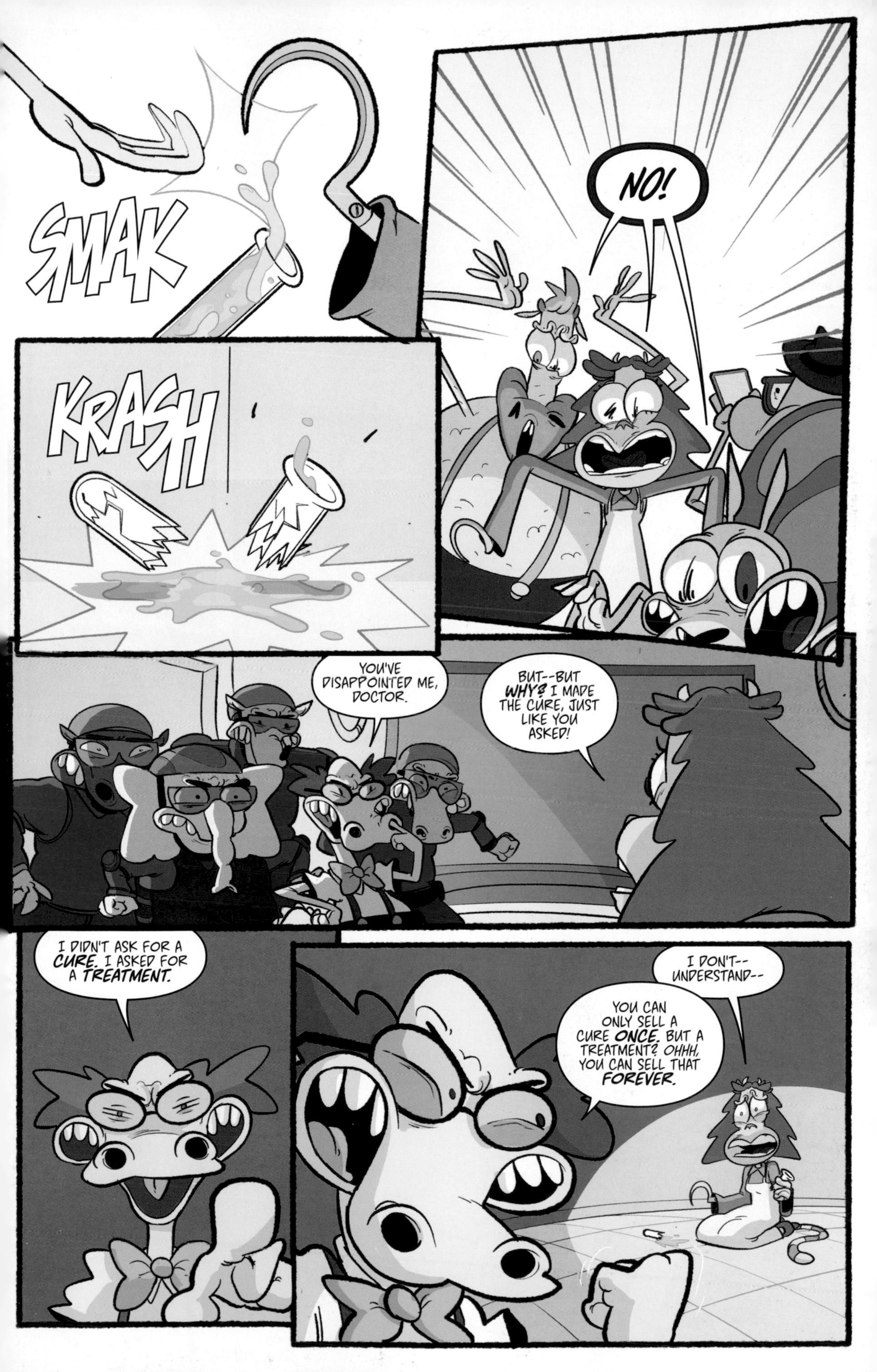
SMAK
NO!
KRASH
YOU'VE DISAPPOINTED ME, DOCTOR.
BUT--BUT WHY? I MADE THE CURE, JUST LIKE YOU ASKED!
I DIDN'T ASK FOR A CURE. I ASKED FOR A TREATMENT.
I DON'T--UNDERSTAND--
YOU CAN ONLY SELL A CURE ONCE. BUT A TREATMENT? OHHH, YOU CAN SELL THAT FOREVER.

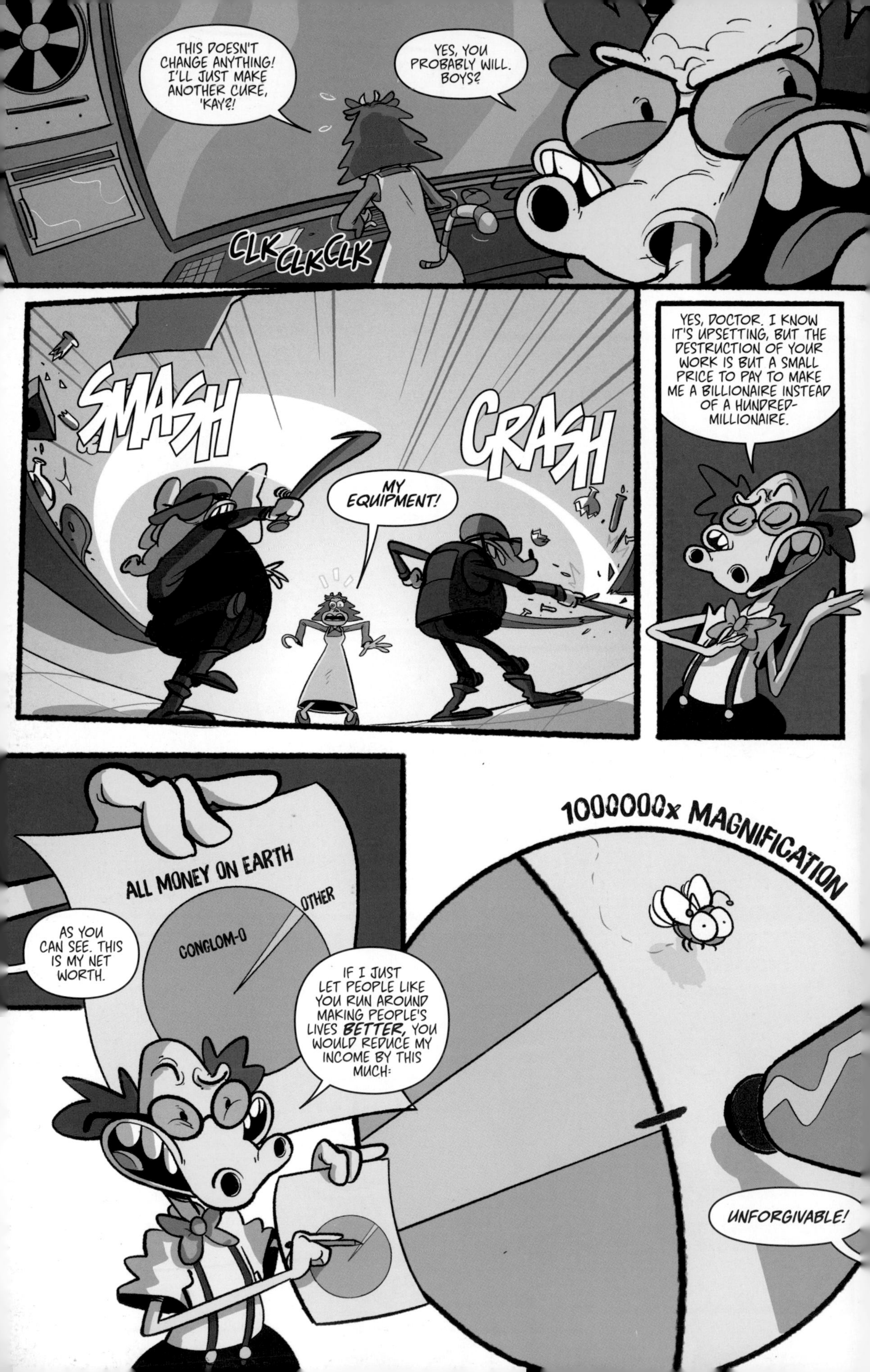
THIS DOESN'T CHANGE ANYTHING! I'LL JUST MAKE ANOTHER CURE, 'KAY?!
YES, YOU PROBABLY WILL. BOYS?
CLK CLK CLK
SMASH
MY EQUIPMENT!
CRASH
YES, DOCTOR. I KNOW IT'S UPSETTING, BUT THE DESTRUCTION OF YOUR WORK IS BUT A SMALL PRICE TO PAY TO MAKE ME A BILLIONAIRE INSTEAD OF A HUNDRED-MILLIONAIRE.
ALL MONEY ON EARTH
CONGLOM-O
OTHER
AS YOU CAN SEE. THIS IS MY NET WORTH.
IF I JUST LET PEOPLE LIKE YOU RUN AROUND MAKING PEOPLE'S LIVES BETTER, YOU WOULD REDUCE MY INCOME BY THIS MUCH:
1000000x MAGNIFICATION
UNFORGIVABLE!

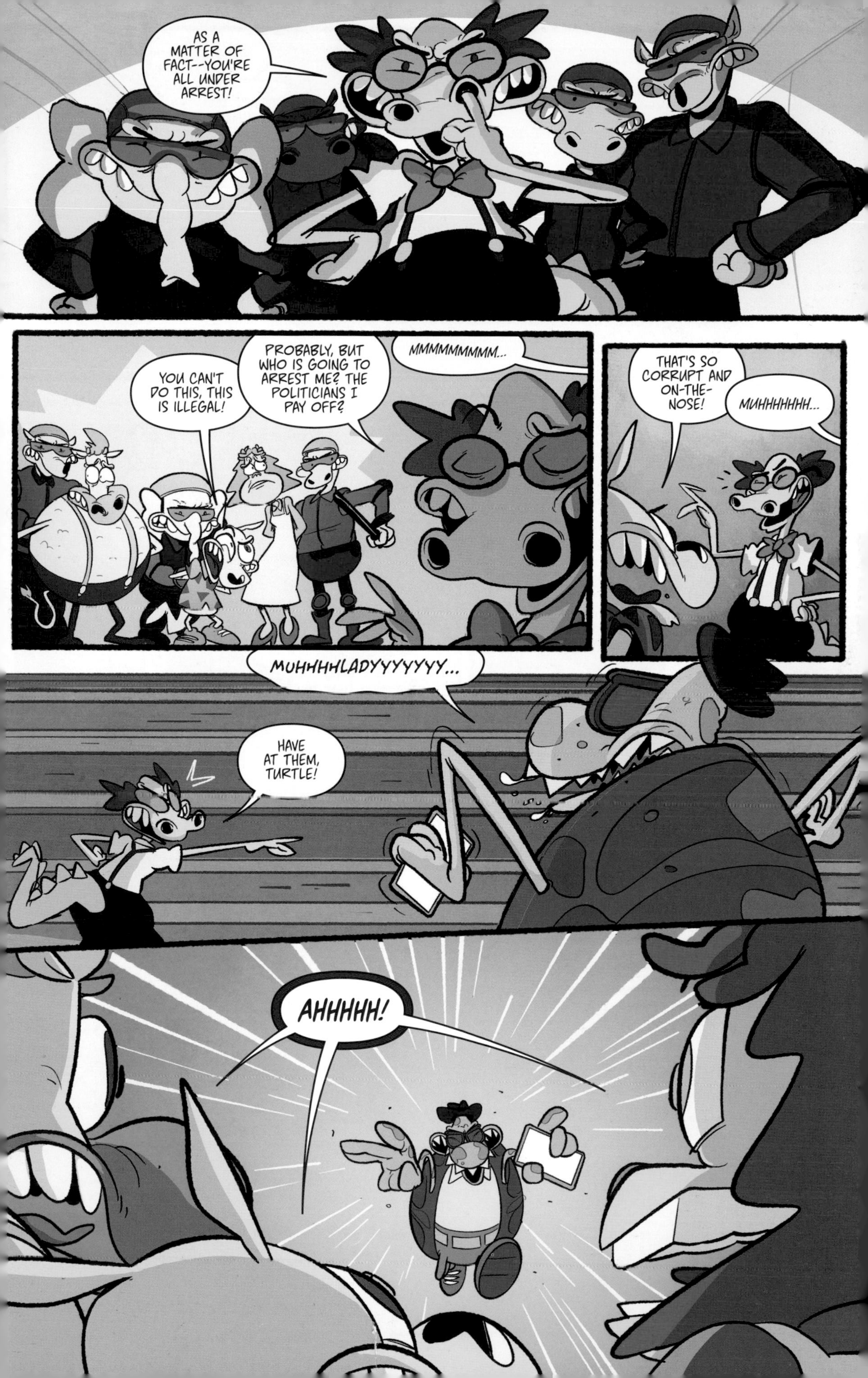
AS A MATTER OF FACT--YOU'RE ALL UNDER ARREST!
YOU CAN'T DO THIS, THIS IS ILLEGAL!
PROBABLY, BUT WHO IS GOING TO ARREST ME? THE POLITICIANS I PAY OFF?
MMMMMMMMM...
THAT'S SO CORRUPT AND ON-THE-NOSE!
MUHHHHHHH...
MUHHHHLADYYYYYY...
HAVE AT THEM, TURTLE!
AHHHHH!

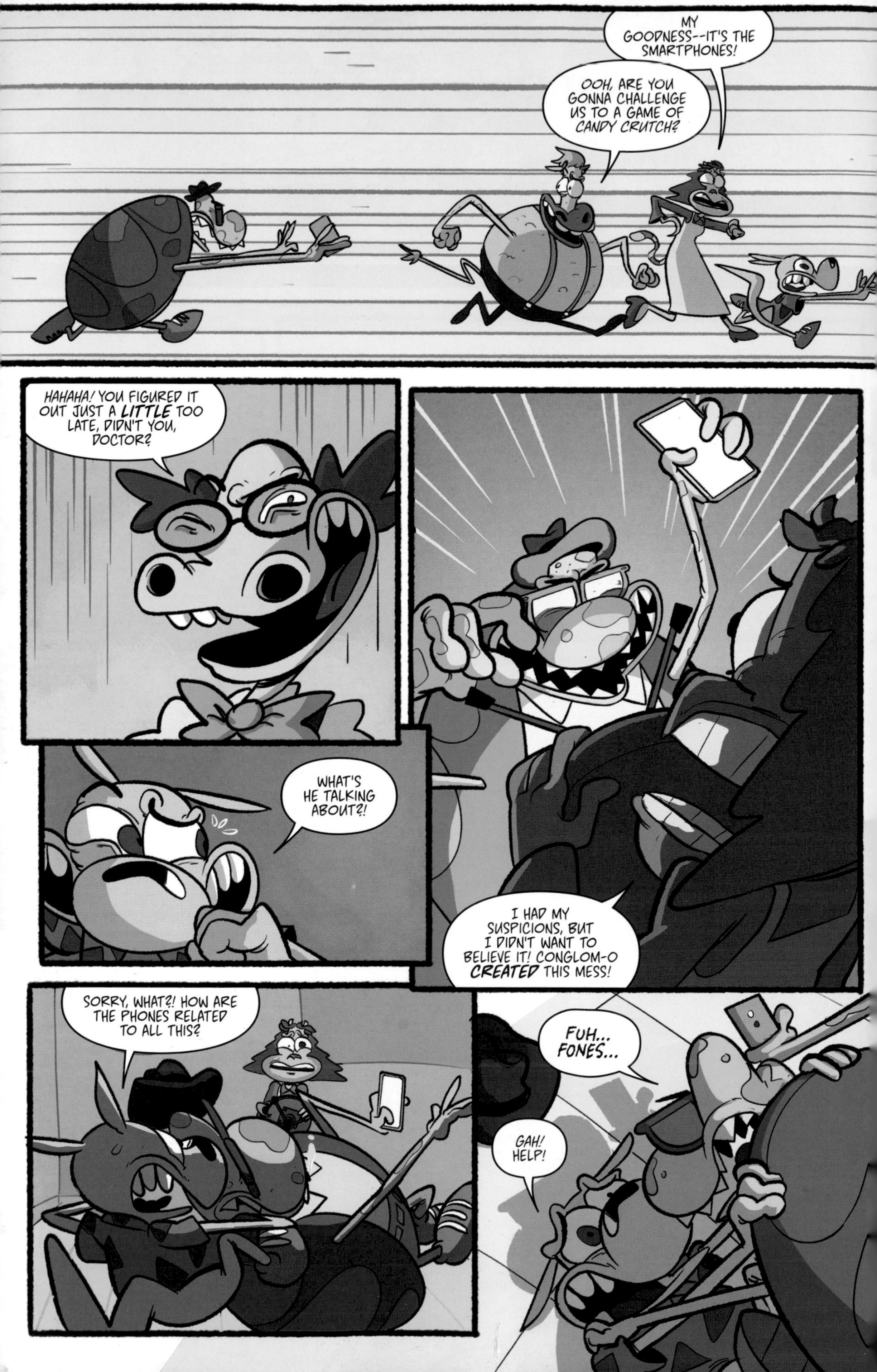
MY GOODNESS--IT'S THE SMARTPHONES!
OOH, ARE YOU GONNA CHALLENGE US TO A GAME OF CANDY CRUTCH?
HAHAHA! YOU FIGURED IT OUT JUST A LITTLE TOO LATE, DIDN'T YOU, DOCTOR?
WHAT'S HE TALKING ABOUT?!
I HAD MY SUSPICIONS, BUT I DIDN'T WANT TO BELIEVE IT! CONGLOM-O CREATED THIS MESS!
SORRY, WHAT?! HOW ARE THE PHONES RELATED TO ALL THIS?
FUH... FONES...
GAH! HELP!

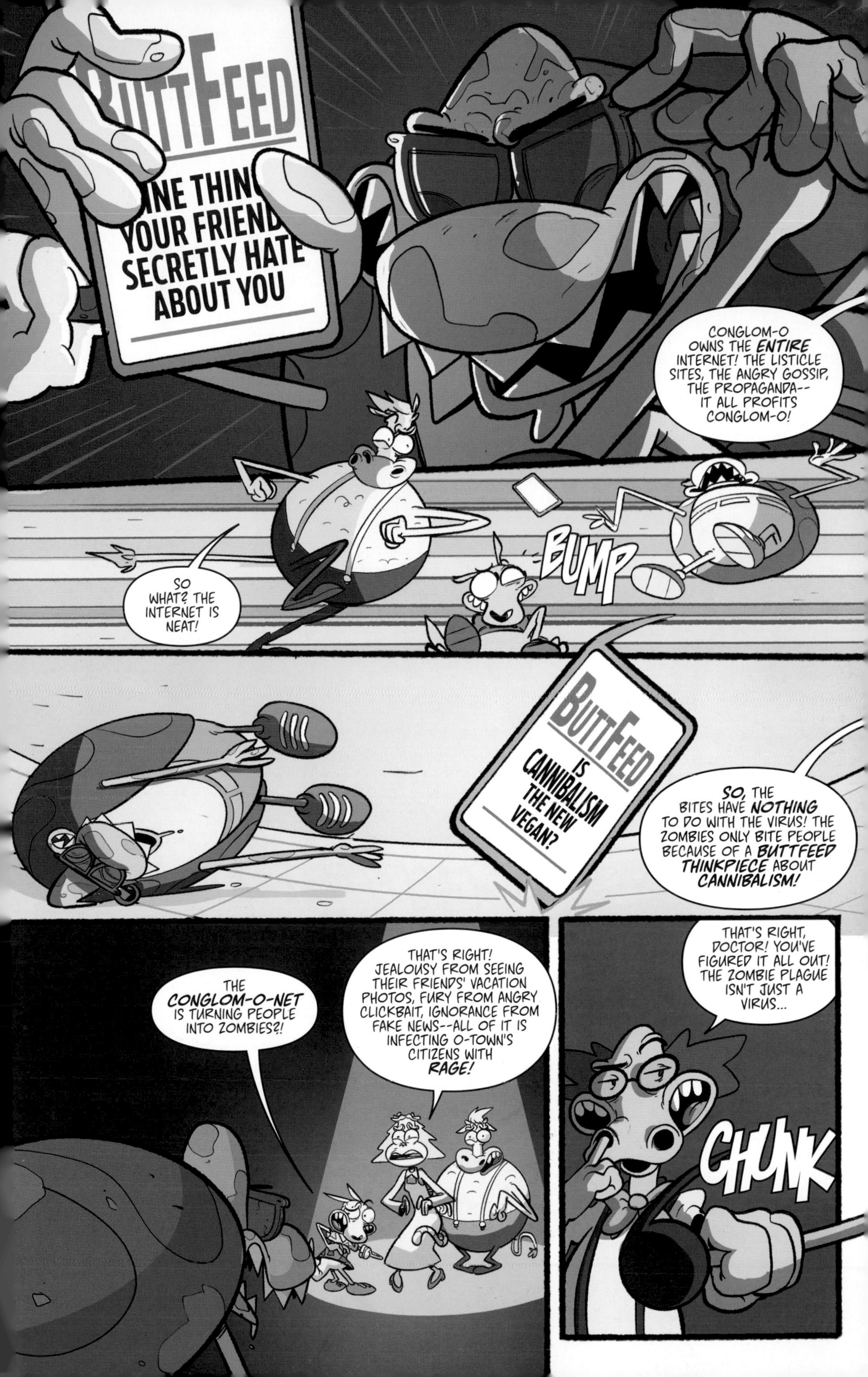
BUTTFEED
ONE THING YOUR FRIENDS SECRETLY HATE ABOUT YOU
CONGLOM-O OWNS THE ENTIRE INTERNET! THE LISTICLE SITES, THE ANGRY GOSSIP, THE PROPAGANDA-- IT ALL PROFITS CONGLOM-O!
BUMP
SO WHAT? THE INTERNET IS NEAT!
BUTTFEED
IS CANNIBALISM THE NEW VEGAN?
SO, THE BITES HAVE NOTHING TO DO WITH THE VIRUS! THE ZOMBIES ONLY BITE PEOPLE BECAUSE OF A BUTTFEED THINKPIECE ABOUT CANNIBALISM!
THE CONGLOM-O-NET IS TURNING PEOPLE INTO ZOMBIES?!
THAT'S RIGHT! JEALOUSY FROM SEEING THEIR FRIENDS' VACATION PHOTOS, FURY FROM ANGRY CLICKBAIT, IGNORANCE FROM FAKE NEWS--ALL OF IT IS INFECTING O-TOWN'S CITIZENS WITH RAGE!
THAT'S RIGHT, DOCTOR! YOU'VE FIGURED IT ALL OUT! THE ZOMBIE PLAGUE ISN'T JUST A VIRUS...
CHUNK

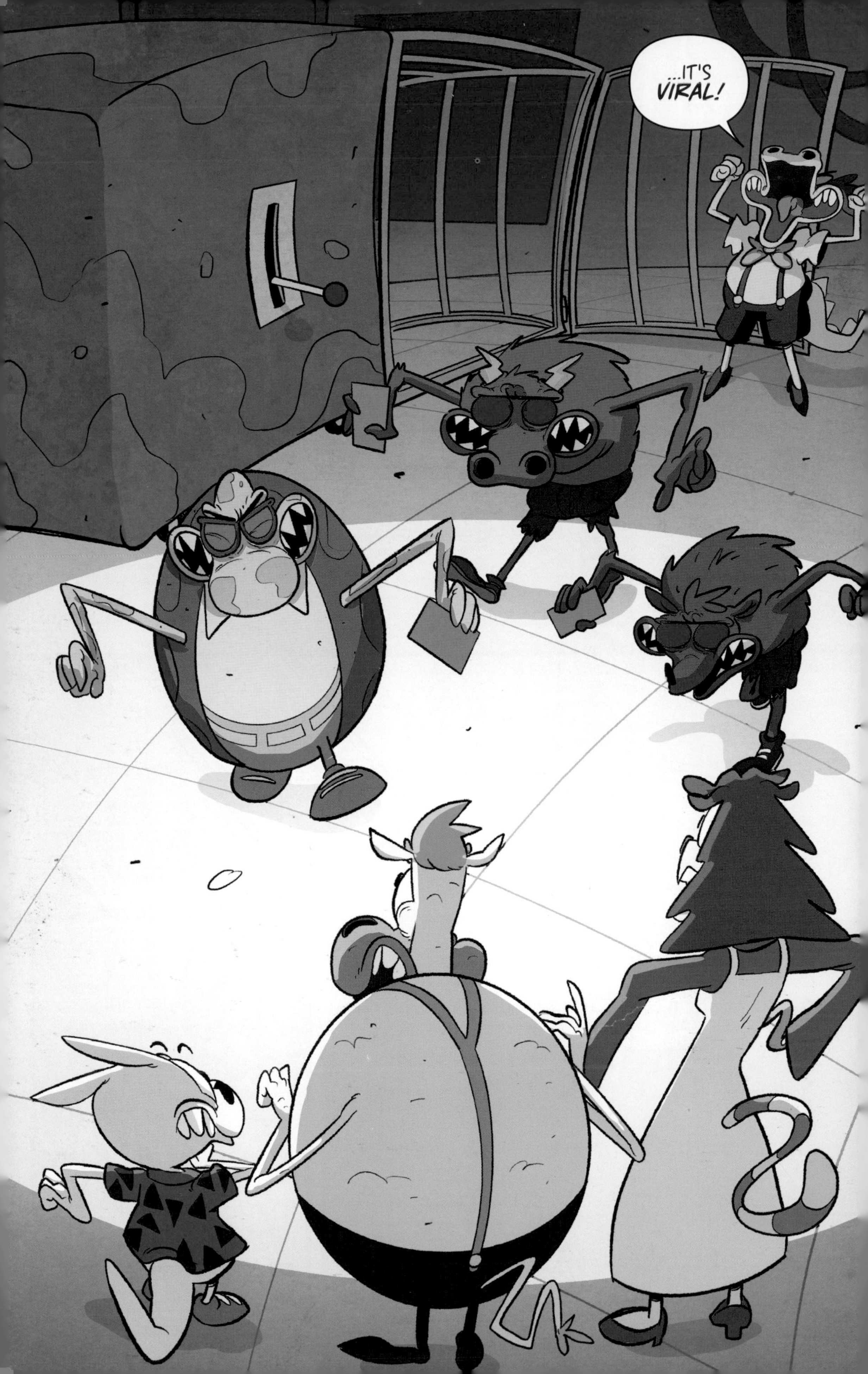
...IT'S VIRAL!

CHAPTER
FOUR

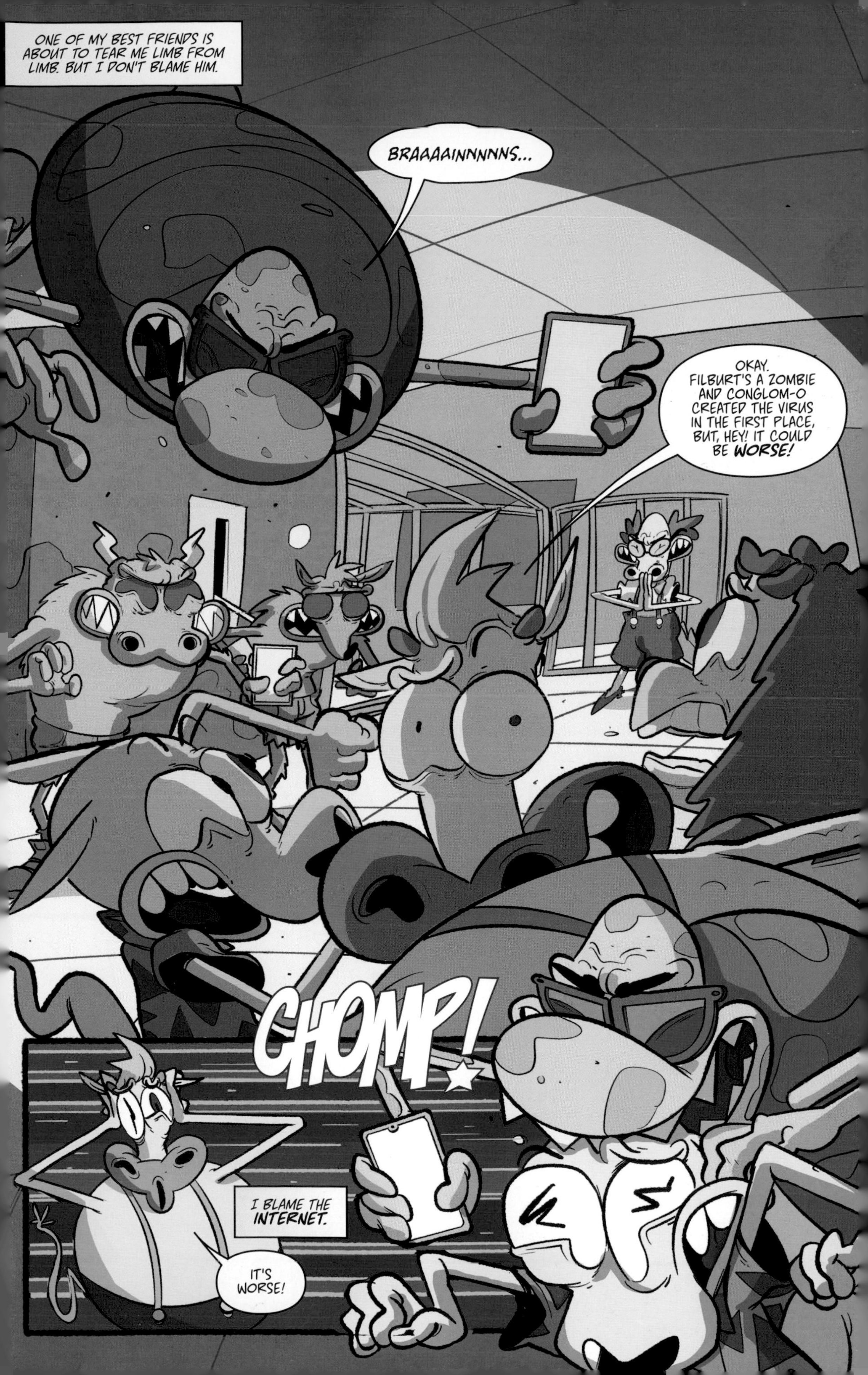
ONE OF MY BEST FRIENDS IS ABOUT TO TEAR ME LIMB FROM LIMB. BUT I DON'T BLAME HIM.
BRAAAAINNNNNS...
OKAY. FILBURT'S A ZOMBIE AND CONGLOM-O CREATED THE VIRUS IN THE FIRST PLACE, BUT, HEY! IT COULD BE **WORSE!**
CHOMP!
I BLAME THE **INTERNET.**
IT'S WORSE!

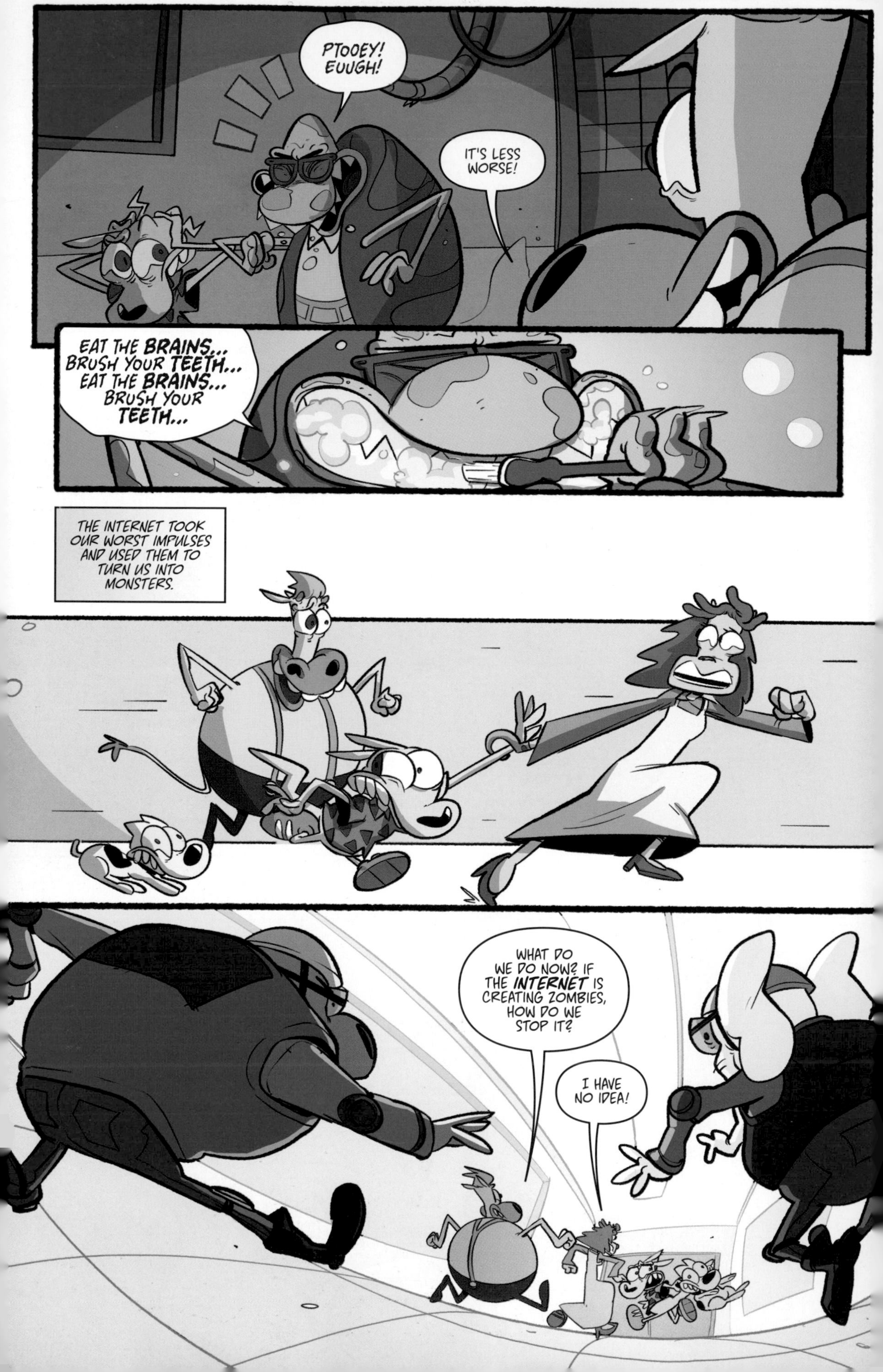
PTOOEY! EUUGH!
IT'S LESS WORSE!
EAT THE BRAINS... BRUSH YOUR TEETH... EAT THE BRAINS... BRUSH YOUR TEETH...
THE INTERNET TOOK OUR WORST IMPULSES AND USED THEM TO TURN US INTO MONSTERS.
WHAT DO WE DO NOW? IF THE INTERNET IS CREATING ZOMBIES, HOW DO WE STOP IT?
I HAVE NO IDEA!

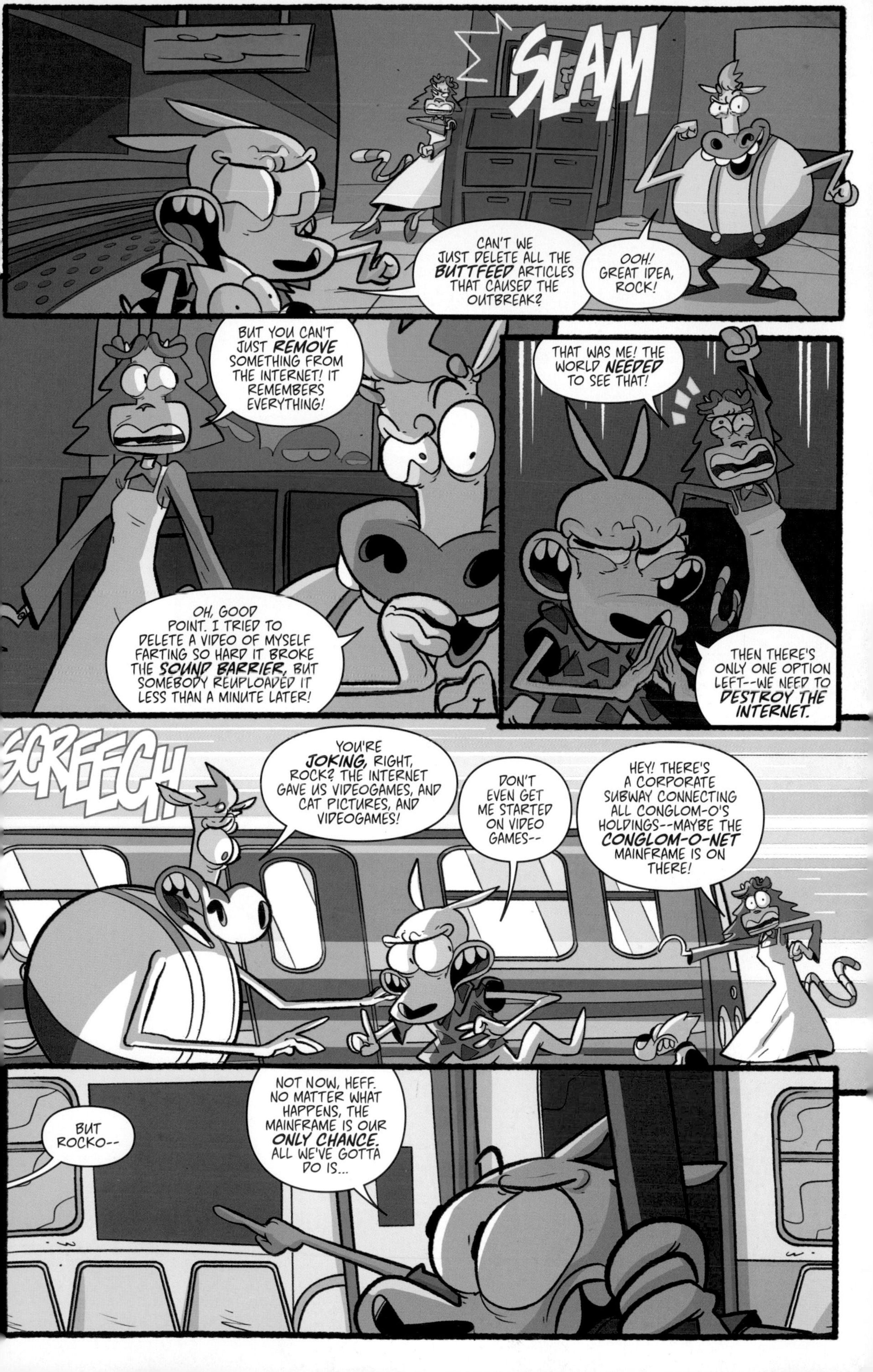
SLAM
CAN'T WE JUST DELETE ALL THE BUTTFEED ARTICLES THAT CAUSED THE OUTBREAK?
OOH! GREAT IDEA, ROCK!
BUT YOU CAN'T JUST REMOVE SOMETHING FROM THE INTERNET! IT REMEMBERS EVERYTHING!
OH, GOOD POINT. I TRIED TO DELETE A VIDEO OF MYSELF FARTING SO HARD IT BROKE THE SOUND BARRIER, BUT SOMEBODY REUPLOADED IT LESS THAN A MINUTE LATER!
THAT WAS ME! THE WORLD NEEDED TO SEE THAT!
THEN THERE'S ONLY ONE OPTION LEFT--WE NEED TO DESTROY THE INTERNET.
SCREECH
YOU'RE JOKING, RIGHT, ROCK? THE INTERNET GAVE US VIDEOGAMES, AND CAT PICTURES, AND VIDEOGAMES!
DON'T EVEN GET ME STARTED ON VIDEO GAMES--
HEY! THERE'S A CORPORATE SUBWAY CONNECTING ALL CONGLOM-O'S HOLDINGS--MAYBE THE CONGLOM-O-NET MAINFRAME IS ON THERE!
BUT ROCKO--
NOT NOW, HEFF. NO MATTER WHAT HAPPENS, THE MAINFRAME IS OUR ONLY CHANCE. ALL WE'VE GOTTA DO IS...

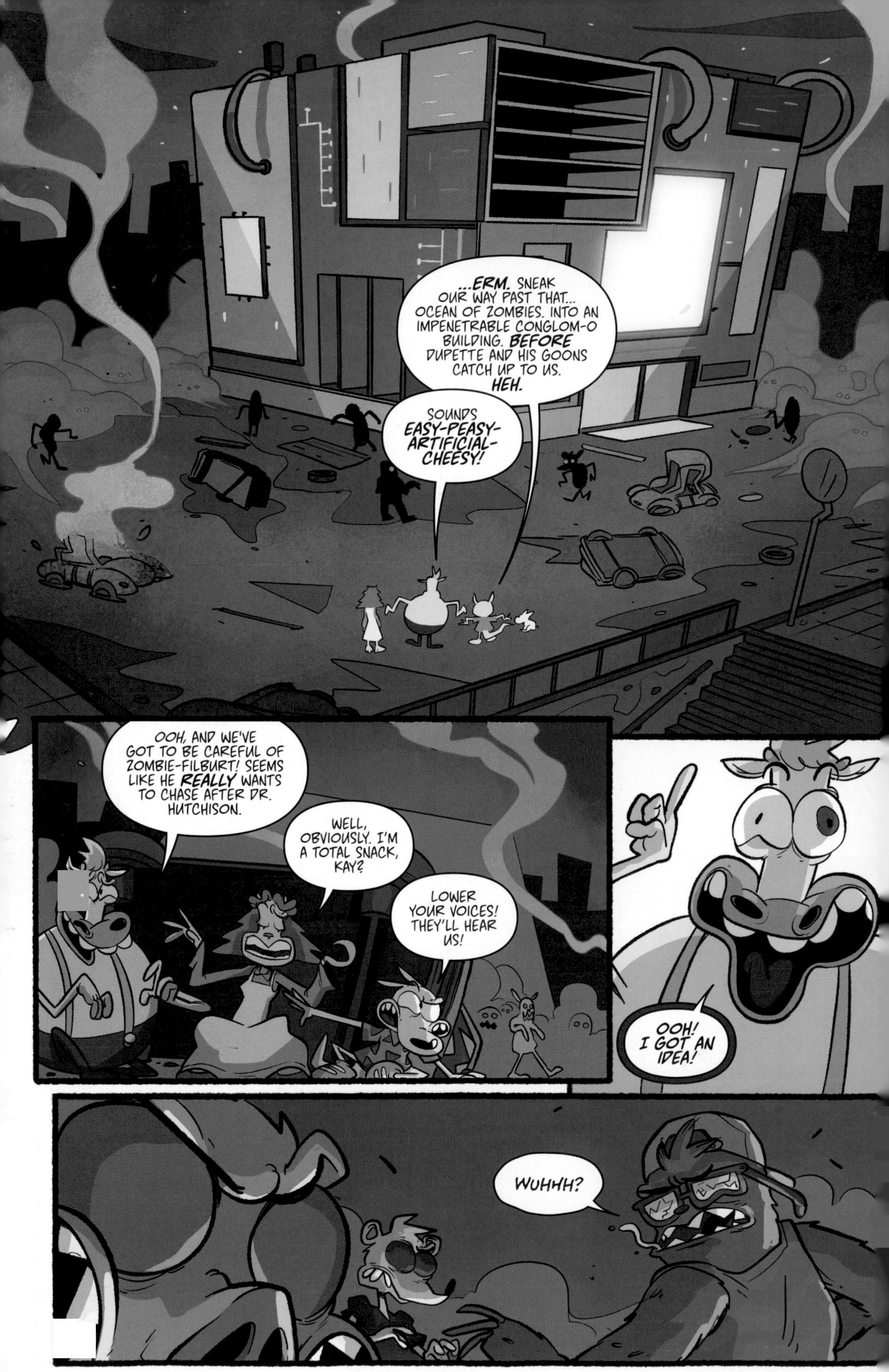
...ERM. SNEAK OUR WAY PAST THAT... OCEAN OF ZOMBIES. INTO AN IMPENETRABLE CONGLOM-O BUILDING. BEFORE DUPETTE AND HIS GOONS CATCH UP TO US. HEH.
SOUNDS EASY-PEASY-ARTIFICIAL-CHEESY!
OOH, AND WE'VE GOT TO BE CAREFUL OF ZOMBIE-FILBURT! SEEMS LIKE HE REALLY WANTS TO CHASE AFTER DR. HUTCHISON.
WELL, OBVIOUSLY. I'M A TOTAL SNACK, KAY?
LOWER YOUR VOICES! THEY'LL HEAR US!
OOH! I GOT AN IDEA!
WUHHH?

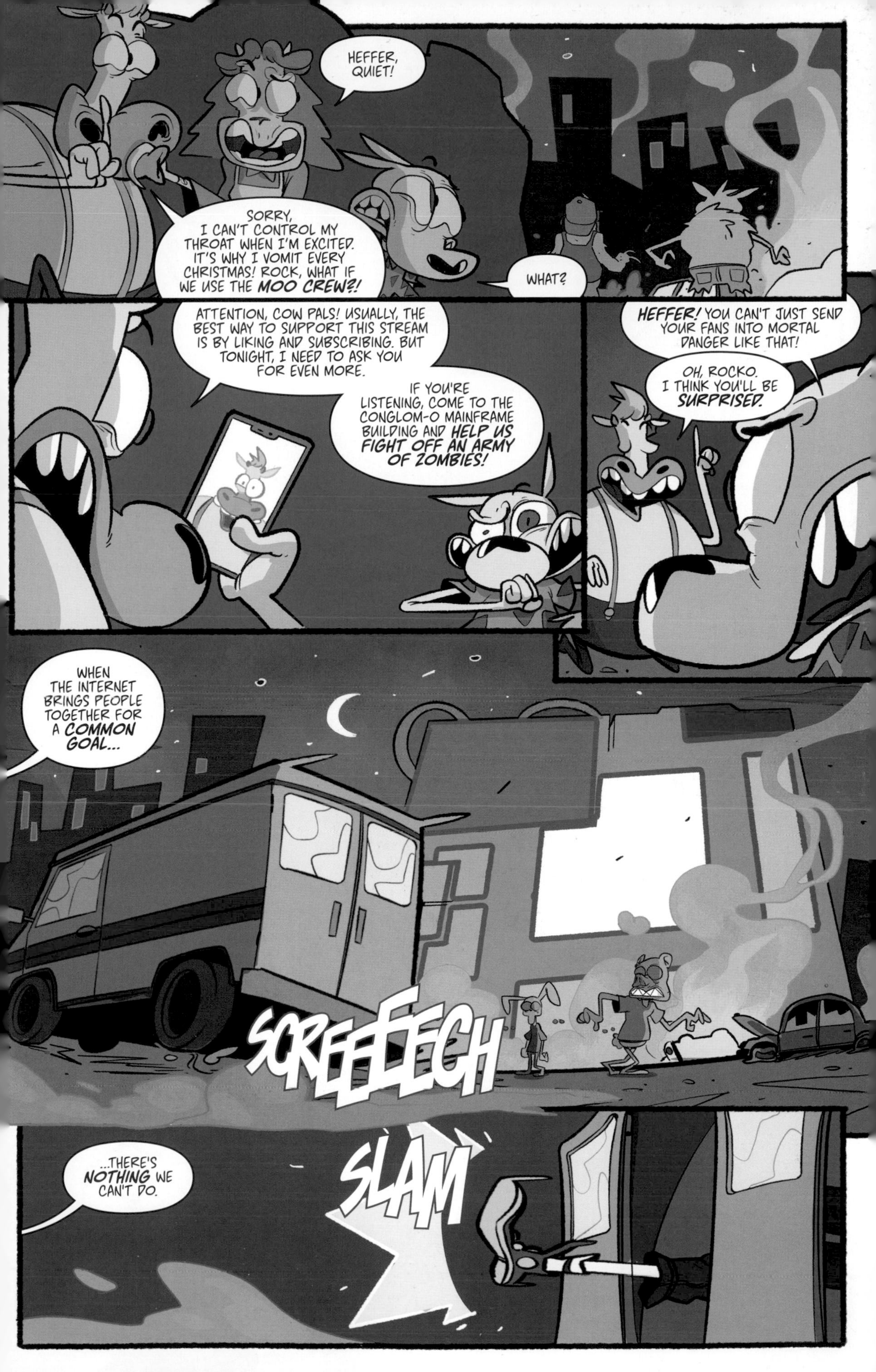
HEFFER, QUIET!
SORRY, I CAN'T CONTROL MY THROAT WHEN I'M EXCITED. IT'S WHY I VOMIT EVERY CHRISTMAS! ROCK, WHAT IF WE USE THE MOO CREW?!
WHAT?
ATTENTION, COW PALS! USUALLY, THE BEST WAY TO SUPPORT THIS STREAM IS BY LIKING AND SUBSCRIBING. BUT TONIGHT, I NEED TO ASK YOU FOR EVEN MORE.
IF YOU'RE LISTENING, COME TO THE CONGLOM-O MAINFRAME BUILDING AND HELP US FIGHT OFF AN ARMY OF ZOMBIES!
HEFFER! YOU CAN'T JUST SEND YOUR FANS INTO MORTAL DANGER LIKE THAT!
OH, ROCKO. I THINK YOU'LL BE SURPRISED.
WHEN THE INTERNET BRINGS PEOPLE TOGETHER FOR A COMMON GOAL...
SCREEEECH
SLAM
...THERE'S NOTHING WE CAN'T DO.

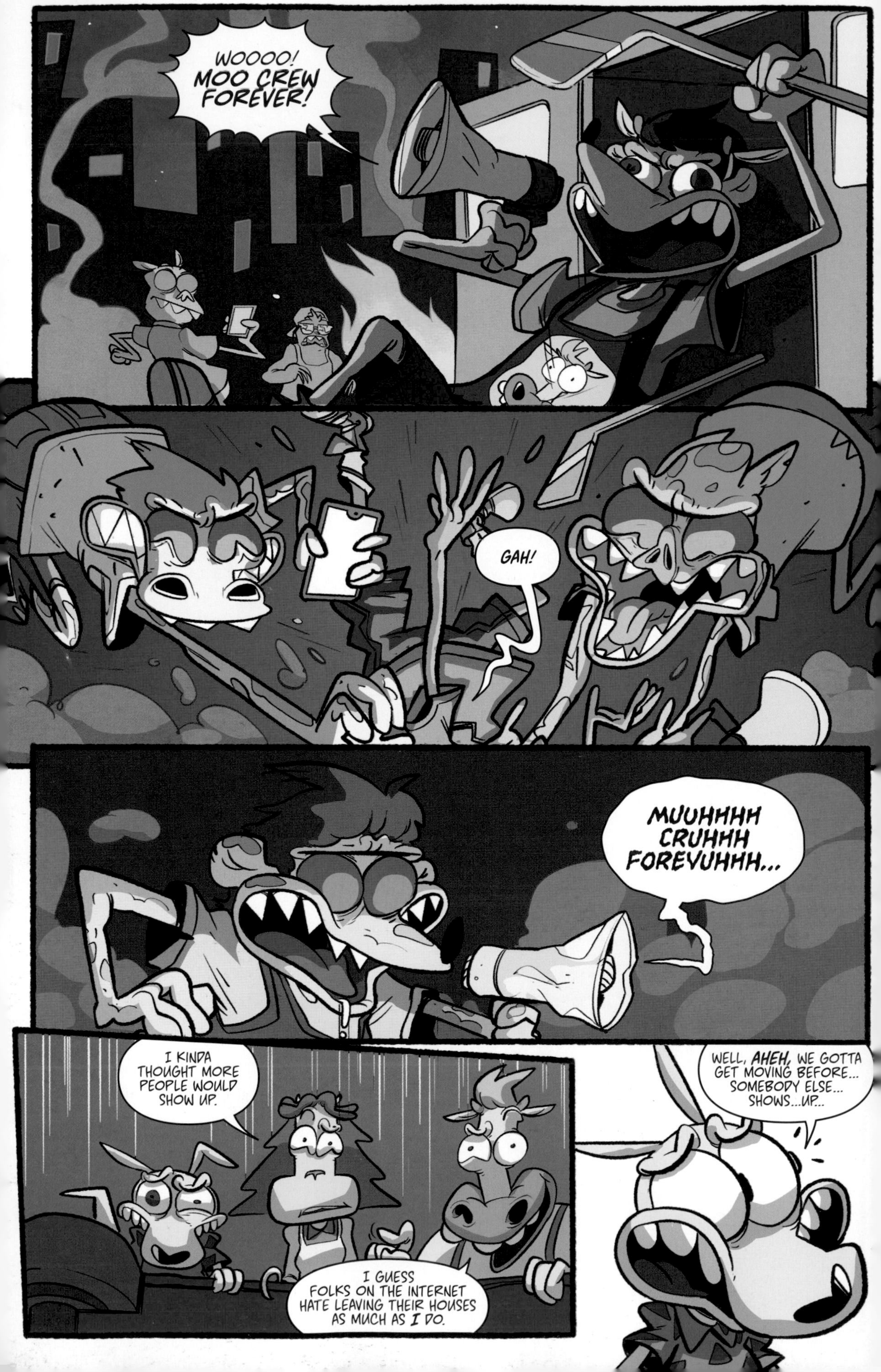
WOOOO! MOO CREW FOREVER!
GAH!
MUUHHHH CRUHHH FOREVUHHH...
I KINDA THOUGHT MORE PEOPLE WOULD SHOW UP.
I GUESS FOLKS ON THE INTERNET HATE LEAVING THEIR HOUSES AS MUCH AS I DO.
WELL, AHEH, WE GOTTA GET MOVING BEFORE... SOMEBODY ELSE... SHOWS...UP...

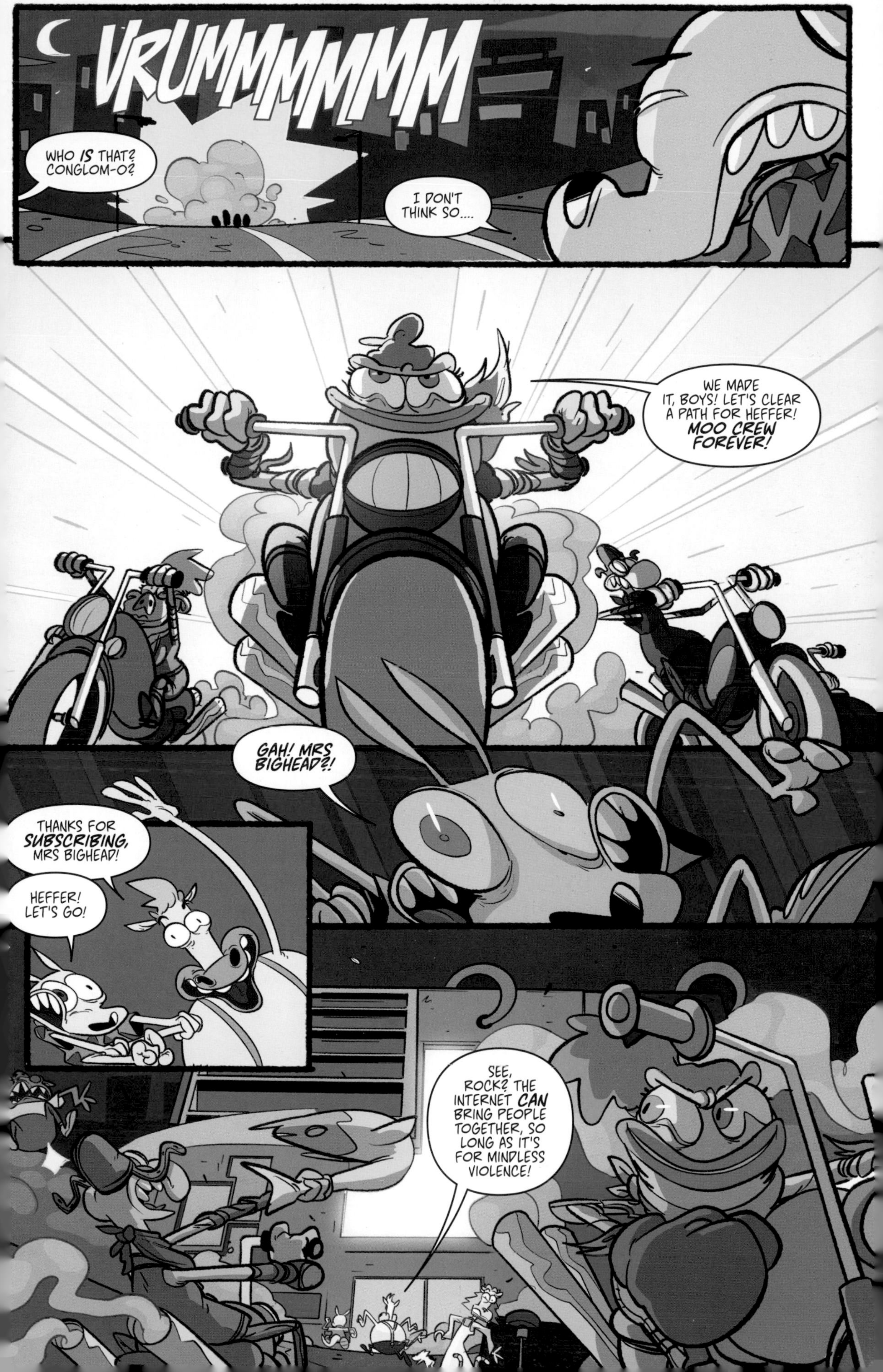
VRUMMMMMMM
WHO IS THAT? CONGLOM-O?
I DON'T THINK SO....
WE MADE IT, BOYS! LET'S CLEAR A PATH FOR HEFFER! MOO CREW FOREVER!
GAH! MRS BIGHEAD?!
THANKS FOR SUBSCRIBING, MRS BIGHEAD!
HEFFER! LET'S GO!
SEE, ROCK? THE INTERNET CAN BRING PEOPLE TOGETHER, SO LONG AS IT'S FOR MINDLESS VIOLENCE!

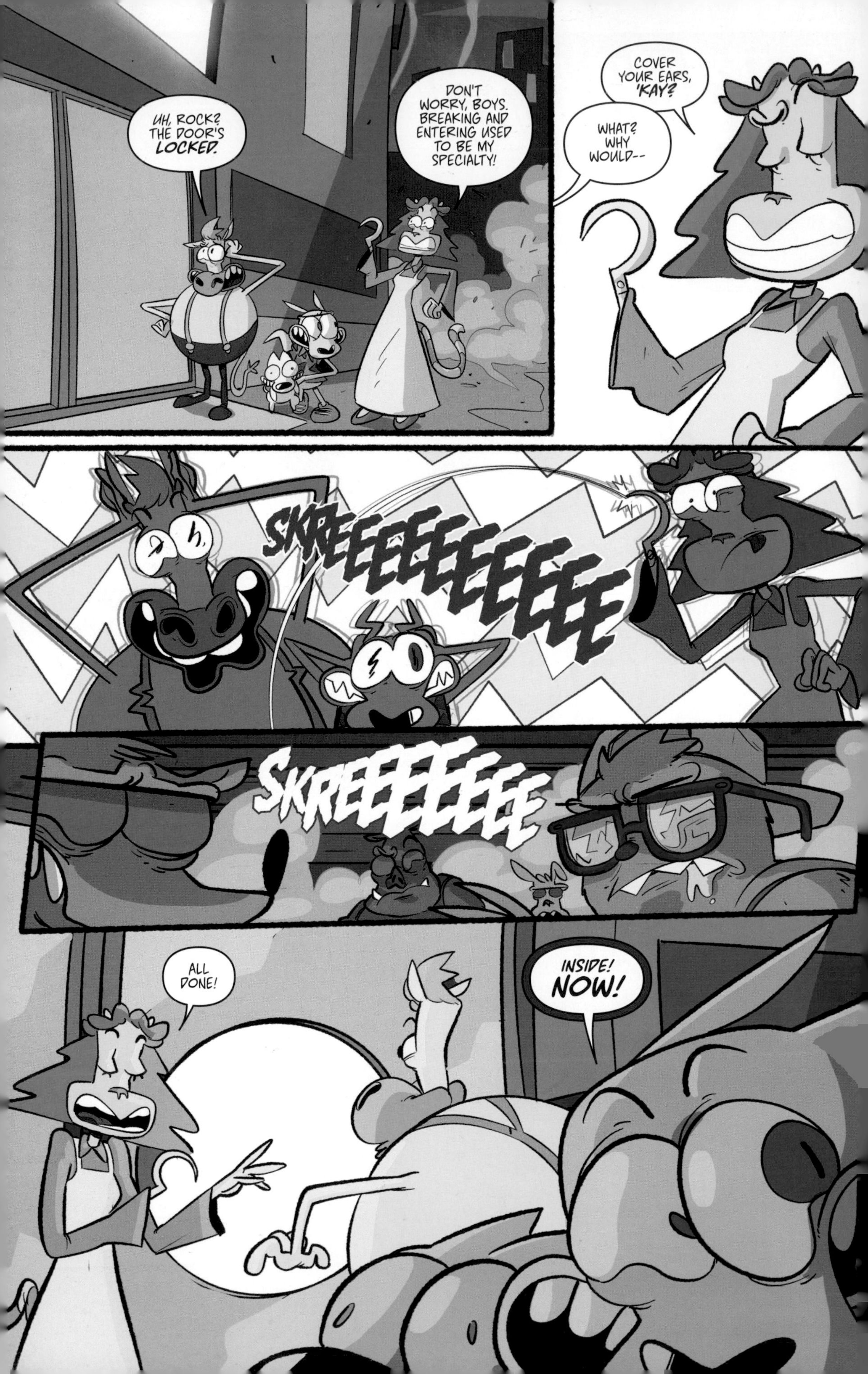
UH, ROCK? THE DOOR'S LOCKED.
DON'T WORRY, BOYS. BREAKING AND ENTERING USED TO BE MY SPECIALTY!
COVER YOUR EARS, 'KAY?
WHAT? WHY WOULD--
SKREEEEEEEEEEEE
SKREEEEEEEEEE
ALL DONE!
INSIDE! NOW!

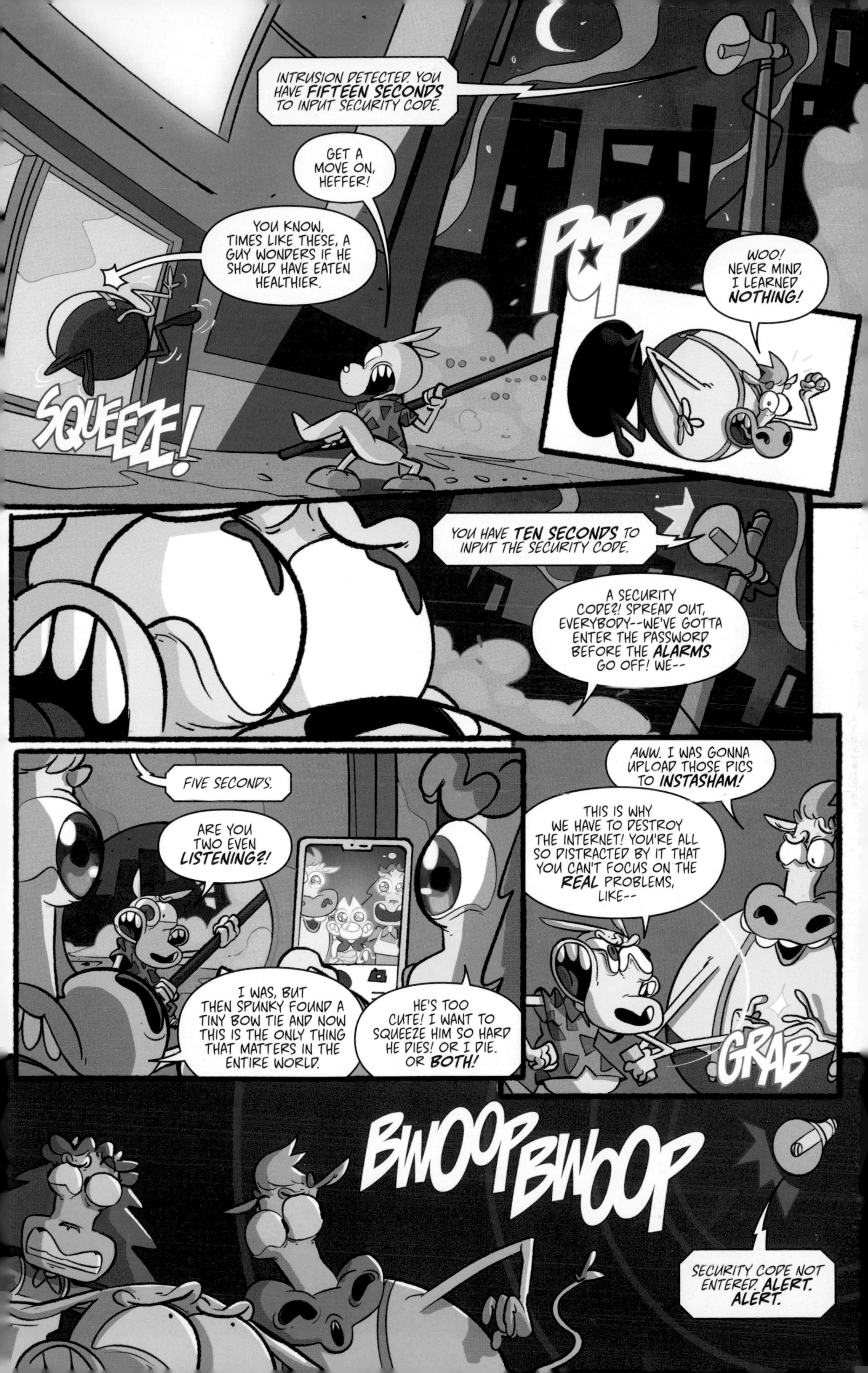
INTRUSION DETECTED. YOU HAVE FIFTEEN SECONDS TO INPUT SECURITY CODE.
GET A MOVE ON, HEFFER!
YOU KNOW, TIMES LIKE THESE, A GUY WONDERS IF HE SHOULD HAVE EATEN HEALTHIER.
SQUEEZE!
POP
WOO! NEVER MIND, I LEARNED NOTHING!
YOU HAVE TEN SECONDS TO INPUT THE SECURITY CODE.
A SECURITY CODE?! SPREAD OUT, EVERYBODY--WE'VE GOTTA ENTER THE PASSWORD BEFORE THE ALARMS GO OFF! WE--
FIVE SECONDS.
ARE YOU TWO EVEN LISTENING?!
I WAS, BUT THEN SPUNKY FOUND A TINY BOW TIE AND NOW THIS IS THE ONLY THING THAT MATTERS IN THE ENTIRE WORLD.
HE'S TOO CUTE! I WANT TO SQUEEZE HIM SO HARD HE DIES! OR I DIE. OR BOTH!
AWW. I WAS GONNA UPLOAD THOSE PICS TO INSTASHAM!
THIS IS WHY WE HAVE TO DESTROY THE INTERNET! YOU'RE ALL SO DISTRACTED BY IT THAT YOU CAN'T FOCUS ON THE REAL PROBLEMS, LIKE--
GRAB
BWOOP BWOOP
SECURITY CODE NOT ENTERED. ALERT. ALERT.

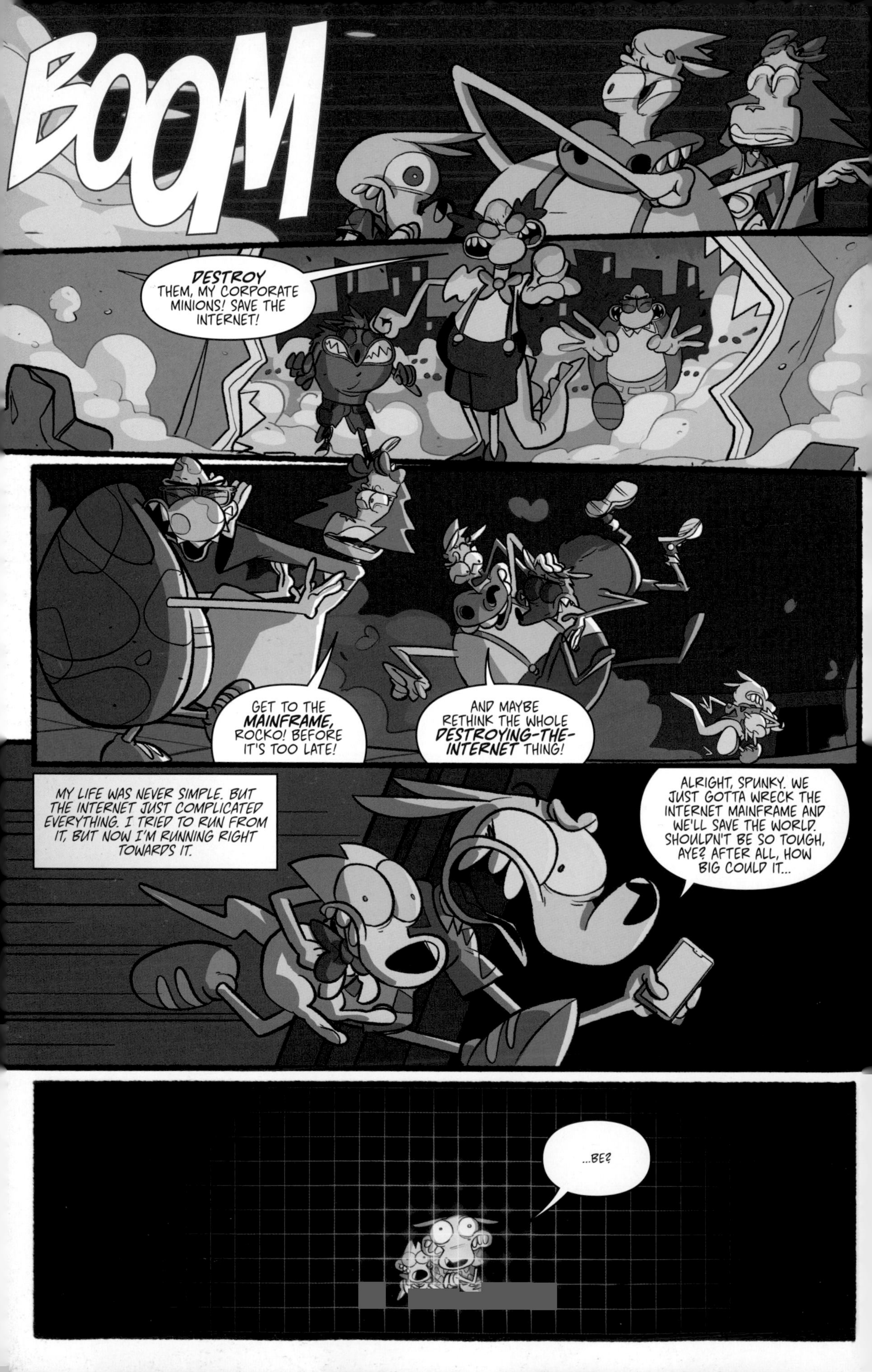
BOOM
DESTROY THEM, MY CORPORATE MINIONS! SAVE THE INTERNET!
GET TO THE MAINFRAME, ROCKO! BEFORE IT'S TOO LATE!
AND MAYBE RETHINK THE WHOLE DESTROYING-THE-INTERNET THING!
MY LIFE WAS NEVER SIMPLE. BUT THE INTERNET JUST COMPLICATED EVERYTHING. I TRIED TO RUN FROM IT, BUT NOW I'M RUNNING RIGHT TOWARDS IT.
ALRIGHT, SPUNKY. WE JUST GOTTA WRECK THE INTERNET MAINFRAME AND WE'LL SAVE THE WORLD. SHOULDN'T BE SO TOUGH, AYE? AFTER ALL, HOW BIG COULD IT...
...BE?

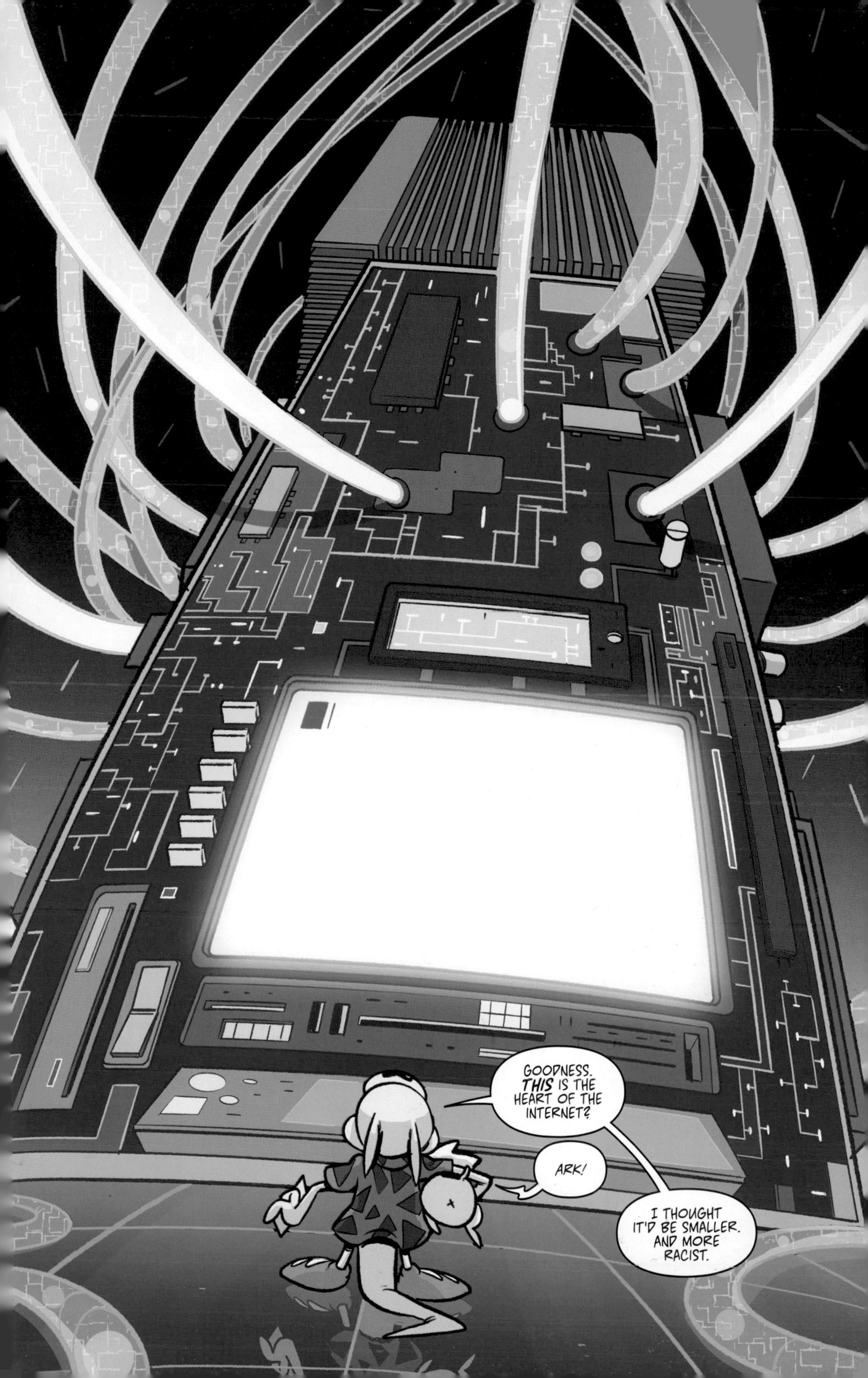
GOODNESS. THIS IS THE HEART OF THE INTERNET?
ARK!
I THOUGHT IT'D BE SMALLER. AND MORE RACIST.

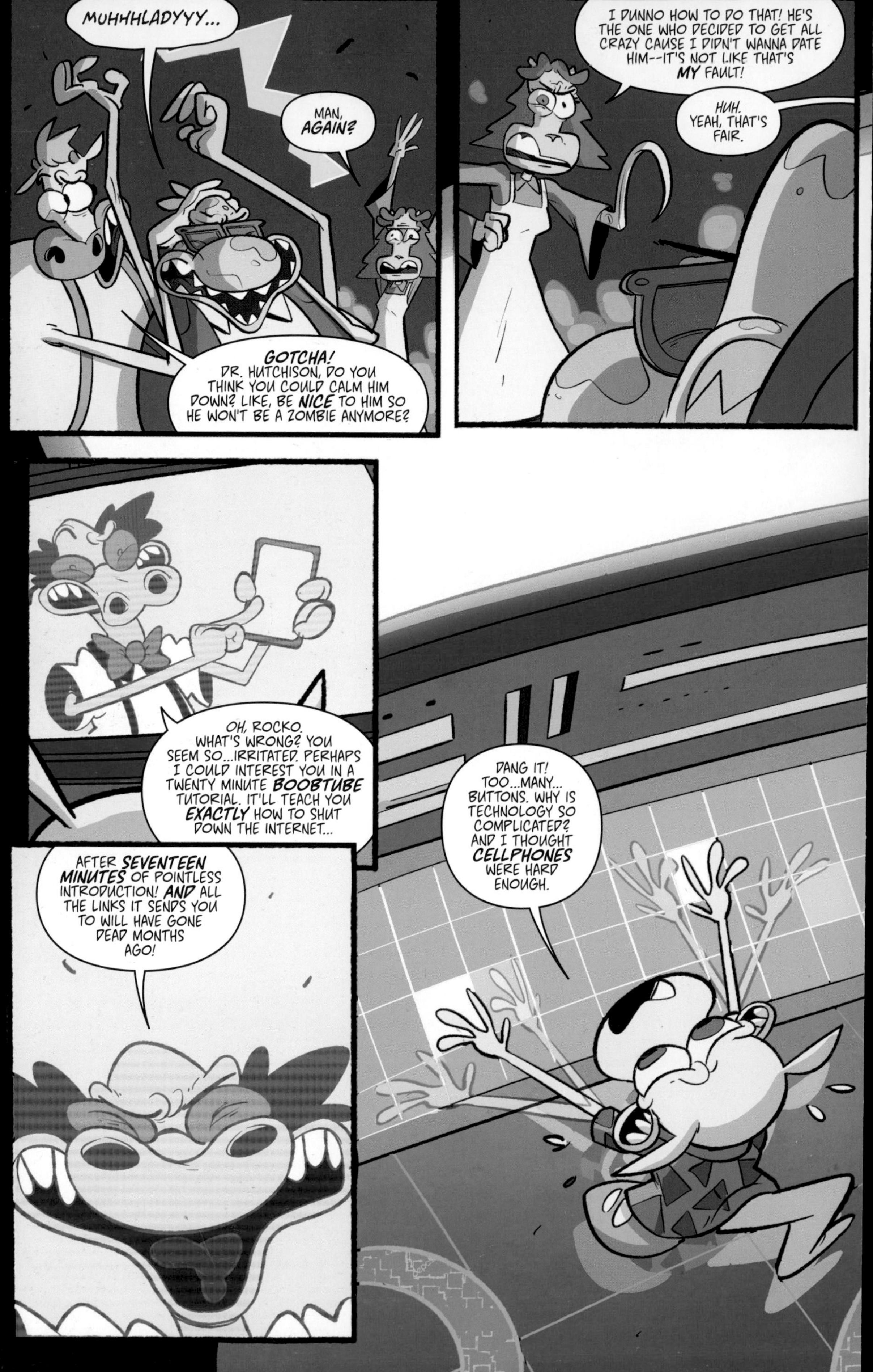
MUHHHLADYYY...
MAN, AGAIN?
GOTCHA! DR. HUTCHISON, DO YOU THINK YOU COULD CALM HIM DOWN? LIKE, BE NICE TO HIM SO HE WON'T BE A ZOMBIE ANYMORE?
I DUNNO HOW TO DO THAT! HE'S THE ONE WHO DECIDED TO GET ALL CRAZY CAUSE I DIDN'T WANNA DATE HIM--IT'S NOT LIKE THAT'S MY FAULT!
HUH. YEAH, THAT'S FAIR.
OH, ROCKO. WHAT'S WRONG? YOU SEEM SO...IRRITATED. PERHAPS I COULD INTEREST YOU IN A TWENTY MINUTE BOOBTUBE TUTORIAL. IT'LL TEACH YOU EXACTLY HOW TO SHUT DOWN THE INTERNET...
DANG IT! TOO...MANY... BUTTONS. WHY IS TECHNOLOGY SO COMPLICATED? AND I THOUGHT CELLPHONES WERE HARD ENOUGH.
AFTER SEVENTEEN MINUTES OF POINTLESS INTRODUCTION! AND ALL THE LINKS IT SENDS YOU TO WILL HAVE GONE DEAD MONTHS AGO!

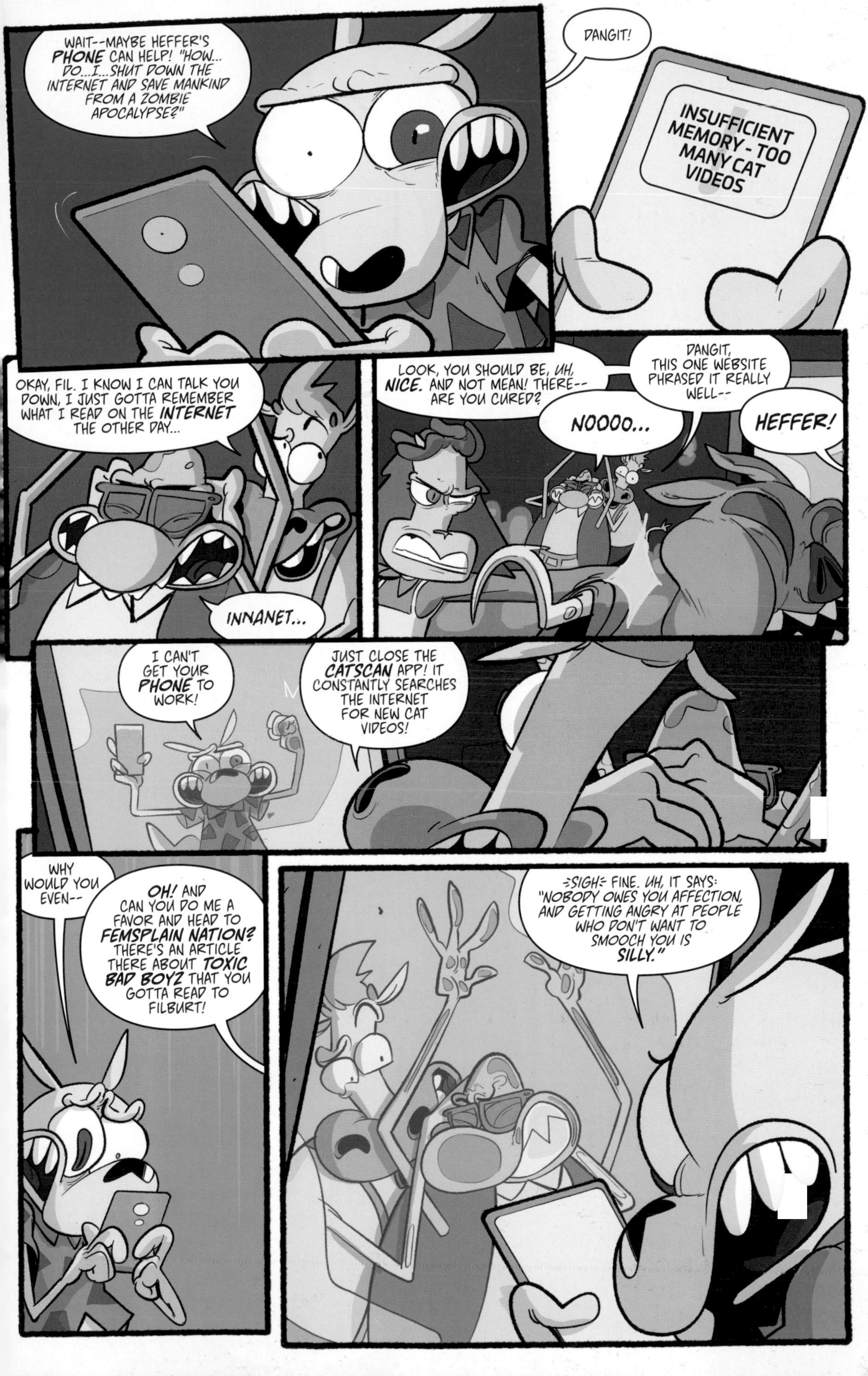
WAIT--MAYBE HEFFER'S PHONE CAN HELP! "HOW... DO...I...SHUT DOWN THE INTERNET AND SAVE MANKIND FROM A ZOMBIE APOCALYPSE?"
DANGIT!
INSUFFICIENT MEMORY - TOO MANY CAT VIDEOS
OKAY, FIL. I KNOW I CAN TALK YOU DOWN, I JUST GOTTA REMEMBER WHAT I READ ON THE INTERNET THE OTHER DAY...
INNANET...
LOOK, YOU SHOULD BE, UH, NICE. AND NOT MEAN! THERE--ARE YOU CURED?
DANGIT, THIS ONE WEBSITE PHRASED IT REALLY WELL--
NOOOO...
HEFFER!
I CAN'T GET YOUR PHONE TO WORK!
JUST CLOSE THE CATSCAN APP! IT CONSTANTLY SEARCHES THE INTERNET FOR NEW CAT VIDEOS!
WHY WOULD YOU EVEN--
OH! AND CAN YOU DO ME A FAVOR AND HEAD TO FEMSPLAIN NATION? THERE'S AN ARTICLE THERE ABOUT TOXIC BAD BOYZ THAT YOU GOTTA READ TO FILBURT!
=SIGH= FINE. UH, IT SAYS: "NOBODY OWES YOU AFFECTION, AND GETTING ANGRY AT PEOPLE WHO DON'T WANT TO SMOOCH YOU IS SILLY."

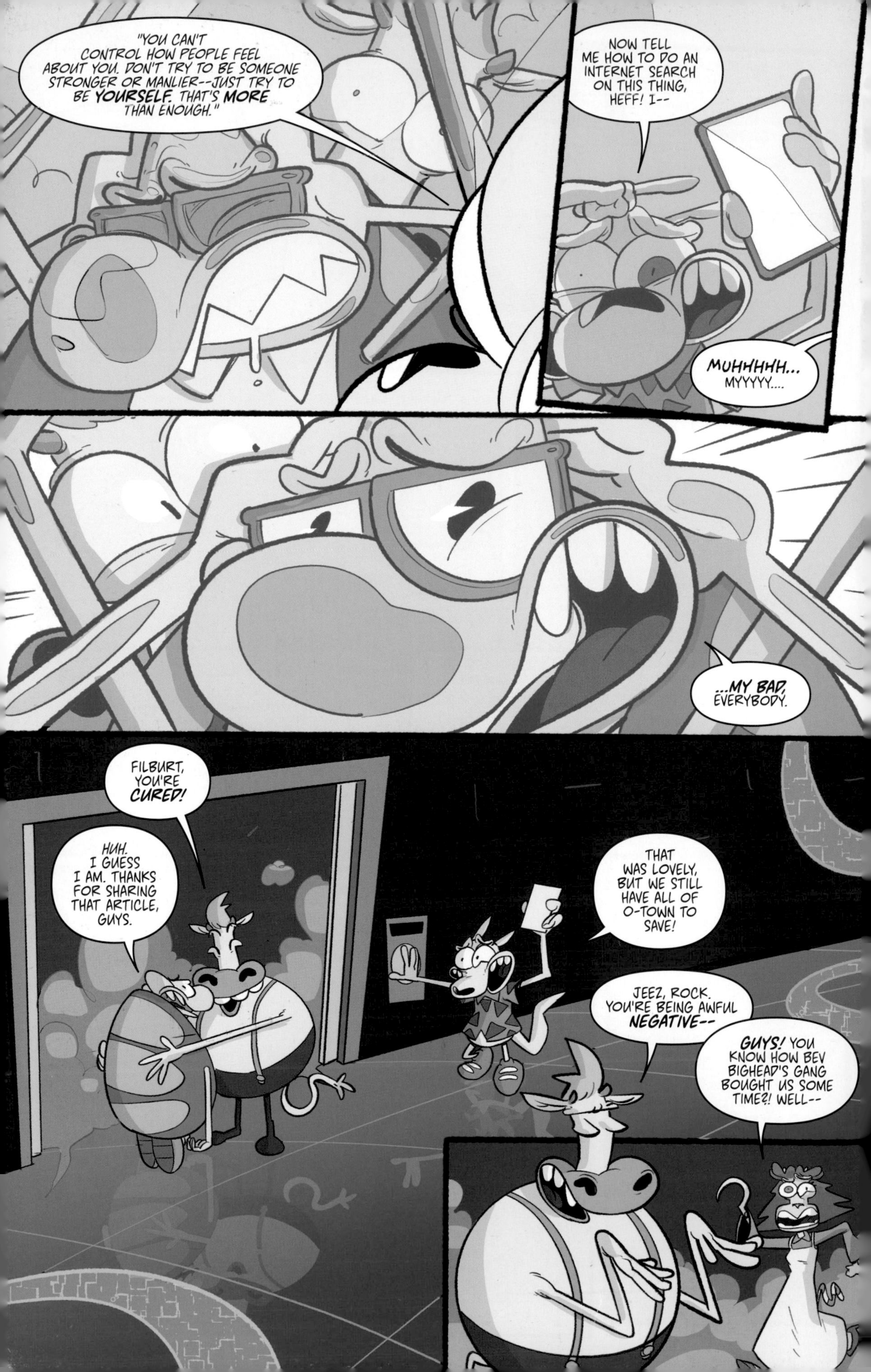
"YOU CAN'T CONTROL HOW PEOPLE FEEL ABOUT YOU. DON'T TRY TO BE SOMEONE STRONGER OR MANLIER--JUST TRY TO BE **YOURSELF.** THAT'S **MORE** THAN ENOUGH."
NOW TELL ME HOW TO DO AN INTERNET SEARCH ON THIS THING, HEFF! I--
MUHHHHH... MYYYYY....
...MY BAD, EVERYBODY.
FILBURT, YOU'RE ***CURED!***
HUH. I GUESS I AM. THANKS FOR SHARING THAT ARTICLE, GUYS.
THAT WAS LOVELY, BUT WE STILL HAVE ALL OF O-TOWN TO SAVE!
JEEZ, ROCK. YOU'RE BEING AWFUL ***NEGATIVE--***
GUYS! YOU KNOW HOW BEV BIGHEAD'S GANG BOUGHT US SOME TIME?! WELL--

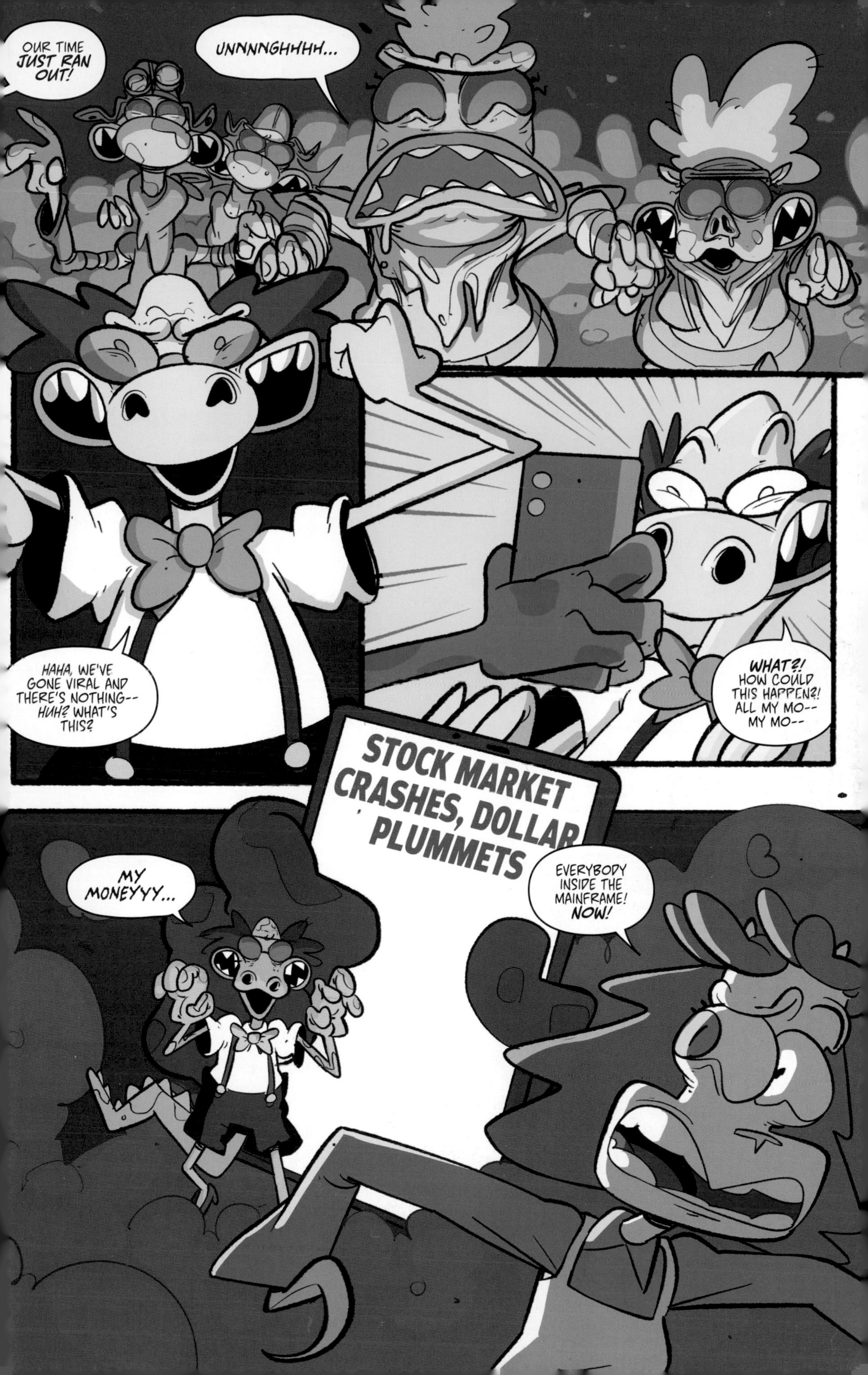
OUR TIME JUST RAN OUT!
UNNNNGHHHH...
HAHA, WE'VE GONE VIRAL AND THERE'S NOTHING-- HUH? WHAT'S THIS?
WHAT?! HOW COULD THIS HAPPEN?! ALL MY MO-- MY MO--
STOCK MARKET CRASHES, DOLLAR PLUMMETS
MY MONEYYY...
EVERYBODY INSIDE THE MAINFRAME! NOW!

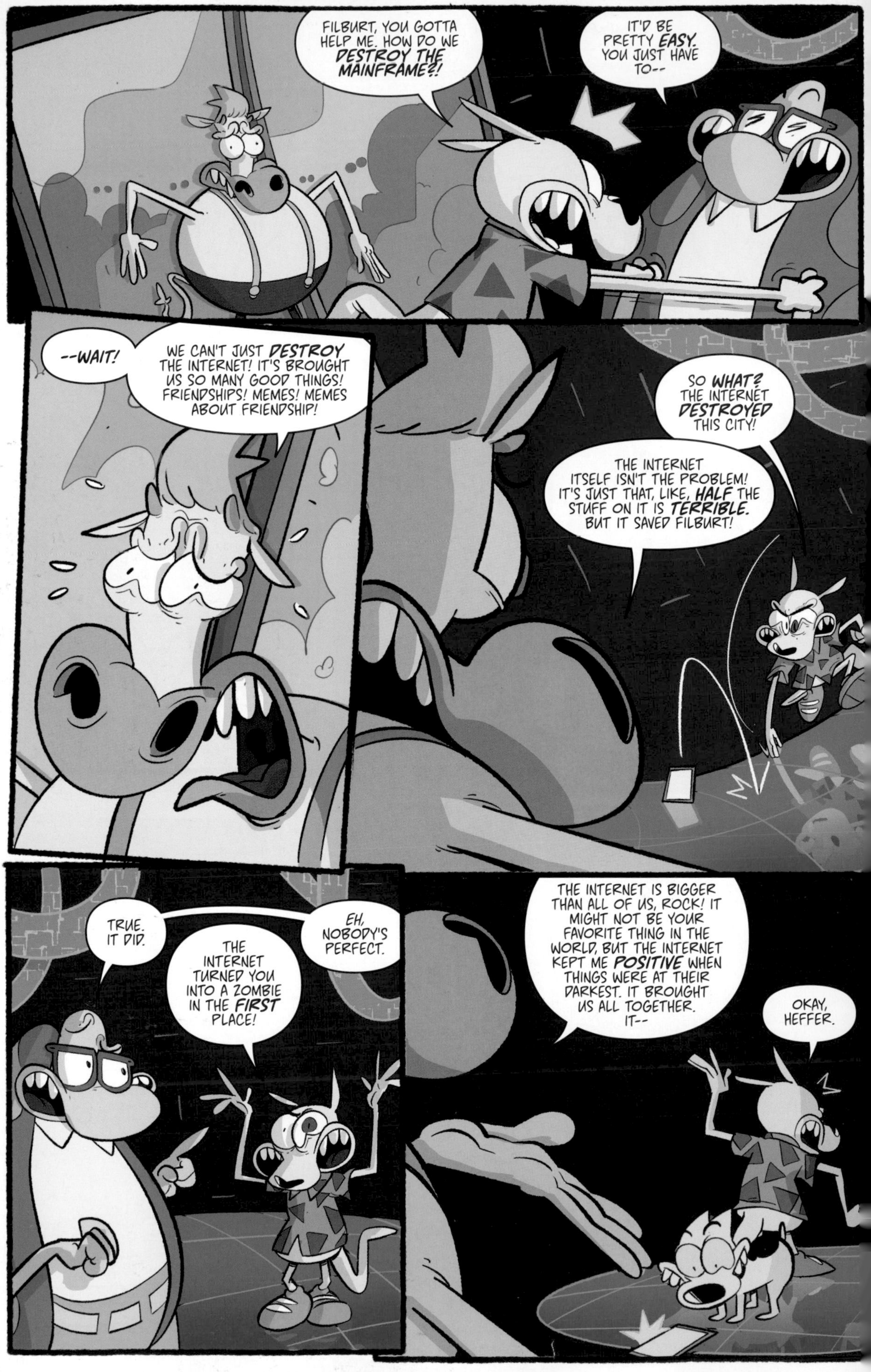

FILBURT, YOU GOTTA HELP ME. HOW DO WE DESTROY THE MAINFRAME?!
IT'D BE PRETTY EASY. YOU JUST HAVE TO--
--WAIT!
WE CAN'T JUST DESTROY THE INTERNET! IT'S BROUGHT US SO MANY GOOD THINGS! FRIENDSHIPS! MEMES! MEMES ABOUT FRIENDSHIP!
SO WHAT? THE INTERNET DESTROYED THIS CITY!
THE INTERNET ITSELF ISN'T THE PROBLEM! IT'S JUST THAT, LIKE, HALF THE STUFF ON IT IS TERRIBLE. BUT IT SAVED FILBURT!
TRUE. IT DID.
THE INTERNET TURNED YOU INTO A ZOMBIE IN THE FIRST PLACE!
EH, NOBODY'S PERFECT.
THE INTERNET IS BIGGER THAN ALL OF US, ROCK! IT MIGHT NOT BE YOUR FAVORITE THING IN THE WORLD, BUT THE INTERNET KEPT ME POSITIVE WHEN THINGS WERE AT THEIR DARKEST. IT BROUGHT US ALL TOGETHER. IT--
OKAY, HEFFER.

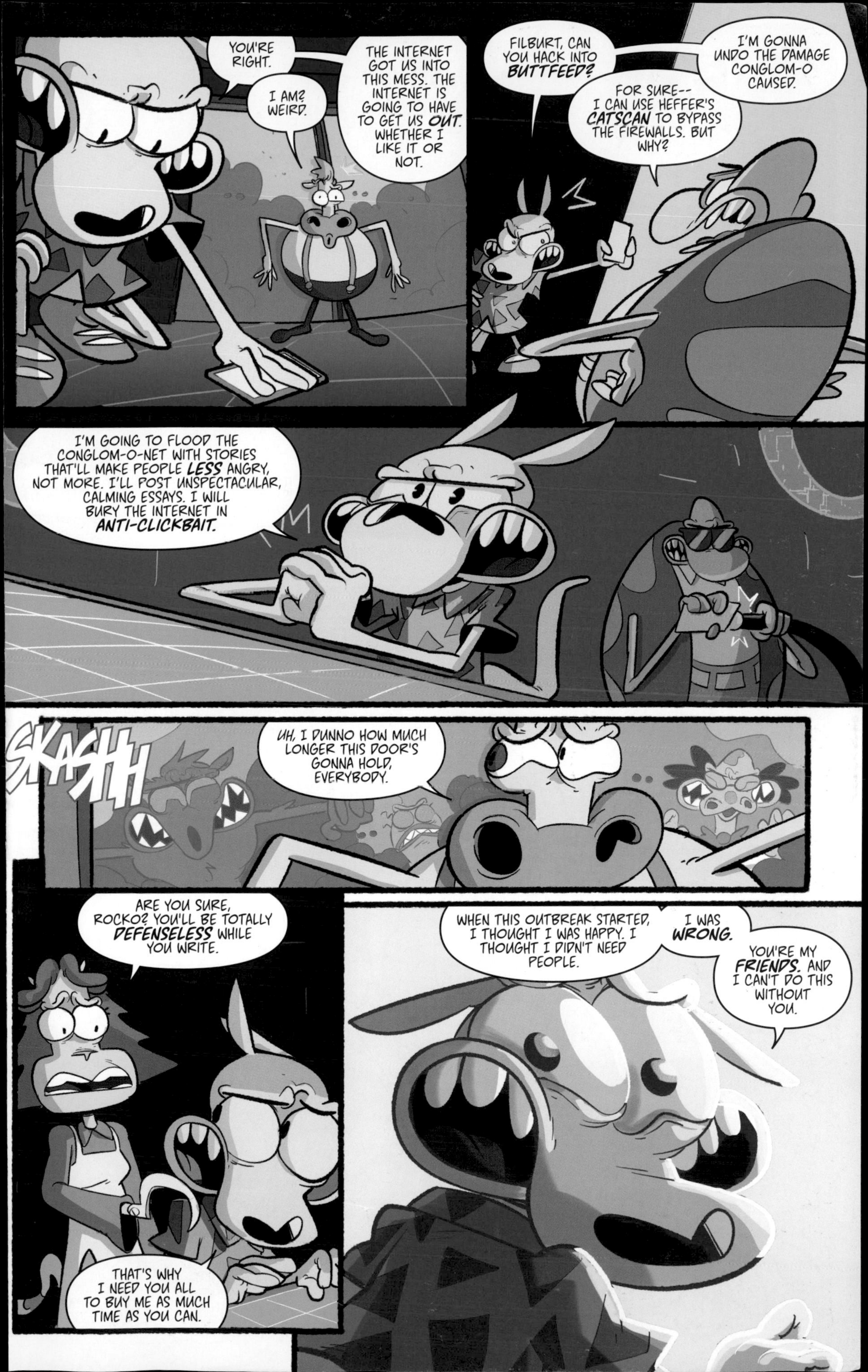
YOU'RE RIGHT.
I AM? WEIRD.
THE INTERNET GOT US INTO THIS MESS. THE INTERNET IS GOING TO HAVE TO GET US OUT. WHETHER I LIKE IT OR NOT.
FILBURT, CAN YOU HACK INTO BUTTFEED?
I'M GONNA UNDO THE DAMAGE CONGLOM-O CAUSED.
FOR SURE-- I CAN USE HEFFER'S CATSCAN TO BYPASS THE FIREWALLS. BUT WHY?
I'M GOING TO FLOOD THE CONGLOM-O-NET WITH STORIES THAT'LL MAKE PEOPLE LESS ANGRY, NOT MORE. I'LL POST UNSPECTACULAR, CALMING ESSAYS. I WILL BURY THE INTERNET IN ANTI-CLICKBAIT.
SKASHH
UH, I DUNNO HOW MUCH LONGER THIS DOOR'S GONNA HOLD, EVERYBODY.
ARE YOU SURE, ROCKO? YOU'LL BE TOTALLY DEFENSELESS WHILE YOU WRITE.
THAT'S WHY I NEED YOU ALL TO BUY ME AS MUCH TIME AS YOU CAN.
WHEN THIS OUTBREAK STARTED, I THOUGHT I WAS HAPPY. I THOUGHT I DIDN'T NEED PEOPLE.
I WAS WRONG.
YOU'RE MY FRIENDS. AND I CAN'T DO THIS WITHOUT YOU.

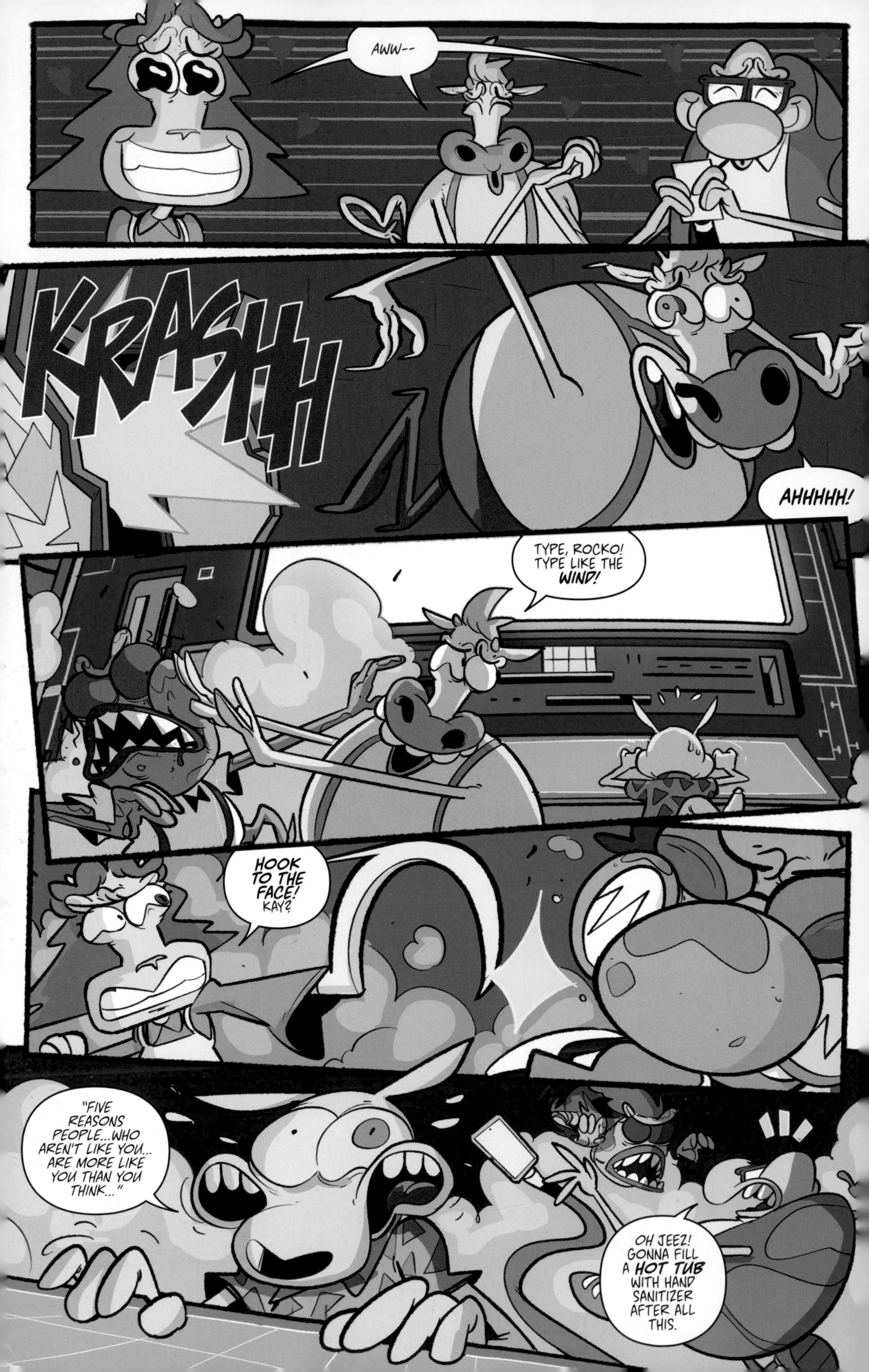
AWW--
KRASHH
AHHHHH!
TYPE, ROCKO! TYPE LIKE THE WIND!
HOOK TO THE FACE! KAY?
"FIVE REASONS PEOPLE...WHO AREN'T LIKE YOU... ARE MORE LIKE YOU THAN YOU THINK..."
OH JEEZ! GONNA FILL A HOT TUB WITH HAND SANITIZER AFTER ALL THIS.

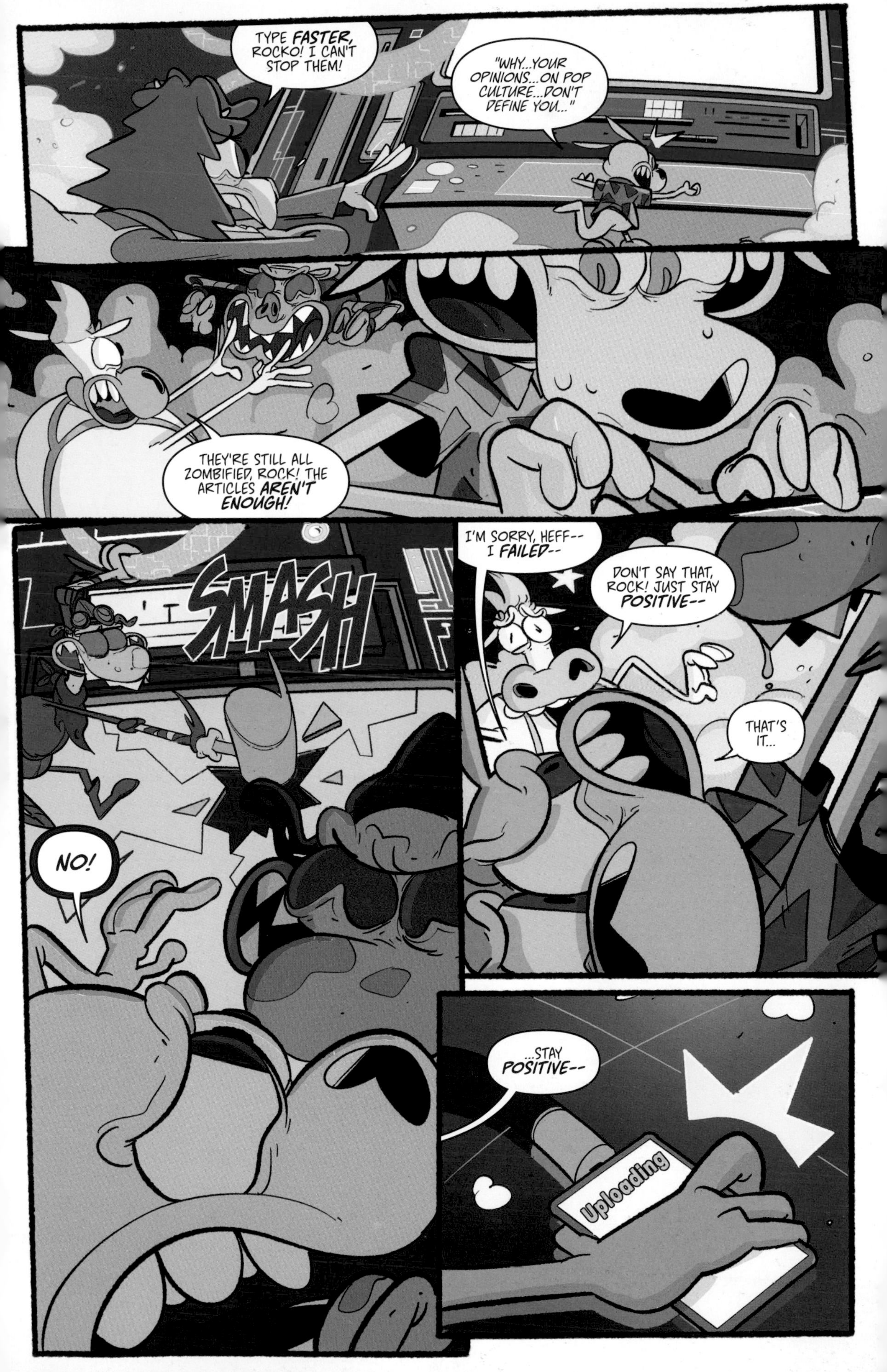
TYPE **FASTER**, ROCKO! I CAN'T STOP THEM!
"WHY...YOUR OPINIONS...ON POP CULTURE...DON'T DEFINE YOU..."
THEY'RE STILL ALL ZOMBIFIED, ROCK! THE ARTICLES **AREN'T ENOUGH!**
SMASH
NO!
I'M SORRY, HEFF-- I **FAILED**--
DON'T SAY THAT, ROCK! JUST STAY **POSITIVE**--
THAT'S IT...
...STAY **POSITIVE**--
Uploading

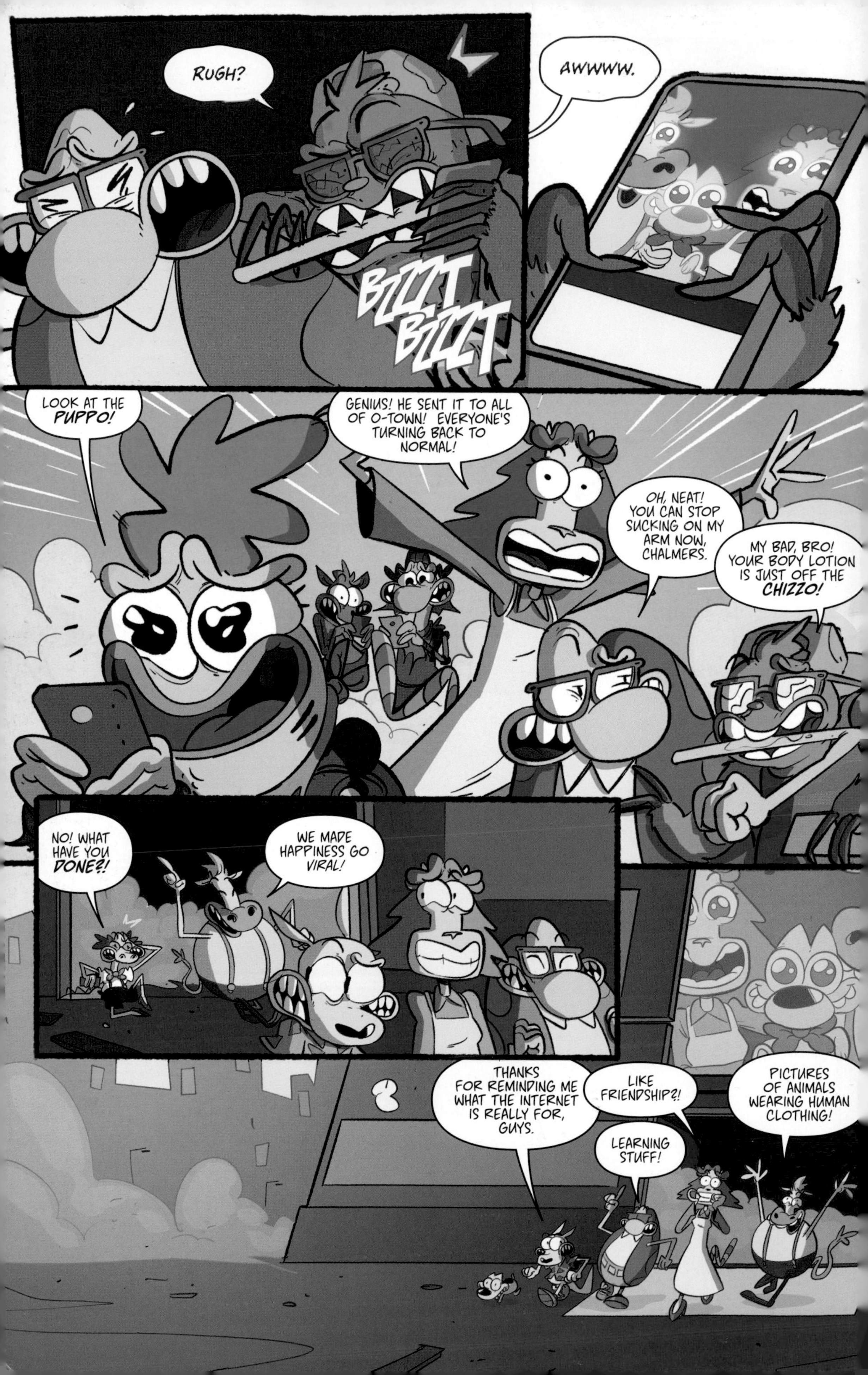
RUGH?
BZZZT BZZZT
AWWWW.
LOOK AT THE PUPPO!
GENIUS! HE SENT IT TO ALL OF O-TOWN! EVERYONE'S TURNING BACK TO NORMAL!
OH, NEAT! YOU CAN STOP SUCKING ON MY ARM NOW, CHALMERS.
MY BAD, BRO! YOUR BODY LOTION IS JUST OFF THE CHIZZO!
NO! WHAT HAVE YOU DONE?!
WE MADE HAPPINESS GO VIRAL!
THANKS FOR REMINDING ME WHAT THE INTERNET IS REALLY FOR, GUYS.
LIKE FRIENDSHIP?!
LEARNING STUFF!
PICTURES OF ANIMALS WEARING HUMAN CLOTHING!

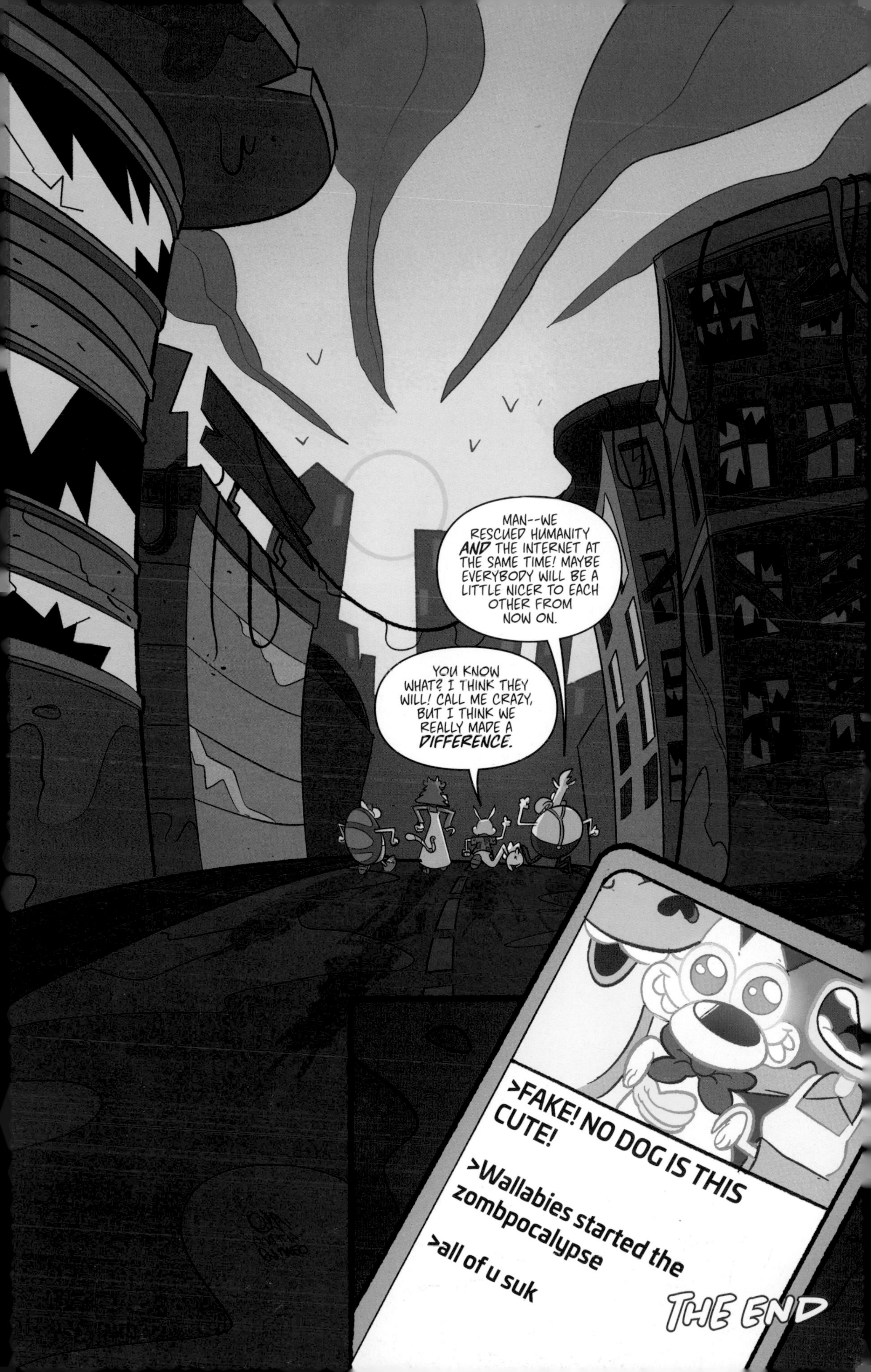

MAN--WE RESCUED HUMANITY **AND** THE INTERNET AT THE SAME TIME! MAYBE EVERYBODY WILL BE A LITTLE NICER TO EACH OTHER FROM NOW ON.
YOU KNOW WHAT? I THINK THEY WILL! CALL ME CRAZY, BUT I THINK WE REALLY MADE A **DIFFERENCE.**
>FAKE! NO DOG IS THIS CUTE!
>Wallabies started the zombpocalypse
>all of u suk
THE END

COVER

GALLERY

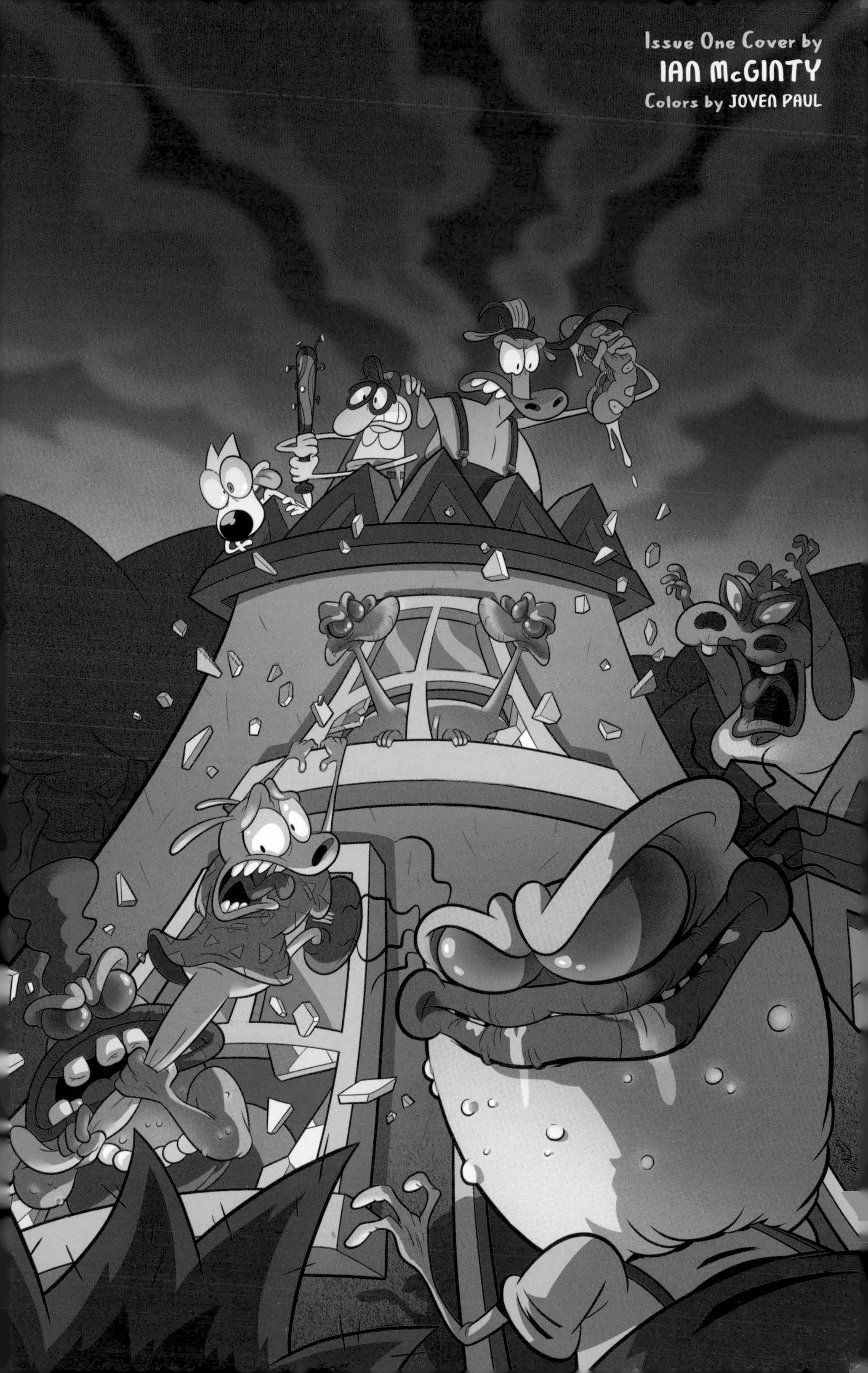

Issue One Cover by
IAN McGINTY
Colors by **JOVEN PAUL**

Issue One Variant Cover by
JORGE CORONA

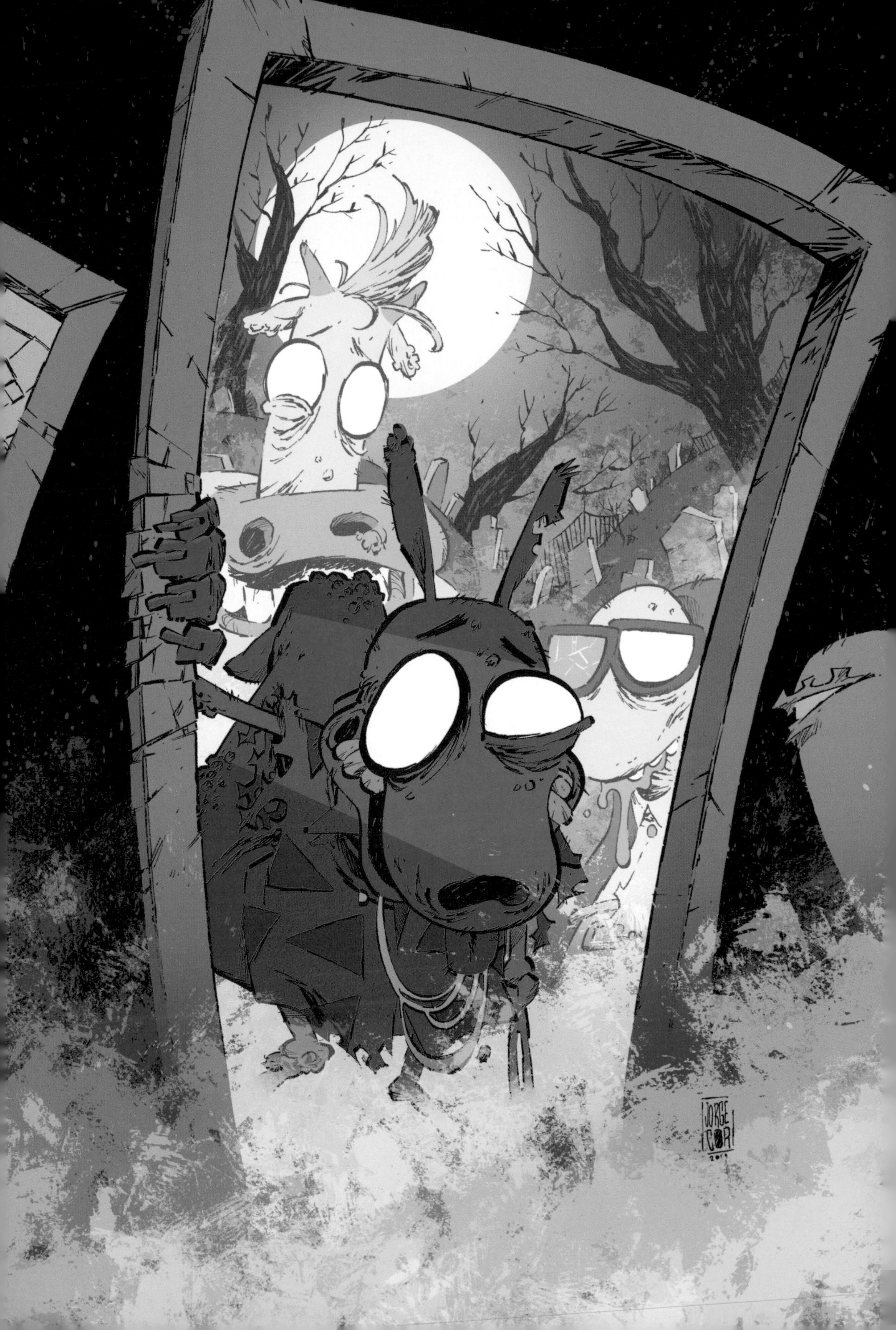

Issue One Connecting Cover by
JOEY McCORMICK

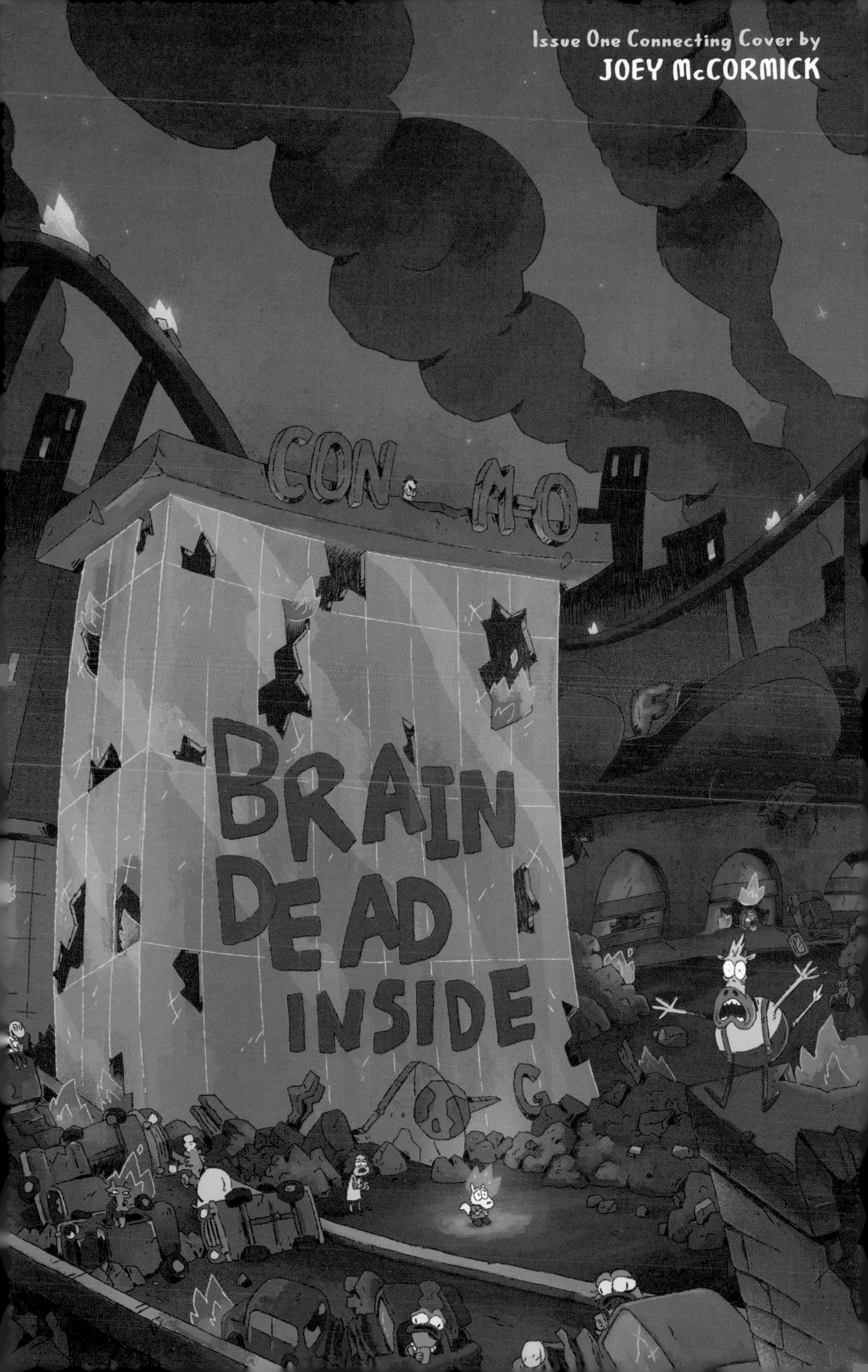
CON M-O
BRAIN DEAD INSIDE

Issue Two Cover by
IAN McGINTY
Colors by JOVEN PAUL

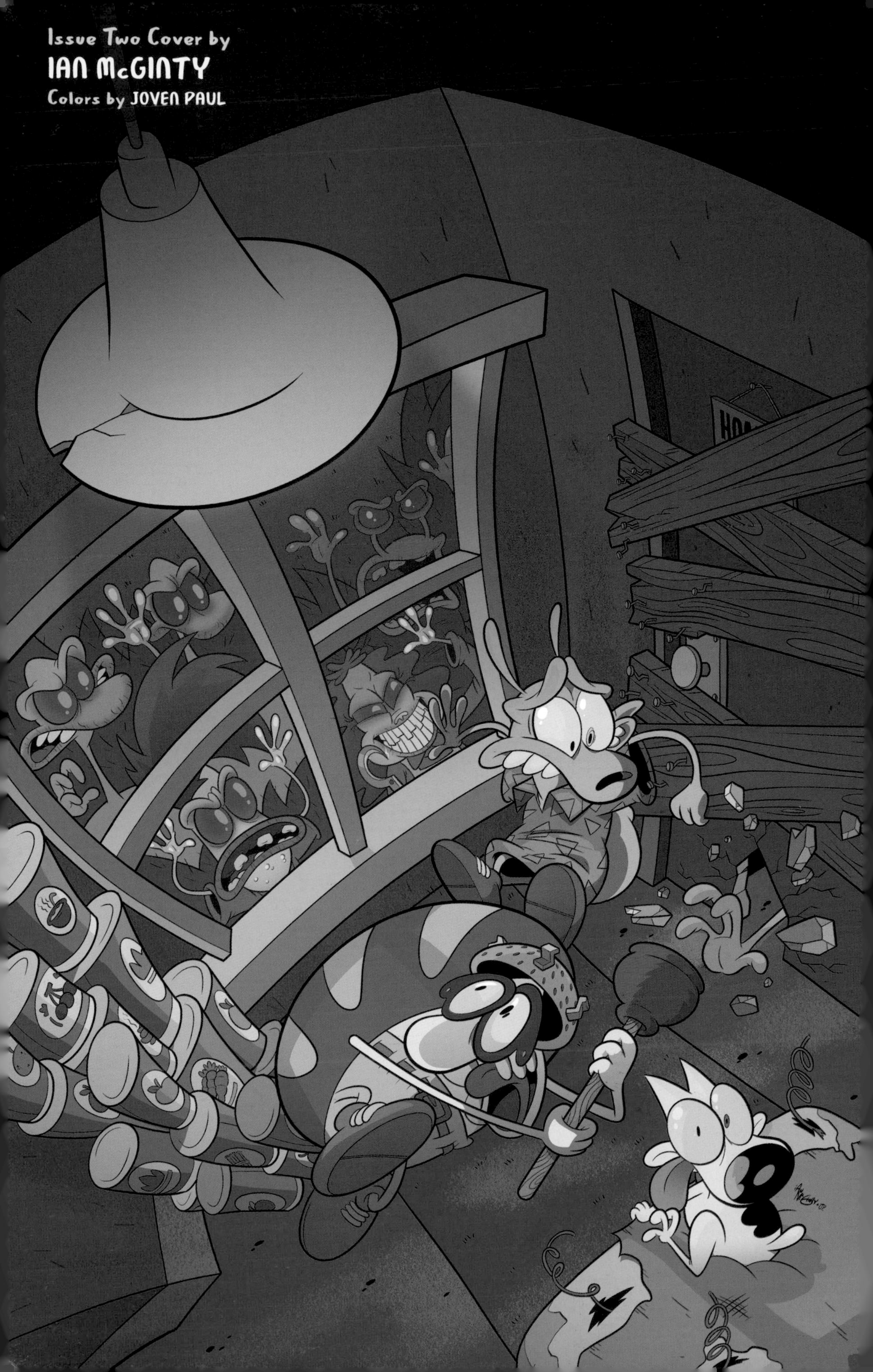

Issue Two Connecting Cover by
JOEY McCORMICK

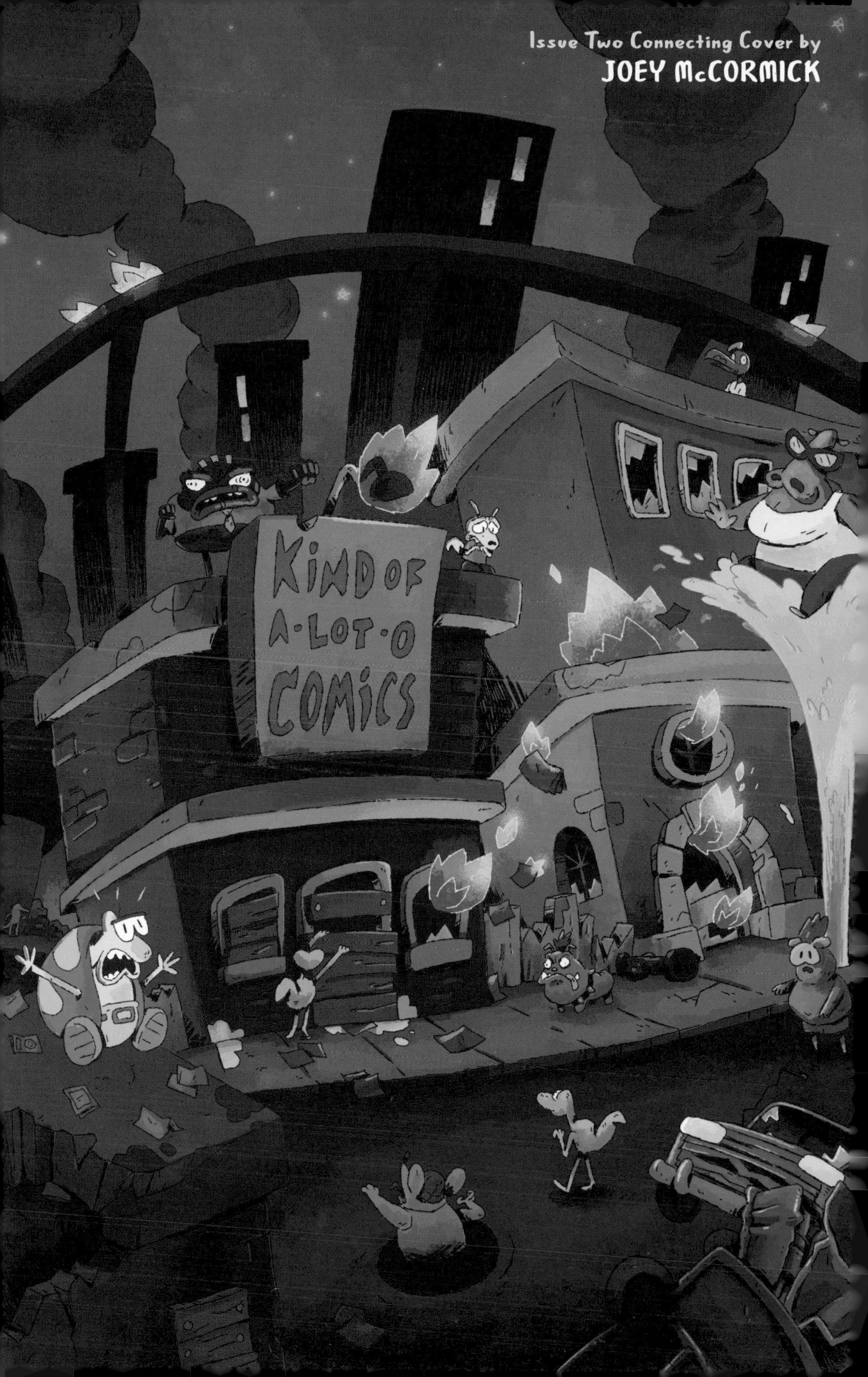
KIND OF A-LOT-O COMICS

Issue Three Cover by

IAN McGINTY

Colors by JOVEN PAUL

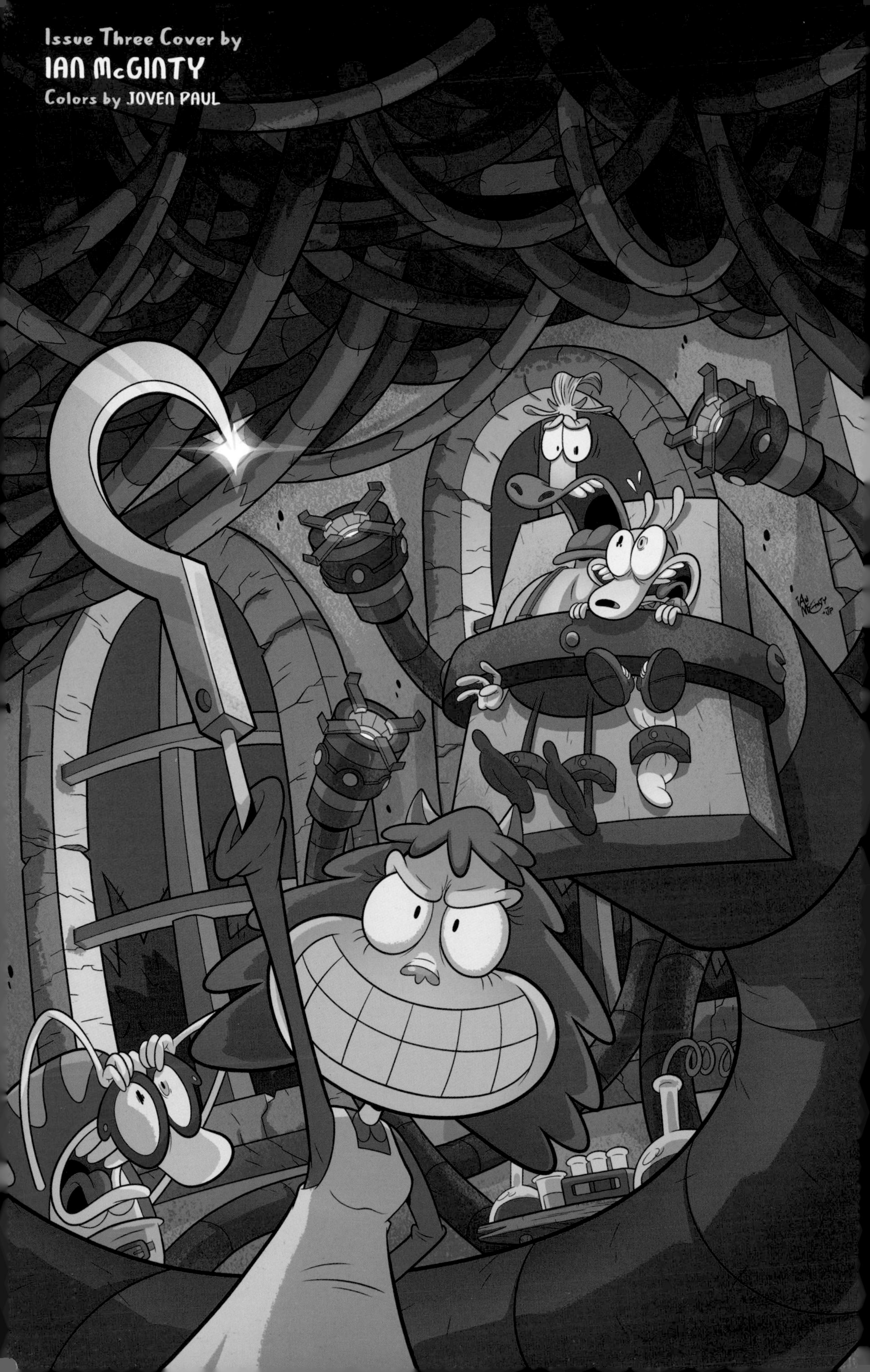

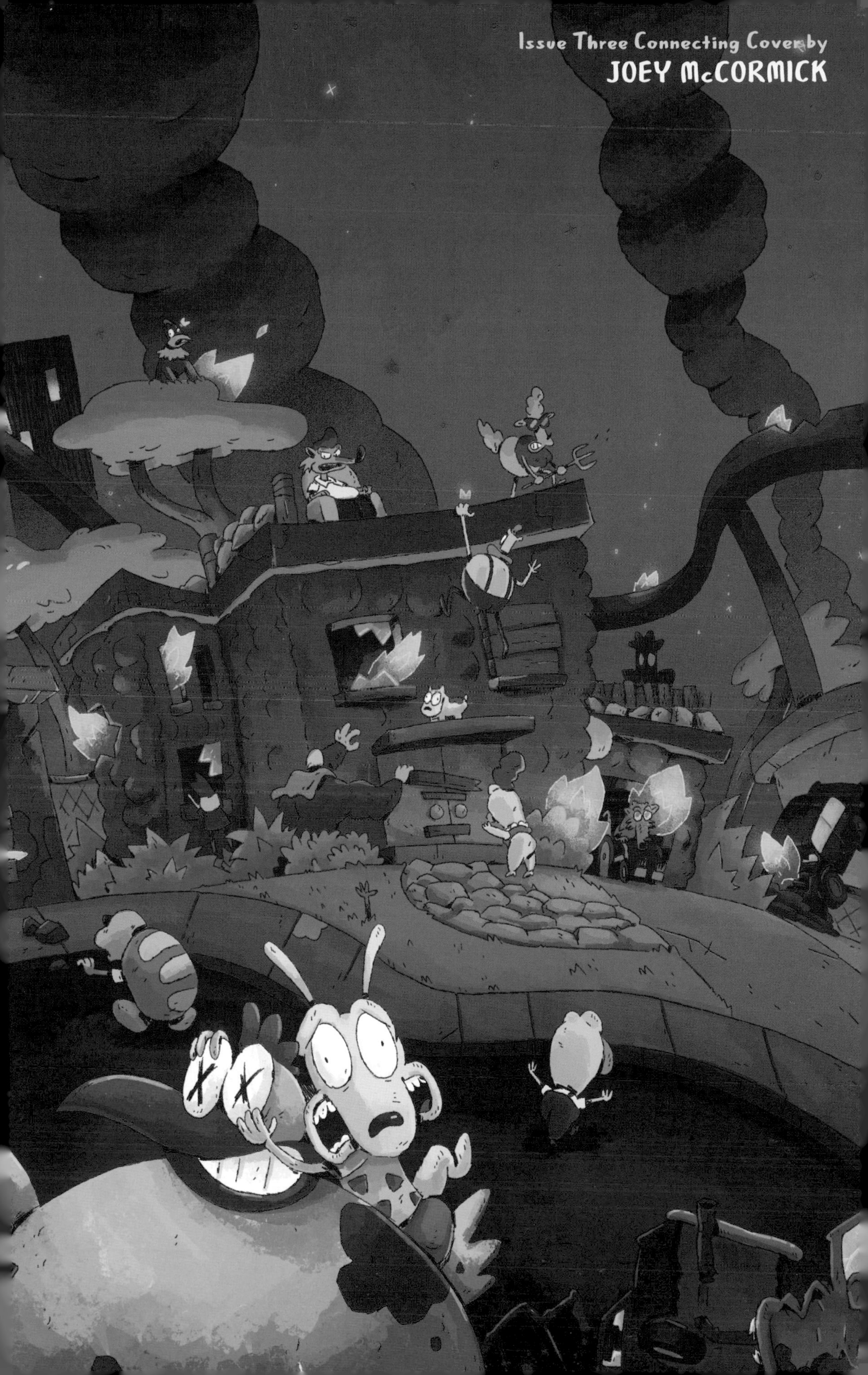

Issue Three Connecting Cover by
JOEY McCORMICK

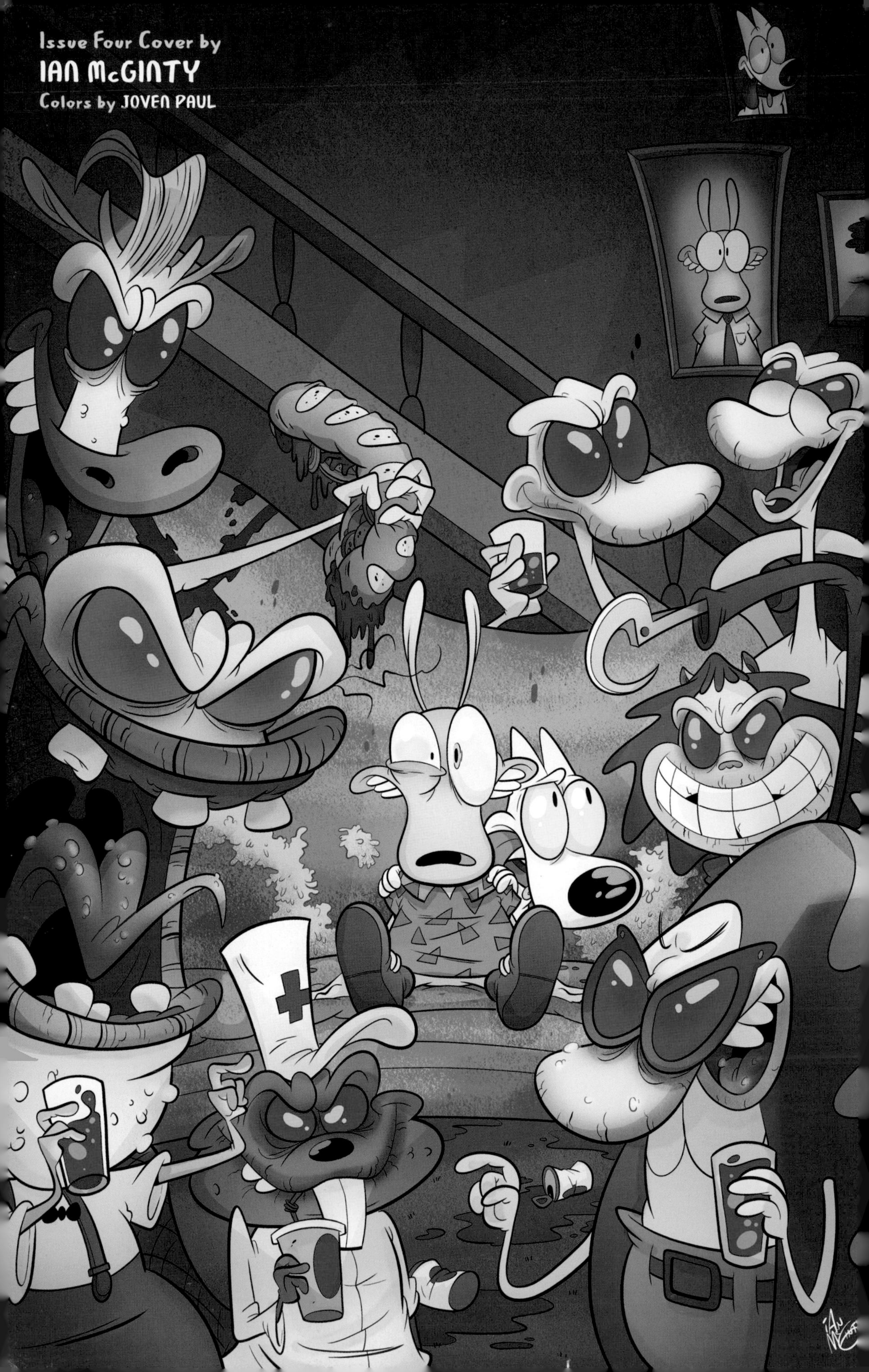

Issue Four Cover by
IAN McGINTY
Colors by JOVEN PAUL

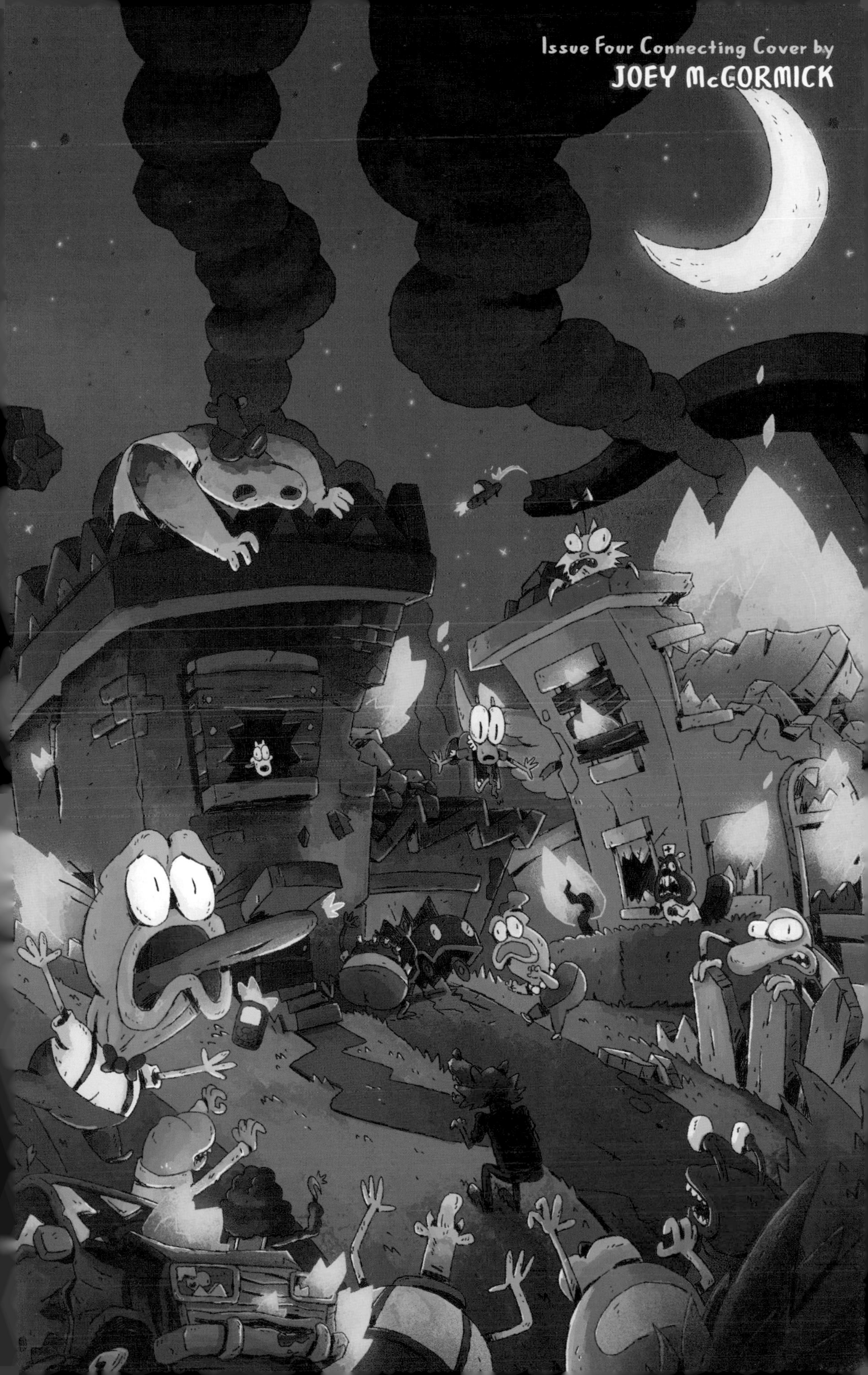
Issue Four Connecting Cover by
JOEY McCORMICK

Connecting Covers by
JOEY McCORMICK

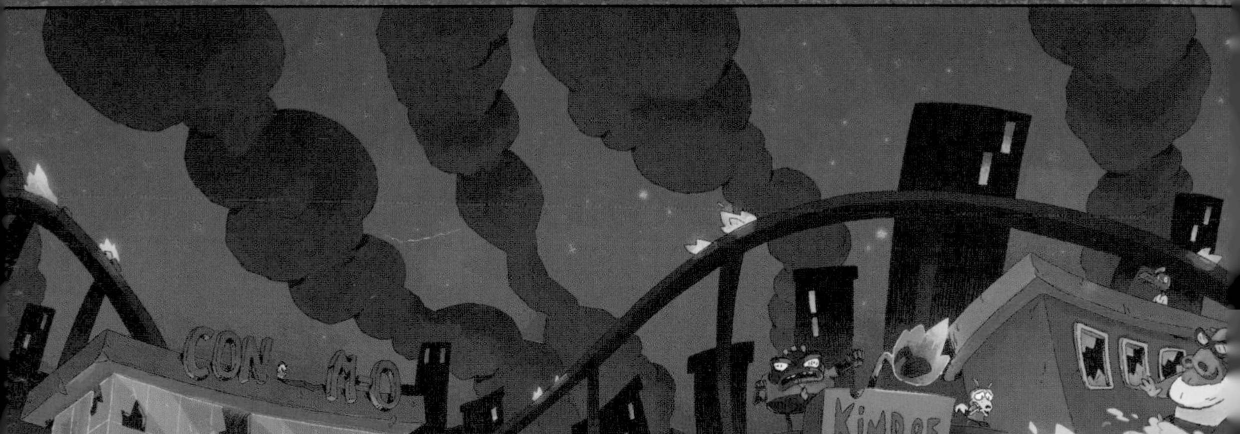
CON MO
BRAIN DEAD INSIDE
KIND OF A-LOT-O COMICS

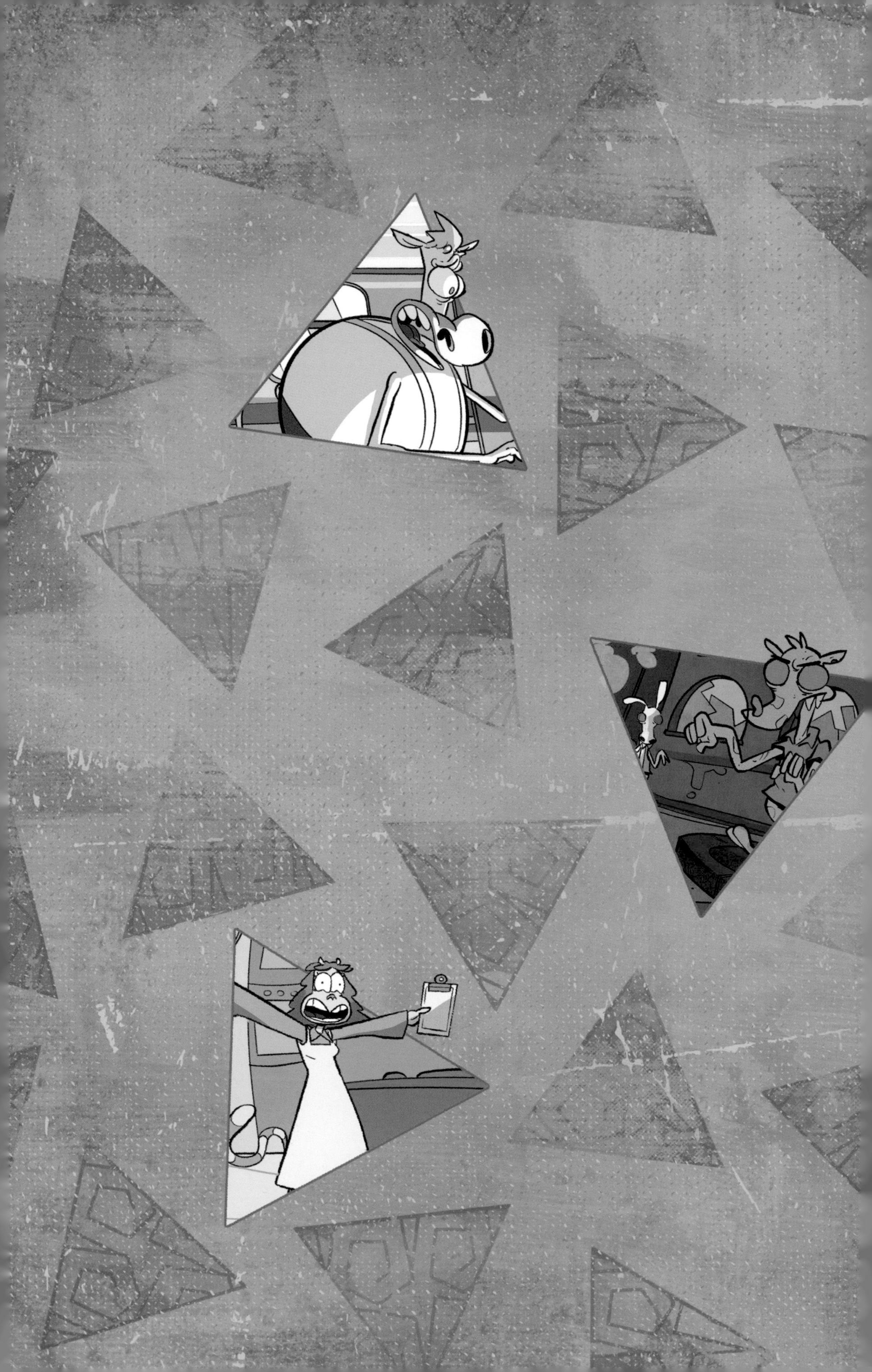

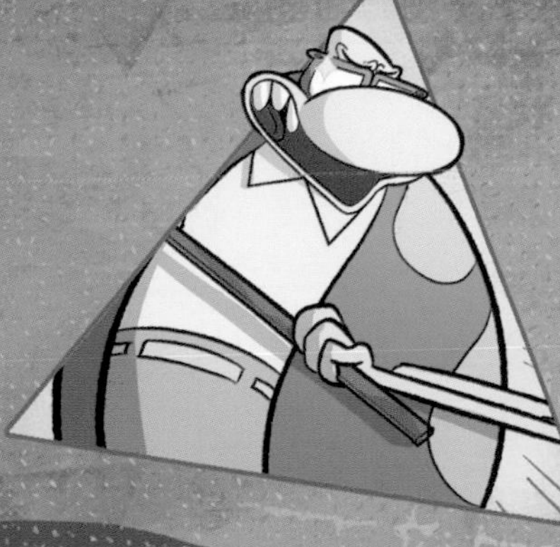

SCRIPT TO PAGE

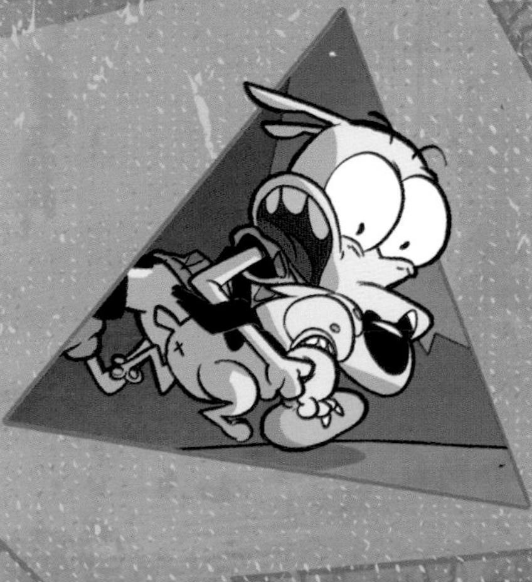

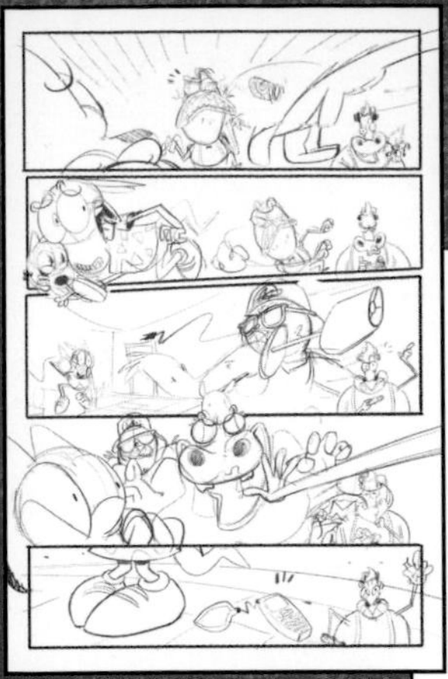

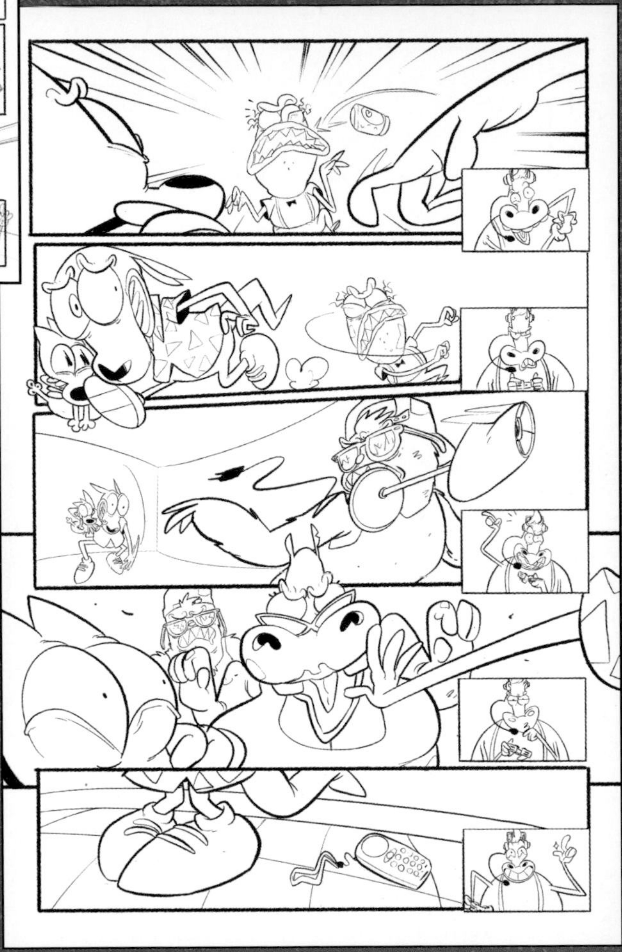

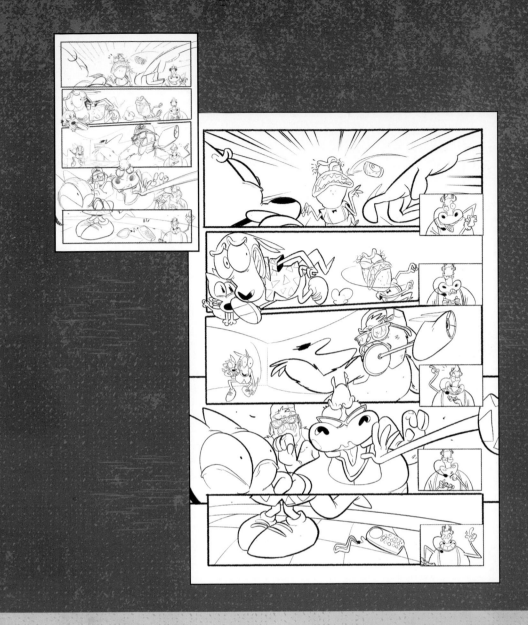

ISSUE ONE: PAGE FOURTEEN

PANEL ONE: Until mentioned otherwise, the following panels have a tiny Heffer on the bottom left corner of the screen, in the same way that streamers put a little image of themselves on the bottom of their own streams. The gag here is that Heffer's old recording is sorta commentating on Rocko's fight as if it's a videogame. Rocko throws the can of black licorice jelly beans at Ed, but it bounces off harmlessly.

SFX: donk

HEFFER: Alright, let's get started!

PANEL TWO: Rocko, still holding Spunky, dodges away from Ed, barely getting out of the way of Ed's hands as he grasps for Rocko. Stream-Heffer looks like he's in the zone playing this game.

HEFFER: So, it's real important you don't let the bad guys touch you. That'll sap a ***lot*** of health.

PANEL THREE: Rocko throws a lamp at zombie Chalmers, but misses completely. Stream Heffer raises a finger, like he's got an idea.

    HEFFER: Then, you gotta find a **weapon**, so you can fight back.

PANEL FOUR: The zombies have cornered Spunky and Rocko -- they're about to be killed. Stream Heffer is thinking to himself.

    HEFFER: It can't just be **any** weapon, though--it's gotta be something dependable. Something sturdy.

PANEL FIVE: Rocko looks down and sees his phone, still on the ground from when he threw it. Stream Heffer snaps his fingers -- he's got an idea.

    HEFFER: Something **classic**.

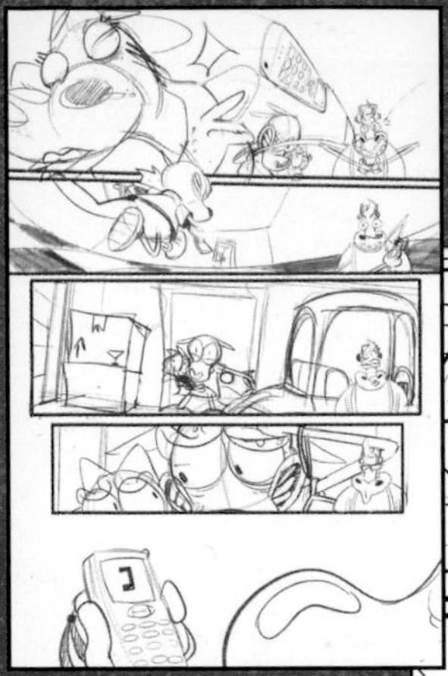

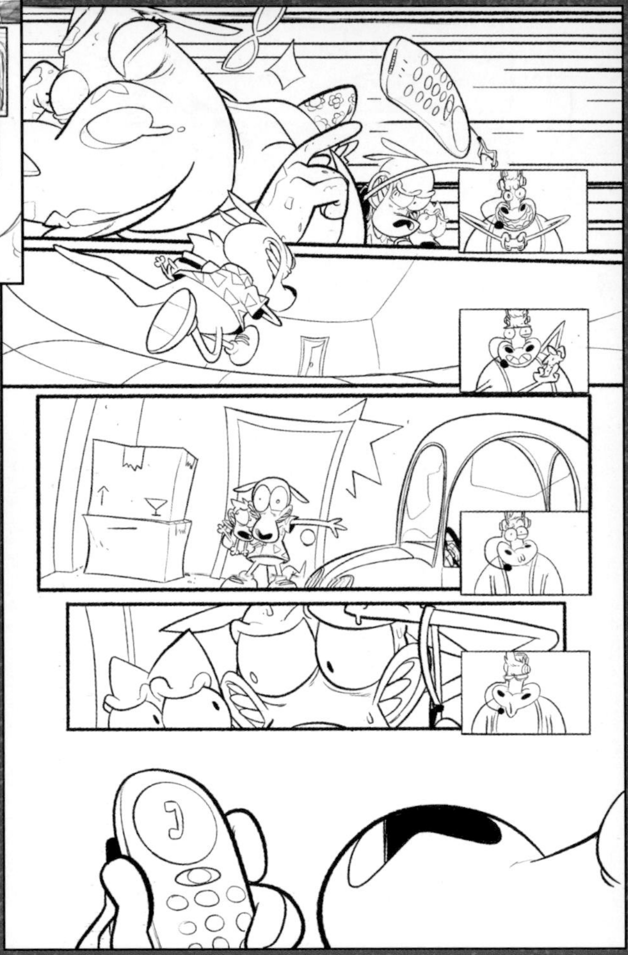

ISSUE ONE: PAGE FIFTEEN

PANEL ONE: Rocko SMACKS Gladys Hippo with his phone (he wields it like a flail, holding it by the wrist strap) and nearly spins her head all the way around, it's so dang powerful. Stream Heffer is psyched!

SFX: WHOK

ROCKO: Sorry, Ms. Hippo!

HEFFER: Yes! ***Critical hit!***

PANEL TWO: Rocko and Spunky run toward the open door to the garage, make an escape. Stream Heffer is excited!

HEFFER: Now, let's make our ***escape!***

PANEL THREE: Rocko slams the door to the garage shut behind he and Spunky. Stream Heffer breathes a sigh of relief. Rocko's car is here.

HEFFER: Yes! We're ***safe*** for now.

PANEL FOUR: Rocko wipes his brow. Stream Heffer looks really bored.

ROCKO: Spunky...I think I'm gonna give up meditation.

HEFFER: Dialog scene coming up. *BO-RING!*

PANEL FIVE: Stream Heffer is gone. Rocko looks down at his phone, which is still playing audio from the recorded stream.

HEFFER: Anyway, that's it for tonight. As always, if anyone out there has heard anything about a turtle named **Filburt** or a wallaby named *Rocko*, shoot me a message.

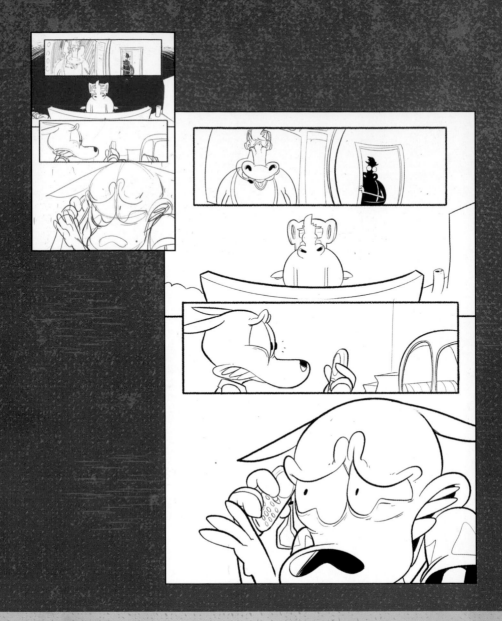

ISSUE ONE: PAGE SIXTEEN

PANEL ONE: In the background, slightly darkened (so we can't see that he's been bit) Heffer walks away from his parents' bedroom, toward frame. In the foreground, we see the old video of Heffer on his computer. The dialog comes from the Heffer on the computer, not the real Heffer.

   HEFFER: Not gonna lie--it's been kinda lonely since the outbreak started. But hanging out with you folks online has helped a lot.

PANEL TWO: Repeat of an earlier panel in the comic -- a wide panel of Heffer sitting in his very lonely living room, lit by the light of the computer monitor. The computer, and not him, is still the one talking.

   HEFFER: We all get bummed out sometimes, and if the internet is good for one thing, it's reminding you that you don't have to go through the bummer stuff alone.

PANEL THREE: Rocko looks at his phone, sad. He's clearly misjudged Heffer.

ROCKO: Oh jeez, Heff.

HEFFER (COMING FROM PHONE): Hey, Rocko! I'm back.

PANEL FOUR: Rocko puts the phone up to his ear.

ROCKO: I'm sorry, Heffer, I --

HEFFER (COMING FROM PHONE): About what? You were totally right--

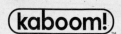